Instructional Design for

Action Learning

Instructional Design for Action Learning

GERI McARDLE

AMACOM
American Management Association
New York • Atlanta • Brussels • Chicago • Mexico City • San Francisco
Shanghai • Tokyo • Toronto • Washington, D.C.

Bulk discounts available. For details visit:
www.amacombooks.org/go/specialsales
Or contact special sales:
Phone: 800-250-5308
Email: specialsls@amanet.org
View all the AMACOM titles at: www.amacombooks.org

Library of Congress Cataloging-in-Publication Data

McArdle, Geri E. H.
Instructional design for action learning / Geri McArdle.
p. cm.
Includes bibliographical references and index.
ISBN-13: 978-0-8144-1566-5
ISBN-10: 0-8144-1566-0
1. Instructional systems—Design. 2. Educational technology. I. Title.
LB1028.38.M33 2011
371.3—dc22

2010004417

About AMA
American Management Association (www.amanet.org) is a world leader in talent development, advancing the skills of individuals to drive business success. Our mission is to support the goals of individuals and organizations through a complete range of products and services, including classroom and virtual seminars, webcasts, webinars, podcasts, conferences, corporate and government solutions, business books and research. AMA's approach to improving performance combines experiential learning—learning through doing—with opportunities for ongoing professional growth at every step of one's career journey.

Printing number
10 9 8 7 6 5 4 3 2 1

Contents

Preface

This book presents numerous thought-stimulating examples of active-oriented learning techniques that you can apply to your training design and delivery. If you apply these techniques and strategies to your training design and presentation, that training will stick! Specific strategies will show you how to do the following:

- Create trainings that are fun and memorable.
- Write learner-based trainings that guarantee success for each learner performance.
- Develop learning activities that match the need, learning style, and level of understanding of the participants.
- Use learning strategies that encourage learners to build on their experiences.
- Plan ongoing training activities that evaluate learner mastery during the entire learning event.
- Design blended and accelerated learning strategies that strengthen learning transfer back on the job.
- Identify methods that accurately measure training results.

What Are the Six Components of Creating Training?

Once you determine that a training need exists, there are six components, as shown in Figure P-1, that are considered the tools of the training trade, to guide you through the steps to create the training. These are the basis for the chapters in this book.

Chapter 1. Define the Training Need

Identify the skills and competencies that will improve job performance. Training needs information can be gathered from surveys, interviews,

Figure P-1. Training design model.

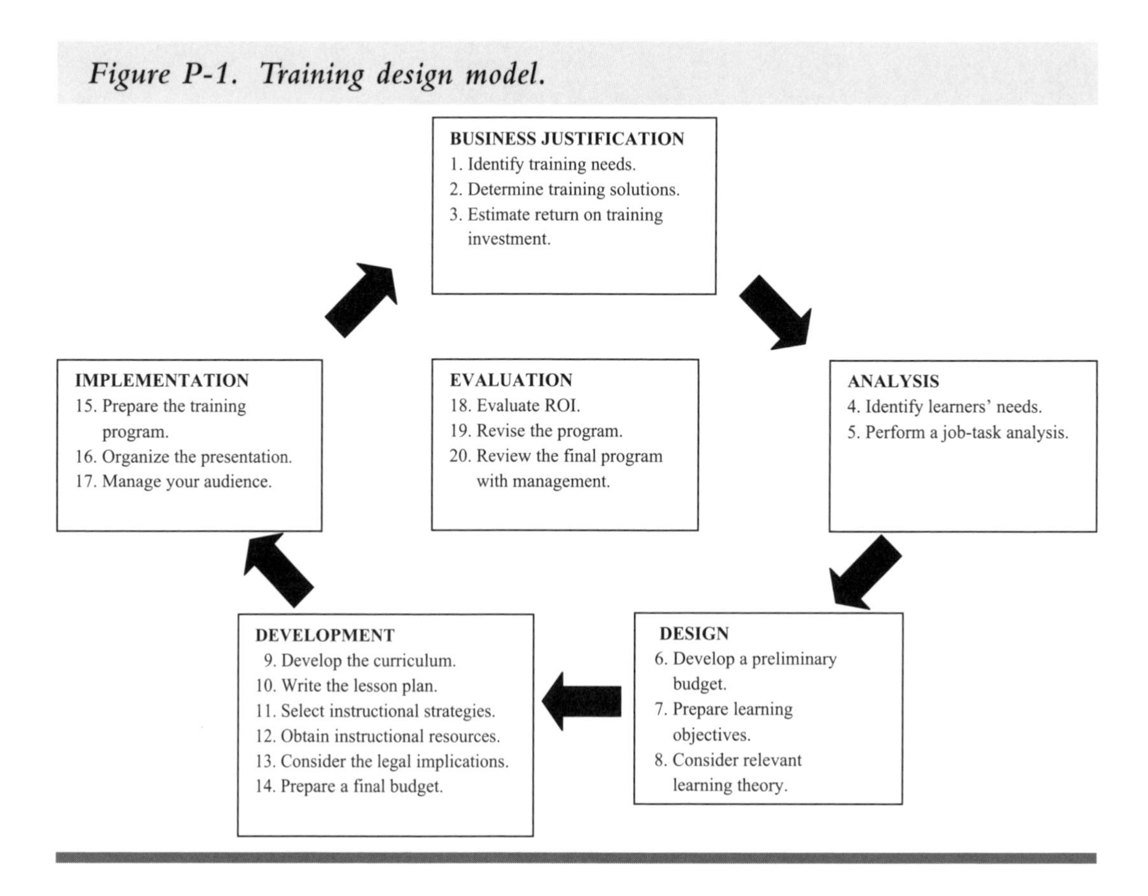

job and performance analyses, and employee and management feedback. When gathering information about the targeted group, determine if the learning should be more specialized and focused on a particular profession or function. Also, does the learning need occur at the individual level, team level, or organization level?

Chapter 2. Design the Learning to Fit the Need

Devise a program plan, and use methods that best facilitate the needed learning. Once you have identified the training needs, set the program objectives to meet these needs. When you write the program objectives, keep in mind that there are two types of objectives: knowledge based and behavioral based. Knowledge-based objectives show that participants have acquired information, theories, or facts. Behavioral-based objectives show that participants have acquired skills.

Objective statements should contain action verbs and be measurable. Once you have developed the objective statement, select training methods that reflect adult learning principles. Remember, your methods must be focused and interesting. Your goal is to convey the content clearly and to make sure it applies to the job. Participants should be able to apply their own experience and use what they have learned to solve real-world problems. Frequently used methods include small- and large-group discussions, readings, case studies, group presentations, pre- and post-work, videos, games, and simulations.

Chapter 3. Prepare to Conduct the Training

Ensure that you have the knowledge and an approachable style needed to foster learners' understanding of the training topics. Trainers and facilitators are expected to be authorities in the programs they lead. But keep in mind that your job is to facilitate learning and not to show off your expertise. Ask participants to show what they have learned and apply the subject matter to their work experiences whenever possible. Encourage participants to support and respond to other participants' perspectives.

It is important to develop your expertise and learn how to benchmark organizations' use of skills, competencies, and knowledge by reading, talking to colleagues, and attending professional meetings. If you can, observe and co-facilitate before you lead a training program. This allows you to familiarize yourself with the program, typical participants, frequent problems, common questions, and applications of the topic to the workplace. Once you have the knowledge, you need to make sure you have an approachable style. While knowing the content will help you be more approachable, focusing on developing that knowledge in others will also make you more approachable. Let others have the last word whenever possible to avoid arguments. Acknowledge that others have a right to their opinions, and only rebut challenges to the subject matter if absolutely necessary. Simply ask learners to keep an open mind. If it's relevant, show how the training topic relates to your own work experiences. Show learners how the topic relates to your own responsibilities and problems.

Chapter 4. Set the Scene for Learning

The program logistics and setting should be optimal for learning. If possible, always check the room setup well ahead of the training. The physical setting can enhance or detract from a participant's learning. Though you will not always have complete control over the physical setting, do what is possible to ensure that it is conducive for learning. Make sure all visuals can be seen from all seats in the room. If there are major features of the rooms that are disruptive and cannot be controlled, acknowledge them. Make suggestions for how you might try to work around them, and be open to any suggestions. Also, make sure you have enough handouts for each participant, and, if possible, have extra copies.

Chapter 5. Implement the Training

Follow the program plan closely. Let learners know that you are available during breaks, lunches (if possible), and after the program for one-on-one and small-group issues. Participants want you to know your topic yet not be the only source of authority in the classroom. Authority derives from worthwhile experience, and participants want acknowledgment that their experience can contribute to understanding the subject. Know-it-alls are never popular, rarely make good teachers, and never make good trainers. Trainers must invite engagement.

Remember, participants often plan to check on important business and personal issues at breaks and lunch. Therefore, don't deviate from the schedule unless you have to, and if you do, announce that if there are matters that need to be attended to, people may step out for a few minutes. Keep a copy of the program timeline handy to remind you of the schedule and maintain a knowledgeable, supportive, and approachable style.

Chapter 6. Measure the Effectiveness

Always distribute and collect learner evaluations of program objectives, content, methods, and instructor effectiveness. Follow-up studies will allow you to measure the difference in learners' performance after the training. You can also compare their performance to the performance of those who were not enrolled in the program.

Evaluations of program effectiveness range from collecting questionnaires given to participants at the end of a program to sophisticated (and often expensive) designs using control groups and cost-benefit analyses. Most programs place more emphasis on immediate evaluations made by participants at the end of the program. Remember, evaluation sheets should also ask for reactions to the usefulness of the program to the participants' jobs.

In addition, this chapter focuses on blended learning and e-learning strategies. Technology has allowed learning to be delivered to different geographical locations to accompany trainees, whether they are at work or home, and to be completed using a personal computer.

What Are the Main Points of the Book?

This book presents four themes that provide the focus to be used as a writing target when you design and develop training programs. The four themes occurring in the book are as follows:

1. Use the six components each time you create a training program.
2. Create trainings that engage learners and appeal to all learner styles and learning levels.
3. Facilitate small and large training groups effectively and with ease.
4. Identify and manage difficult learning situations (people) when conducting training.

How Is This Book Different?

The book is organized around the classic instructional system design (ISD) model. The ISD model is the "tool of the training practice" and is used to design and develop trainings. The four steps of the model are:

1. Identify need.
2. Design a training outline.
3. Develop course material.
4. Implement training.

Each chapter of the book presents a specific step in the ISD model, plus two additional steps: managing the setting and evaluating the training. The design and development approach of this book reflects a systems outlook. The book presents comprehensive training strategies and techniques using a step-by-step approach so that the directions are easy to follow.

A *system* is defined as a set of concepts that work together to perform a particular function. An organization is a system or a collection of systems. Every job in an organization is used by a system to produce a product or service.

Instructional Design for Action Learning

CHAPTER ONE

Define the Training Need

The goal of doing a training needs assessment (TNA) is to determine whether a need exists, who needs training, and what tasks need to be trained. When conducting the TNA, it is important to remember to include managers, trainers, and employees. At one time, just trainers and training instructional designers were concerned with the TNA process. Today, as training becomes increasingly used by companies to achieve their strategic goals, upper and middle managers are involved in the assessment process as well.

Employees often can feel confident of their abilities to perform on the job and lack any motivation to improve their performance. A properly designed and implemented training program will instill both confidence and motivation in the people you train. Training based on a specific context and on techniques specific to the workplace will demonstrate that change is not only possible but also desirable, and thus will motivate employees to change and improve even more. If you conduct some front-end assessments and design your training based on your assessment results, you should be able to make final adjustments before the training begins.

When there is no time to conduct a training needs analysis, you can obtain information quickly in the following ways:

- Phone a contact person who is familiar with the participants.
- Use the audience analysis and the problem analysis profile sheets.
- Introduce yourself, and ask the participants some key questions. Trust the responses to be representative, and treat the people as if they were a sample of a large group.
- Ensure that you receive relevant materials (e.g., surveys, meeting notes, records).
- Contact other trainers who have worked with the group to get their opinions and impressions.
- Talk to participants who arrive early, and obtain whatever information you can.
- Design some activities at the beginning of the program so you can assess the group.

How Do You Get Started?

Here's an overview of the six steps that you will use to design and conduct a TNA:

1. Plan a preliminary and formal data-gathering session. Involve management early in the process; by doing this, everyone benefits. Management is often the driving force behind a TNA, and you must have their support before beginning an analysis. The training project agreement (shown in Figure 1-1) represents such support. By conducting a TNA in an environment that fosters mutual respect and honesty, you give yourself every advantage for reaching an agreement with management about the outcome.

Figure 1-1. Sample training project agreement.

Training Project Agreement

Project Name: ____________________

Project Manager: ____________________

Client Project Manager: ____________________

Sponsor: ____________________

Overview

Description of Project: ____________________

____

Description of Project Outcome: ____________________

Work Plan

Project Start Date: __________ Printed Material Review Date: __________

Pilot Test Date: __________

Course Outline Review Date: __________ Course Release Date: __________

External Resources Required: ____________________

Limitations or Constraints: ____________________

Assumptions and Contingencies: ____________________

Project Manager	Sponsor	Client
__________	__________	__________

2. Identify the types of data to gather. It saves time and money to determine if training is an appropriate response to a perceived problem. Providing training simply because it was requested does not guarantee success. You must decide if the situation calls for training. You must also establish the following:

- How will the proposed training affect the audience?
- How will the proposed training be accepted by the audience, supervisors, and management?
- How will the training affect the entire organization?

3. Create well-stated questions. Questions guide the analysis process. Defining the problem clearly is critical to developing a successful training. Answers to the following two questions help define the area of need:

- Why do or don't people perform well?
- What performance level is desired?

4. Gather the information. It is important to examine knowledge, skills, and attitudes (KSAs) in the analysis. The work environment is an important factor in the process; so, too, is examining individuals' KSAs about their tasks, jobs, bosses, and organizations. Together, these factors influence your decision about whether to provide training. For example, they might show that the problem has to do with an environmental situation (e.g., poor lighting) or that it is the result of unrealistic deadlines, not inefficient training.

5. Prepare and analyze the data. It is important to differentiate between the two types of responses:

- Training, which teaches an immediate job skill
- Education, which provides theories, content, and knowledge to be applied in the future

6. Develop a presentation to show your findings. You may decide to share your preliminary findings by either a brief written report or a presentation. The format you choose depends on you and the organization.

The specific message you want to deliver with either communication is that you will deliver training that has been identified as a need and that you are using the following three indicators to measure individual and organizational performance:

- What should and does the organization consider baseline skills?
- What is the group intelligence of the individuals, groups, departments, and organizations?
- What is the expected change in performance?

Who Conducts the Training Needs Analysis?

A trainer or consultant performs a TNA to collect and document information concerning any of the following three issues:

1. Performance problems
2. Anticipated introduction of a new system, task, or technology
3. Organization's desire to benefit from a perceived opportunity

Here, you will get a clear idea of the need, look at possible remedies, and report on the findings to management before deciding on the best solution. A TNA often reveals the need for well-targeted training. However, keep in mind that training is not always the best way to close a gap between the organization's goals and its actual performance.

Needs always exist, and training is not always the solution. Below is a list of items that point to the root causes of performance problems:

- Unclear performance expectations and poor or no performance feedback
- Lack of tools, resources, or materials to do the job
- Inadequate financial rewards
- Poor match between employees' skills and the requirements of the job
- Lack of job security

Where Does the Training Needs Analysis Fit?

Conducting a TNA is a systematic process based on specific information-gathering techniques. Each stage builds off the last; the findings of one stage will affect and help shape the next stage. There is no easy formula for carrying out this process. Each particular situation requires its own mix of observing, probing, analyzing, and deducing.

In many ways, the TNA process is like detective work: you follow up on every lead, check every piece of information, and examine every alternative before drawing any conclusions. Only then can you be sure you have the evidence on which to base a sound strategy for problem-solving a performance issue.

How Do You Manage the Training Needs Analysis Process?

It's important to have realistic expectations for this process. Just what can you expect from a TNA? Find out if you've got the right idea by taking the quiz in Table 1-1.

A TNA begins with a snapshot of the current situation. You probably won't need a telephoto lens for this part of the process, but you do need to look closely and objectively at both the operations and the people whom the coming changes will affect. Once you have a clear picture of what needs to change, you can assemble your task group and continue with the TNA.

The TNA process consists of four basic steps:

Step 1: Surveillance

Step 2: Investigation

Step 3: Analysis

Step 4: Report

Table 1-1. Training needs analysis quiz.

DIRECTIONS: Examine each of the following 12 statements and determine if the TNA can give you that information.

Can a TNA provide . . .

1.	A clear definition of the roles within the organization?	Yes	No
2.	A clear direction and vision for the organization?	Yes	No
3.	A clear mission statement?	Yes	No
4.	Better customer service?	Yes	No
5.	Better interpersonal skills within the organization?	Yes	No
6.	Improved communication within the organization?	Yes	No
7.	Improved managerial skills within the organization?	Yes	No
8.	Improved operations?	Yes	No
9.	Improved sales?	Yes	No
10.	New managerial knowledge?	Yes	No
11.	New systems and procedures?	Yes	No
12.	New technical knowledge?	Yes	No

(Note: Only statement 6 should be marked "Yes.")

Step 1: Surveillance

As you embark on a formal TNA, you need an accurate idea of the situation. This preliminary step is an opportunity to determine if a need exists. Once you identify a need, you must determine the type of need.

To define the needs, you should consider the magnitude of each need. There are two levels, as shown in Table 1-2: micro and macro.

Table 1-3 shows examples of the two types of needs.

Once you determine the type of problem, the next thing to think about is how to define the gaps that exist between what is happening and what is desired.

Table 1-2. Levels of needs.

Micro Need	An isolated need that affects only a small number of individuals or a small segment of the organization—for example, training on Web page designs; not everyone in an organization designs Web pages.
Macro Need	A need that affects everyone in the organization—for example, all employees are required to complete sexual harassment training.

Table 1-3. Examples of micro and macro needs.

Micro Needs	Macro Needs
A new employee needs to understand critical job elements.	All employees need a benefits orientation.
A two-person unit has a piece of lab equipment installed.	All employees are expected to submit their time sheets online.
A supervisor is having problems giving employee feedback.	All first-line supervisors have been asked to initiate performance appraisal discussions.

Step 1a: Define the Gap

When a performance need exists or an organizational need surfaces, the first decision most managers make is to train the problem away. However, it's important to consider other methods, too. Before thinking about a training program, you must determine if training is the appropriate response to the problem.

There are other good reasons to conduct a TNA before actually developing a training program. When you design training activities, it is extremely helpful to obtain case material directly from the workplace or participants' individual work situations. That way, you can base your designs on real situations that participants face rather than on simulated material.

To determine the gap, you must ascertain the current level of performance and then define the desired state of performance. Of course, you won't see all of the needs by yourself. You will need to observe the day-to-day operations of the organization and interact with people at all levels, from the production line to management.

In many cases, a manager will bring a performance or training need to you. However, if you are not faced with an immediate problem, and you would like to provide training, you can begin with a macro scan of the organization. Here are two questions to help you get started.

1. What results does the organization currently achieve?
2. How do the actual results compare with the expected results?

Or, if a performance problem is involved, you should determine how the performance has changed from the past and what the desired performance is.

Figure 1-2 is a worksheet to help you make an initial assessment of current and desired results. You will gather more detailed data later on,

Figure 1-2. Worksheet for needs and performance gap analysis.

DIRECTIONS: Answer the following questions to determine the nature of the training problem.

Question	Response
1. Why this problem?	
2. Whose need is it, and who is involved?	
3. What is the problem?	
4. When did this problem become a need?	
5. Where did the problem begin?	
6. What is the best way to solve this problem?	

in Step 2. For now, you'll want to concentrate on identifying needs, not developing solutions. Look for trends. When you compare the organization's needs with the employees' perceptions, the issues will emerge.

During surveillance, you should regularly review the situation in your organization. Automatically circulated documents that provide state-of-the-organization themes or issues will give you an up-to-date, broad picture of what is happening, and you can begin scanning for performance problems and training opportunities.

In addition, make an effort to maintain informal contacts with individuals throughout the organization. Regularly assess the attitudes and feelings of the organization's staff, even if your assessment is subjective. Stay abreast of all policies, procedures, and standards relating to work performance.

An easy way to find useful material is simply to ask the potential participants to identify their needs. Going directly to the participants for the information gives them a role in designing and developing the training. Also, they usually appreciate being involved, and this increases the program's likelihood of success.

If you cannot collect information directly from each person in your target audience, consider the following two options:

1. Send a questionnaire to participants before meeting them. This gives you the opportunity to tell them about yourself and your plans for the upcoming program, and to learn about them.
2. Phone or visit some of the participants for an interview. By learning more about them and what they expect from the training, you can better focus the course content. It also minimizes any potential awkwardness when you meet in the classroom.

The sample audience analysis profile in Table 1-4 will help you formulate your questions and record employees' responses.

The employees' responses will help you complete the problem analysis profile; Table 1-5 is a typical problem analysis profile.

Table 1-4. Sample audience analysis profile.

Area	Questions	Findings
Education	Range of school experience	High school
	Native language	English
	Average reading level	10th grade
Work Experience	Existing skills or knowledge related to proposed training	Basic
	Variation of work experience levels	1–10 years in field
Training	Motivation	High
	Recent training experience	Basic introductory courses
	Effect on current job	Minimal to concern
	Degree of accountability	High: mistakes are easily identified
Delivery	Number of people to be trained	Three districts
	Location of people to be trained	Headquarters

Without the overall picture, you could overemphasize one need at the expense of others, wasting resources.

Once you have defined the gap, you'll need to get some assistance in conducting a preliminary needs survey. In this step, you gather input from various constituencies that will be critical to your TNA. You might want to organize a task force; if so, you can start organizing your task force by doing the following:

- Ask around to find out who is interested in joining the task force.
- Select members from multiple departments.
- Help the group appoint a contact person.

When you select your team, choose members who know and care about the situation and also some people who do not care but should.

Table 1-5. Sample problem analysis profile.

Performance Area	Accounts receivable
Performance Goal	All reps should exhibit proficiency. Use upgrading for coding billings
Current Performance	30% staff exhibit appropriate competency; 50% to be trained and tested
Gap Between Goal and Performance	50% to be trained at all locations

Causes	**Findings**
Do employees have the skills and knowledge to meet the performance goals?	No, only 50% at headquarters
Do employees know the performance standards or expectations?	Yes, announced in bulletin
Do employees receive feedback about their performance?	Yes
Do employees have the necessary resources to perform?	Yes, will provide required training
Do employees receive appropriate incentives to perform?	Yes, profit sharing per group performance

Also, try to identify a champion, a person committed to training who you can call upon for support and resources. You will need this support later to get through critical points in the TNA.

Step 1b: Organize the Data

The next step is to organize the information you have gathered so far.

- Sort the information into categories.
- Separate training issues from nontraining issues. For example, some problems you find might be related to a policy issue such as the organization's compensation package.

- Identify content or training topic issues.
- Determine whether an issue is a hands-on skill issue.

For the most part, training needs are performance related, such as helping employees do their jobs better, orienting new employees, or

Training Assessment Worksheet

The list below organizes the kinds of information that would be useful to you when beginning to design your training program. Use this worksheet as a checklist to ensure that you are considering all of the training needs of the trainees. Make a copy of this worksheet, and use it during the training to guide you to achieve the trainer's stated goals.

Information Desired

1. Participants' stated need
2. Nature of the participants' work
3. Participants' knowledge
4. Participants' skills
5. Participants' attitudes
6. Conditions affecting participant involvement

Methods Desired

Observation

Questionnaire

Key consultation

Printed media

Interview

Group discussion

Tests

keeping employees informed of technical and procedural changes. Some training activities also provide employees with an opportunity to develop their skills and knowledge, usually in connection with performance-related needs. Once you classify the needs by types, organize and prioritize each list.

Step 1c: Prioritize the Training Needs

Review your list of needs, and rank each of the needs based on the cost of training to meet them versus the cost of ignoring the needs. Alternatively, you can carry out a cost–benefit analysis for each need or cluster of needs. Use these questions to help sort the data you gathered during this preliminary needs investigation:

- What will a solution cost?
- How much time will the solution take to resolve?
- What is the cost of ignoring the problem?

Next, make a list of priorities and corresponding suggested actions for each priority entry. You can present this list to management to help you gain their support of your proposed solution.

Remember, a top priority for senior management is the bottom line. They will mostly be looking at the bottom line and the solution's overall contribution to the organization. Line managers are interested in evaluating solutions based on their costs in terms of lost or delayed production, employees' time, and possible overtime. Little will be accomplished without management support.

Your goal before the meeting is to write a well-defined problem statement. The pre-meeting guide in Figure 1-4 will help you organize your presentation. As you prepare, consider the following four factors:

1. **Time:** It's important to have a good idea of how long your analysis phase will take. It's a planned process that takes time to design and conduct; if there are many complex issues, the process will take longer.

Figure 1-3. Pre-meeting worksheet.

Needs Assessment Client Meeting #1

Date: ______________________________

Place: ______________________________

Time: ______________________________

Contact: ______________________________

Position: ______________________________

Training issue(s): ______________________________

____

Guiding questions or topics: ______________________________

____

Next steps: ______________________________

____

2. **Need:** The assessment process requires resources. Make sure management understands the process and why it's a necessary investment in the design process.
3. **Time Lines:** Don't spend all of your valuable time in the assessment process. Make sure you develop an appropriate and reasonable time line for the conducting and reporting phase of the TNA process.
4. **Cause and Effect:** Look for situations in which one situation affects another, and look for root causes. Separate problems from symptoms.

When you have your material ready, schedule the meeting. Don't forget to invite other staff, if appropriate.

Use Figure 1-5 as a guide during the meeting with management to help you stay on track. It is designed to assist you in recording the deci-

Figure 1-4. Meeting guide.

Needs Assessment Client Meeting #1

About the Target Task	Responses
Organization's performance standards	
Work conditions	
Supervisor's performance expectations	
About the Participants	**Responses**
Stated training needs	
Current performance levels	
Current knowledge levels	
Attitude toward task	
Attitude toward training	
About the Training	**Responses**
Time frame for planning	
Stakeholders	
Conditions under which training will be conducted	
Available resources (e.g., materials, tools)	
Instructor's skills	

sions you and management reach. During this meeting, you must do the following:

- Define the task.
- Agree on the needs.
- State the desired outcome.

- Establish shared responsibility.
- Identify a contact person for the report.
- Record management's commitment to proceed.

Below is a list of categories that you should include in your guide:

1. Description of the target topic: performance standards, work conditions, and supervisor's performance expectations
2. Description of the participants: stated need, current performance levels and knowledge, and attitude toward task and training
3. Description of training session: time frame for planning, stakeholders, conditions under which training will be conducted, available resources, and instructor skills

Step 1d: Complete the Post-Meeting Summary

As soon as possible after the initial meeting, complete the post-meeting summary memo. The memo should request a written commitment to continue the TNA, state agreed-upon allocation of resources, describe the goals you want to achieve, and establish a project time line that lists all of the steps in the needs process. Use the client summary memorandum in Figure 1-6 to record your findings. Below is a list of the items that you should think about when preparing the summary:

1. The sources of the information gathered
2. All names of individuals, groups, or documents
3. Indication of whether sources are internal or external to the organization

Step 1e: Draft the Problem Statement

You are now ready to start defining the need and gathering evidence to support the assertion that a need exists. The key element in the preliminary needs analysis process is the problem statement. Use the training needs outline in Table 1-6 to define your training need.

Figure 1-5. Client summary memorandum worksheet.

MEMORANDUM

To: Client
From: Trainer or facilitator
Date: October 16, 20xx
Subject: Needs assessment client meeting

---

1. Statement of Need

(Write a clear statement describing the assessment and training outcomes mutually agreed upon during the meeting.)

---

2. Description of Tasks

(Define the task you perceive to be involved in the needs assessment process.)

---

3. Summary of Analyses

(Summarize the information about the target tasks, the participants, and the training situation that would help management make a commitment to the process and the proposed training outcome.)

---

4. Proposed Plan

(Present your plan for conducting the assessment, including tasks, time line, and budget.)

---

5. Request for Management's Commitment

(Ask for the client's written commitment to the project.)

Table 1-6. Training needs outline.

Source	Internal to Organization	External to Organization
People	Trainers Supervisors Upper-level managers	Trainers Consultants
Jobs	Personal changes (new hires, promotions) Changes in performance standards Analyses of efficiency indexes (e.g., waste, downtime, repairs, quality control)	Professional associations Consultants Government regulations
Organization	Changes in the organization's mission Mergers and acquisitions Change in organizational structure New products and services Analysis or organizational climate (e.g., grievances, absenteeism, turnover, accident)	Government regulations and legislative mandate Consultants Pressure from outside competition Environmental pressures (e.g., political, economic, demographic, technical)

Step 2: Investigation

In this step, you investigate the current circumstances at the organization to decide whether training is appropriate to resolve the need. To do this, you should find out what data are needed, develop appropriate data-collection methods, and collect and analyze the data.

The training needs analysis relies on opinions and information gathered from many sources, including people. Because you'll be getting so much information from so many places, it's important to confirm and check each piece of data to make sure it is valid.

Step 2a: Begin the Investigation

Use the following questions to help establish some guidelines for your investigation:

1. What results does the organization seek?
2. How do these results compare with the organization's key objectives?
3. What contribution does the training department need to make to meet the organization's key objectives?
4. What methods are currently in use to set priorities and justify training targets?
5. How are training results measured?

The outcome of a TNA will be only as good as the data you collect. The data will help you verify that a need exists and can be used for other purposes long after this application. In fact, it may save you time and effort in future endeavors.

Let's look at factors that you should consider for defining what to look for when you begin gathering the appropriate information you need. Here's a suggested process to follow:

► **Establish Your Goal:** Draft a description of what you hope to reveal in your TNA based on your preliminary research findings during the surveillance stage. List your expectations, and note the situation prior to your assessment.

► **Define Your Reporting Needs:** Decide who should receive what information and when. Also, consider at what levels you should gather data. Data collected for the TNA should be on the same level of the organization as the issues involved. It could be the entire organization, subunits, or individuals. By specifying the reporting levels early on in the TNA, you'll be able to collect information at a sufficient level of detail to use in the reports and to make points during the decision-making meetings.

➤ **Identify the TNA Content Areas:** Most applications of TNA emphasize the person component, ignoring the critical roles of the organization and the job components. However, training needs are generated from all three sources.

In the content-level matrix, as shown in Table 1-7, the intersection of each content factor with each organizational level suggests questions or issues that should be addressed in a comprehensive needs analysis. The framework is useful for identifying factors that can influence

Table 1-7. Content-level matrix.

Method	Description	Advantage	Disadvantage
Human resource records	Provide causes regarding performance needs and training issues	Objective	Time-consuming
Accident and safety records	Reveal clusters of problem types by department and position	Quantitative	Do not necessarily document causes
Grievance filings and turnover rates	State problem with employee or immediate supervisor	Documentation	May be related to policy rather than to training
Performance evaluation and meeting ratings	Measured analysis of employees on absolute and relative bases	Document skills and employee progress	Subjective information
Production statistics	Numerical results of output and itemized costs of doing business	Quantitative	Do not always provide a complete picture

performance, and it provides a guide to what kinds of data you will be considering.

Step 2b: Determine the Key Data Sources

When conducting the TNA, you can collect data via questionnaires, surveys, interviews, observations, focus groups, documentation, job descriptions, and policies and procedures. As you proceed with your investigation, remember that you must clearly define a training need before you can solve it. Here are some tips that could help:

- Ask who, what, why, when, and how questions.
- Develop a clear and concise problem statement.
- Document the causes of the problem.
- Identify feelings about the problem.
- Determine who is involved and why.
- Separate facts from opinions.

A majority of the issues that you must address are going to be performance matters; therefore, you should gather data about the person(s) involved, the jobs, the performance levels, and the job expectations.

Step 2c: Collect Data from Key Sources

Now that you have defined the training need, you are ready to collect data to support your initial findings. Here is a list of the potential sources and contacts to use for your investigation, along with questions to focus your research:

1. Investigate all available data.
2. Ask questions of colleagues.
3. Network.
4. Get to know your potential audience.

5. Determine the causes: What kind of need is it?
    - Performance deficiency
    - Skill improvement or development
    - Skill needed for the future
6. Find out who or what is involved: Which does it pertain to?
    - An individual
    - A department
    - A division
    - An organization
7. Determine how the problem can be corrected: Which will you use?
    - Recruiting
    - Coaching
    - Assessing skills or placement
    - Training
    - Organization development (OD) intervention
8. Determine the causes of performance problems.
    - Lack of skill
    - Barriers to achievement
    - Lack of incentives
    - Lack of motivation

When conducting your investigation, you will collect information from several sources. You will encounter both soft and hard data. Hard data are factual and objective, found in reports, accounting records, statistics, and other official documentation. Soft data are subjective and come from observations, group discussions, individual interviews, and opinion surveys.

The following are ways to collect data.

▸ **Questionnaires.** The intention of the questionnaire is to create questions that you would like to have answered. The questionnaire is sent either via e-mail or on paper. Using the questionnaire as a data-collection source is inexpensive. You can collect data from a large number of persons, and the data are easily summarized. The advantages and disadvantages of questionnaires are listed in Table 1-8.

▸ **Interviews.** You can talk with individuals in person or by telephone. Interviews don't just give you information; they can also reveal feelings, opinions, and unexpected insights or suggestions, including potential solutions to needs. But there are disadvantages. Interviews require more time and resources. In addition, you must leave any biases at home,

Table 1-8. Advantages and disadvantages of questionnaires.

Questionnaire Characteristics	Advantages	Disadvantages
Surveys or polls of a random sample of respondents, or an enumeration of an entire population	Reach a large number of people in a short time	Have little provision for free expression of unanticipated responses
Open-ended, projective, forced-choice, priority-ranking formats	Relatively inexpensive	Require substantial time (and technical skills, especially in survey model) to develop effective instruments
Rating scales, either pre-designed of self-generated by one or more respondents, and other alternative forms	Provide opportunity for personal expression without fear of embarrassment	Limited utility in identifying causes or possible solutions
Self-administered (by mail), under controlled or uncontrolled conditions, or with presence of an interpreter or assistant	Yield data that can be easily summarized and reported	Suffer from low return rates (mailed), grudging responses, or unintended or inappropriate respondents

which is not easy. A good interviewer listens well and does not judge, interrupt, nor distort responses.

There are five types of interview formats you should review to determine which best fits your client, the situation, and the type of information you would like to uncover:

1. *Unstructured:* This kind of interview is exploratory. Only the area of interest is chosen for discussion. Interviewers follow their instincts in formulating and ordering questions.
2. *Partially Structured:* The interviewers choose an area for discussion and formulate questions, but the order is up to the interviewer. Interviewers may add questions or modify them as they deem appropriate. Questions are open-ended; responses are recorded almost verbatim.
3. *Semi-Structured:* The questions and their order of presentation are predetermined and open-ended. Interviewers record the essence of each response.
4. *Structured:* The questions are predetermined, and interviewers code responses as they are given.
5. *Totally Structured:* The question order is discussed, and coding is predetermined. Respondents are presented with alternatives for each answer so that the phrasing of responses is structured.

The key to success is defining and developing your training to make sure that the data you gather support a training need (or that the need does not exist). Spend time establishing the reasons for choosing the questions you will ask, and write the questions with care. The model telephone interview shown in Figure 1-6 will help with this.

Computer-assisted telephone interviews use a computer to guide the respondents through the questions. The interview begins with a series of questions that determine whether the person who answered the telephone is part of the target sample. The computer is programmed to end the call if the person is not from the target group.

Figure 1-6. Model telephone interview.

1. Introduce yourself.	Name Where you are located Why you are specifically calling
2. Outline a need in the organization for which you believe training might be appropriate. Be as specific as possible.	What is it? Why is it a problem?
3. Develop short sentences or phrases to ask about the need.	1. 2. 3. 4.
4. Is this a macro or micro need?	What actions are they suggesting?
5. Classify the problem.	a. Do not know (lack of knowledge) b. Cannot do (lack of skill) c. Can do, but aren't motivated to do (lack of good attitude)

Telephone interviews tend to elicit shorter responses than do face-to-face encounters, but this kind of interview has some of the same advantages as face-to-face interviews. This should be the method of choice when results must be obtained in a short time. However, many people are put off by electronic interviewers, so be sure to feel out your potential interviewees before making a decision. You may feel it better to spend your time and money on person-to-person phone interviews, especially if your target sample is small.

➤ **Observations.** Another process to consider for collecting data is observation. One reason to use observation is that it can reveal the context in which performance takes place. Observation can give you valuable nonverbal information about what goes on at what level that may not coincide with a person's verbal opinion. A disadvantage of observation is that you can have an effect on the setting and the way people perform their jobs. Naturally, you will also bring bias to the situation, thus gathering information subjectively rather than objectively.

The use of a question guide is essential in this process. The question guide should be easy to understand and use, and it should consist of a few questions that solicit what is going on now, what would you like to see happening, and what your suggestions are on making the change. Remember to keep the questions short, so that the responses from your interviewee could be yes or no, and if you require a more descriptive response, try to focus the responses to be short and factual.

As you prepare, keep in mind the purpose of the observation. Limit the guide to the parts of the work you're concentrating on, and allow room for both qualitative and quantitative information. Because you must prepare your question guide ahead of the observation, you might overlook useful information, so be sure to leave plenty of space in the guide format to record additional comments. Make sure you gather facts, not opinions.

When you decide what and whom to observe, you can use either suggestions from management or a random sample. Your observations can be covert or overt. If you choose to do a covert observation, which is the most common, you should introduce yourself and then fade into the background. Do not be the center of attention; it can alter your discussions.

To conduct successful observations, do the following:

- Identify what performance aspect you plan to observe.
- Familiarize yourself with the job or system you will observe.
- Design and use a simple, clearly written observation guide.
- Choose an observation method that will provide valid results.
- Blend into the observed environment.
- Be patient.
- Consider both the big picture and the details.
- Follow up.

To help make a decision as to what appropriate observation method to use, review the advantages and disadvantages in Table 1-9.

➤ **Focus Groups.** Here, you will gather information from a select group of people. A focus group consists of multiple interviews with small groups that discuss an assigned question. Focus groups can help determine the significance of a particular situation to various individuals, find the needed range of alternatives from close-ended questions, or determine how people feel about an issue or product.

Focus groups are most successful when the group membership is relatively small and homogeneous. One of the disadvantages of this method

Table 1-9. Advantages and disadvantages of observations.

Observation Types	Advantages	Disadvantages
Technical or nontechnical (time-motion studies vs. behavioral reviews of new board or staff members interacting during meetings)	Minimize interruption of routine work flow or growth activity	Require highly skilled observers with both process and content knowledge (unlike an interviewer who needs, for the most part, only process skills)
Unstructured data collection (as in walking through the company's offices on the lookout for evidence of communication barriers)	Generate on-site data, relevant for identifying situations where training will have an effect	Limited to data collected within the work setting
Normative use (to distinguish between effective and ineffective behaviors, organizational structures, or processes)	Provide important comparison checks between the observer's and the respondent's inferences (when combined with a feedback step)	Can yield subjective data

is that it is difficult to assemble the right mix of people; if your group is widely diverse, some members may not be as willing to open up. Another hurdle is finding a time that fits everyone's schedule.

Once you get everyone together, seat them in a circle. This facilitates spontaneous responses and conversation. To make the most of your focus group, do the following:

- Limit the group to 12 people.
- Use a structured question guide for the discussion.
- Have one group administrator take notes or record responses on a flipchart and another facilitate discussion.
- Audio record responses if you can do so discreetly.
- Arrange the group so members are seated by their rank in the organization (managers and their supervisors should be together).
- Use a variety of group-facilitation tools (e.g., brainstorming, listing by priority) to stimulate responses.

➤ **Documentation.** Several types of organizational documents can provide information about employees. For example, personnel files, accident reports, and customer complaints can help you establish the level of employees' skills and knowledge.

Using documents has several advantages. Mainly, they are an inexpensive needs-analysis tool because the company has already collected the information. There are some disadvantages of using documents, however. They're not necessarily complete because they may have been influenced by the viewpoints of the people who prepared the documentation. It's important to keep this in mind because you must be careful not to generalize from the information you gather. Another problem with documents is that they may be difficult to obtain.

You should work closely with the human resource (HR) manager throughout the process. It is up to that person to establish whether it is appropriate for you to see certain records. For example, reviewing performance appraisal forms may help you identify performance gaps, but these records are confidential and HR may decide not to release them or even discuss them in general terms.

To use documents effectively, you should do the following:

- Explain clearly why you need each document.
- Prepare to make a case for the need to review documents.
- Describe how you will ensure that confidentiality is preserved.
- Review all relevant documents from a random sample.
- Examine documents twice, first to gain a broad perspective and second to identify all relevant aspects of performance.
- Decide whether to share general impressions with the manager who provided access to the documents.

➤ **Job Descriptions.** The job description consists of position duties, responsibilities, reporting relationships, working conditions, and supervisory responsibilities. Job descriptions state the required behaviors, skills (both job and technical), and knowledge. Additionally, these descriptions include required education, certification, and professional work experiences.

➤ **Policies and Procedures.** Every organization has guidelines for managing people and managing work. A policy is a plan of action to guide decisions and achieve rational outcomes. A procedure is a specified series of actions or operations that have to be executed in the same manner to always obtain the same results under the same circumstances (e.g., emergency procedures, safety checks). An advantage of having policies and procedures is their ability to standardize business practices; a disadvantage is that, given the dynamics of the workplace and the diversity of various cultures in the organization, everyone will not agree with those standards regarding work practices, procedures, and treatment.

Step 2d: Obtain Management's Approval to Proceed

Now that you are armed with data that support the need for training, you are ready to get permission from management to proceed. To do this, you should create a client commitment letter, as shown in Figure 1-7.

Step 2e: Determine the Knowledge, Skills, and Attitude

The next step is to determine if KSAs are involved in the performance need. As you conduct your needs analysis, investigating KSAs is critical

Figure 1-7. Sample Client Commitment Letter

Sunshine Corporation
2350 West First Street
Fort Myers, FL 12345
(111) 123-4567

Date:

Ms. Dew Wright, Director
Human Resources Department
1234 The Street
Fort Myers, FL 12345

Dear Ms. Wright:

As president of Sunshine Corporation, I hereby fully support the project's objectives and proposed training outcomes, as stated in your January 25 summary memorandum. Concomitant with this commitment is the agreed-upon availability of resources as requested.

With best wishes for success.

Sincerely yours,

Philip Phillips
President

so you can be sure your need can be solved with training. Explore the following factors that cause performance needs:

- **Lack of Skills and Knowledge to Do the Job:** Can employees do the tasks needed to meet the performance goals?
- **Lack of Specific Standards or Job Expectations:** Do employees know and understand their performance expectations?
- **Lack of Feedback:** Do employees receive constant feedback about their performance?
- **Lack of Necessary Resources to Perform:** Do employees have everything they need to do their jobs adequately?

Step 3: Analysis

Up to this point, you've been finding out what kind of information you'll need, a way to get that information, and then how to actually get it. Now you're ready to analyze what you've found so you can discover what needs to be addressed in the training.

The analysis step provides a clear picture of what issues currently exist. There are three types of analyses that you can perform: goal analysis, organizational analysis, and job/task analysis. Each helps you determine the type of problem, where it exists, and who owns the problem. This section will give you the tools to record and present the findings of your investigation. When you complete this step, you will be able to easily determine the type of need and the best solution.

Until now, your primary focus has been on identifying the need, possible causes, and alternative solutions. Now, the question becomes how to meet the need. To determine whether training or another solution can do that, you must find the root cause of the need, or problem. This is the most critical stage of the needs-analysis process.

If the need is caused by a lack of information, knowledge, or skill, training can solve the problem. If the need is a result of poor communication, lack of feedback, inadequate supervision, inappropriate or inadequate rewards, or inferior procedures, training is not the answer. You must investigate further to ensure that other reasons are not responsible, in whole or in part, for the problem.

If training is a viable solution for meeting the need, the analysis should include the critical KSAs required for optimal performance to be addressed in the training design. Include the following three elements in your analysis before you move ahead with organizing your collected data:

1. Confirm the need for training.
2. Select the methodology for developing the training.
3. Establish exactly what participants need to learn.

Step 3a: Organize the Data

There are three sources of training needs: the people, the job, and the organization. Use the data summary sheet in Table 1-10 to help you make decisions about the appropriateness of training to resolve the problems that you identified during your investigation stage.

Often, the first sign that training might be needed is when a specific need emerges from one of the sources. Once you are aware of the problem, you must decide whether it is:

- Performance related
- Short or long term
- New or recurring
- Affecting a few or many employees
- Urgent, important, or unimportant

The data summary sheet also helps you prepare a well-defined problem statement, determine if the issue is micro or macro, classify the need, and propose a solution.

Table 1-10. Data summary worksheet.

DIRECTIONS: Answer the following questions as they pertain to your organization's need for training.

1. What is the need in the organization for which you believe a training program might be appropriate? Be as specific as possible.
2. Is the need performance-related? Why or why not? (If the need is related to performance, proceed to number 3. If the need is not related to performance, proceed to number 5.)
3. Is this a macro or micro need? What action are you suggesting?
4. Is the need you have identified something your employees
   a. do not know (lack of knowledge)?
   b. cannot do (lack of skill)?
   c. can do, but aren't motivated to do?

   (If it is a lack of knowledge or skill, a training program is an appropriate response. If it is a lack of motivation, proceed to number 5.)
5. What are the possible solutions for meeting the need other than with training?

Step 3b: Analyze the Data

There are three types of analyses to organize needs according to type:

1. Goal analysis
2. Organizational analysis
3. Job analysis

Which method you choose depends upon the category of need you will address, as follows.

➤ **Goal Analysis.** If your goal is to correct a performance need, which could include a specific job/task issue, use the goal-analysis process. Goal analysis is also important when a training program is charged with developing people to serve in new positions, creating a corporate culture, or changing attitudes or beliefs.

Goals analysis requires that you identify key organizational objectives and their behavioral indicators. Behavioral indicators are the abstract qualities (such as feelings) that help a person perform well or badly in a particular position. The objectives and behavioral indicators provide a baseline to measure improvement. Goal analysis ends when you have a complete list of behavioral indicators for each goal. A sample goal analysis is shown in Table 1-11.

Table 1-11. Sample goal analysis.

Performance Problem	Question	Goal
Lack of skills and knowledge to do the job	Can employees do the tasks needed to meet performance goals?	Identify the problem and if it is a training matter, conduct a job/task analysis to determine where the problem exists. Design and deliver training to address the lack of job skill or knowledge, and ensure that employees can perform the task to standard.
Lack of specific standards or job expectations	Do employees know the performance expectations?	If there are no standard performance criteria, work with management to create training to meet standards and establish the behavior necessary to achieve the standards. If employees know the job expectations, address the reasons for poor performance, either through training or through coaching to help them meet the job goals.
Lack of feedback	Do employees receive feedback about their performance?	If employees do not receive feedback, work with supervisors to determine training outcomes and ways in which feedback should be delivered to employees about their job performance.

Training objectives should be clearly stated. They should include the performance issues so the objectives can prove that the participants have learned something. There are two types of objectives, as follows:

Terminal

Statements that describe what a training participant will be able to do at the end of the program, under what conditions, and at what level of competence. Terminal statements describe observable actions.

Enabling

Statements that describe the basic KSAs to be learned. Enabling statements do not necessarily contain a condition statement to execute a final observable action.

▸ **Organizational Analysis.** The second form of analysis is organizational; a sample is shown in Table 1-12. You will use this for gathering information to solve a problem involving the makeup of a company or organization. Answer the following questions to make sure that the training supports the organization's performance standards:

- What are the organization's business goals?
- What are the organization's key products?
- How is the organization structured?
- What are the roles and responsibilities of staff within the organization?
- What resources are available?
- What perceived needs do the organization's members express?
- What is the typical way that people are trained in the organization?
- What general needs exist within the organization that may affect the training?

While these questions can be valuable tools in building an effective training program, they do have their drawbacks. If you suspect that a

Table 1-12. Types of organizational needs analyses.

Type	Description
Organizational needs analysis	The needs of the organization are macro: • Productivity • Personnel structure and job satisfaction • Surviving in a competitive market, etc. Needs are met by organizational interventions.
Group needs analysis	Group needs help to determine the organizational interventions required to meet organization needs.
Individual employee needs analysis	Individual needs are determined by finding out what general knowledge, skills, and abilities are required to work in the organization.
Job needs analysis	Job needs are determined by figuring out the tasks of each job and identifying the skills and knowledge for each task.

performance need exists, use the problem-analysis profile in Table 1-5 to guide your investigation. And don't forget to consider all of the information you have gathered. If you decide to create a data-gathering questionnaire, review the topics presented in Table 1-13.

Once you have organized the information and have entered it on the data summary sheet organizer, as shown in Table 1-14, you can pull it all together before you proceed to Step 4.

▸ **Job Analysis.** Job analysis involves recording information about a particular job and breaking it down into tasks to pinpoint where the training or performance need exists. Start by reviewing job descriptions, observing job performance, and questioning people on the job. The simplified job analysis questionnaire in Table 1-15 can substitute for face-to-face interviewing or serve as a guide when conducting the interviews.

(text continues on page 40)

Table 1-13. Topics for data-gathering questionnaire.

General Questions

1 What is the job role and tasks performed?
2. What are the competencies required for the job or tasks?
3. What is the level of experience in the job?
4. What is the attitude about training?
5. What successes or problems have you encountered performing the job?
6. What is the supervisor's attitude about training?

Performance Problems

1. Is there a lack of skills and knowledge to do the job?
2. Is there a lack of specific standards or job expectations?
3. Is there a lack of feedback?
4. Is there a lack of resources and equipment to do the job?
5. Is there a lack of appropriate consequences for performance?
6. Are there combinations of problems that contribute to poor job performance?

General Information

____ Participant's stated needs

____ The nature of the participant's work

____ Participant's knowledge

____ Participant's skills

____ Participant's attitudes or abilities

____ Conditions affecting participant involvement

____ Methods desired

____ Observations

____ Questionnaires

____ Print media

____ Interviews

____ Consultations

____ Group discussions

____ Tests

____ CBTs

____ Records, reports

____ Simulations

____ Work samples

Table 1-14. Data summary sheet organizer.

Source	Evidence of Need	Skills Set(s)	Education or Training	Priority
Organization	Satellite offices	Coding	Upgrade coding procedure	High
People	Finance staff in billing office of satellite	Analyzing and critical thinking		
Job	Accounts or billing			

Table 1-15. Simplified job analysis questionnaire.

TASK	HOW FREQUENTLY DO YOU PERFORM THIS TASK?			WHERE DID YOU FIRST LEARN HOW TO PERFORM THIS TASK?				HOW CRITICAL IS THIS TASK TO YOUR JOB?			WHAT IS THE BEST WAY TO LEARN THIS TASK?		
	Never	Sometimes	Often	On the job	School	Training	Other	Very	Somewhat	Not Very	On the job	Training	Other
1 Coding			✓	✓				✓			✓		
2													
3													
4													
5													
6													

After you have surveyed a representative sample of your training audience, summarize their responses on the job-analysis profile, as shown in Table 1-16. You now have a general overview of what is or is not happening among groups of people with the same job title, and this overview can help you determine the need.

Table 1-16. Job analysis profile.

Job Title of Training: ______________________________

Write a 30-minute training module.	Define objectives. Develop a topical outline. Decide on instructional strategies. Produce course materials.
Evaluate a 30-minute training session.	Determine level of education. Include test items in design. Determine methods of data collection, analysis, and reporting.

After breaking down the functional responsibilities into tasks, validate the job and the analysis with an advisory group (subject-matter experts, management representatives, and client contacts) to be sure that the job analysis matches the job. Then ask the advisory group to help select the key functions and tasks that will be the focus of your training.

Step 3c: Present the Findings

There are three ways to present your findings visually: check sheets, line graphs, and Pareto charts.

▸ **Check Sheets.** Check sheets, a sample of which is shown in Figure 1-8, are easy to design and use. They use hash marks to show the frequency of a number of events. Starting with a check sheet allows you to decide what events to record, determine the time period for the ob-

Figure 1-8. Sample check sheet.

DELAY	SEPTEMBER				TOTAL
	3	4	5	6	
Missing information	//	/	///	//	8
Policy changes/questions	𝍸	𝍸 //	////	𝍸 ///	24
Input errors	𝍸 ////	𝍸 𝍸 ///	𝍸 //	𝍸 ////	38
Alerts/routing		/	//	/	4
Individual work habits	//	///	//	///	10
Total	18	25	18	23	84

Source: G. McArdle, *Conducting a Needs Assessment* (Menlo Park, CA: Crisp, 1998), p. 64.

servation (e.g., hours, days, months), and develop the format. Information from check sheets is easily transferable to a frequency graph.

➤ **Line Graphs.** A line graph displays trends in a particular activity over a specific time period to identify changes as soon as they occur, a sample of which is shown in Figure 1-9. By noting the change immediately, you can recommend taking prompt action.

Figure 1-9. Sample line graph.

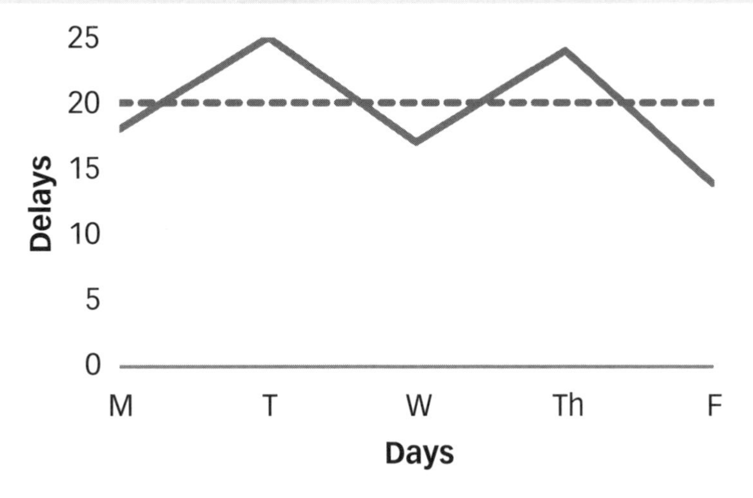

➤ **Pareto Charts.** A Pareto chart, a sample of which is shown in Figure 1-10, is a bar graph that displays the relative importance of different events or needs. The most frequent events or greatest needs (the higher numbers) appear at the end of the chart. The Pareto chart is similar to the check sheet in its ability to identify root causes of problems.

Figure 1-10. Sample Pareto chart.

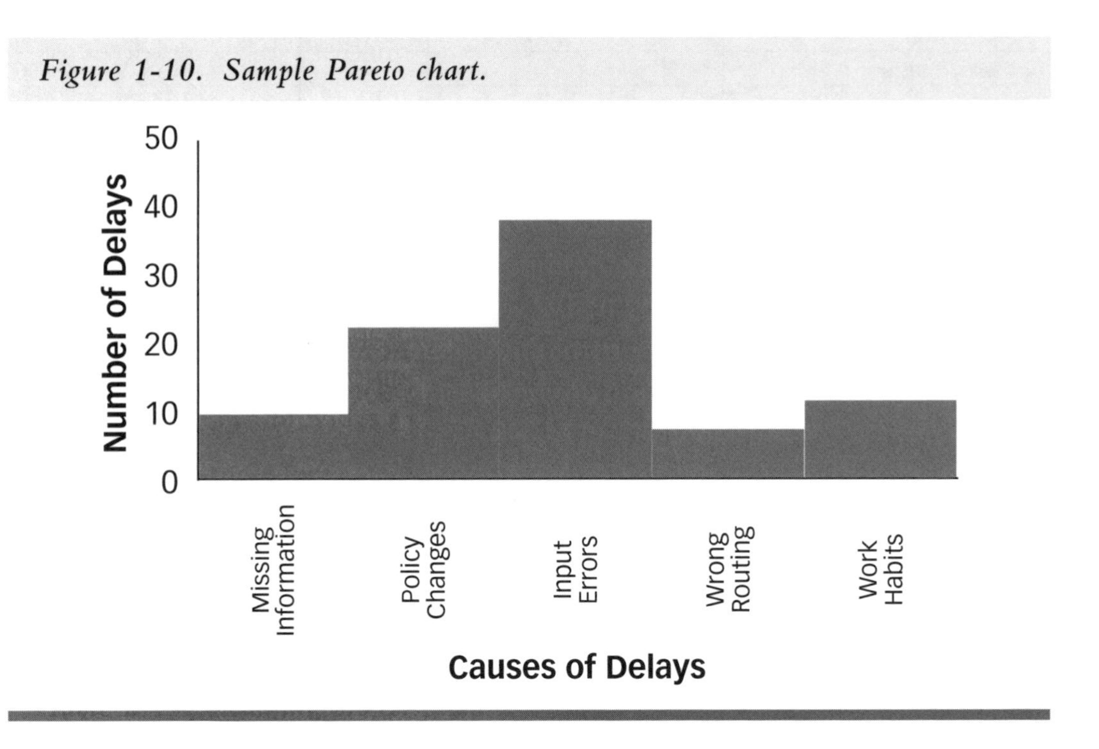

Step 3d: Choose the Trainers

Once the organization has a clear picture of the training priorities, the next step is to decide the best way to meet the identified needs. There are a few routes to make this happen. The organization can design, develop, and deliver the training in-house; it can contract with an outside consultant or vendor to develop the coursework for in-house delivery; it can contract with an outside facility to handle all aspects of the training; or it can purchase a commercially marketed training program and train in-house.

Organizations that don't have a way to train in-house usually look for outside assistance for all but the most basic types of on-the-job training. For organizations that do have internal training staffs, the decision is more complex. Answers to the following questions can help narrow the choice:

- How often will the training be offered?
- How many employees will the training be offered to?
- Does the organization have a content expert with credible delivery skills?
- Will training involve generic skills or a specific technical need?
- What is the trainee job level?
- Will the content of the program involve proprietary or competitive information?

In thinking about the questions, you might consider cost-effectiveness. If training will not be often, using an outside consultant may be most cost-effective. Alternatively, ongoing training needed by many employees may be more cost-effective, if developed and delivered in-house. When training involves technology, equipment, or skills unique to the organization and its jobs, in-house design and delivery may be the only option. For top management, a consultant with a broad range of experience with other companies may enhance the program's credibility.

Support staff and supervisors may be more likely to be onboard with a training program if it is developed and delivered by someone familiar with day-to-day needs. For many types of training, qualified course instructors can be found within the organization. For instance, each executive has expertise in a certain area and most can make time to conduct at least one or two training sessions. Other potential instructors include supervisors and managers, HR personnel (especially those with career counseling or similar experience), and professional employees, particularly ones who have had previous teaching experience.

Also, part- and full-time faculty at area colleges and universities are ideal candidates to recruit as trainers. Depending on the nature of the course, other outside professionals to consider as instructors or guest speakers include consultants, lawyers, psychologists, systems analysts, or efficiency experts. Professional and trade associations, as well as local chambers of commerce, may have the names of experts willing to make presentations.

Step 3e: Design the Training and Course Module

The instructional specifications are your guidelines for content delivery and timing. They are critical components of the module design template. This template organizes all of the necessary training components and serves as a blueprint for development. Once you design your training, you can use this blueprint to evaluate the completed training.

Specifying instructional content is a joint effort between training and subject-matter experts. In this part of the analysis, the trainers and experts will define the critical content of each course module. They will also decide which strategies to use when introducing the content, determining the appropriate learning techniques, providing opportunities for practice, and incorporating the right forms of mediation.

The last stage of Step 3 is to develop a sample training module. This sample module provides a preview of the course content design and treatment. Figure 1-11 shows a 30-minute training module that was designed to teach someone how to record a message on an answering machine. This training module is a result of a training needs assessment.

Figure 1-11. Sample training module.

Module Name: Recording Answering Machine Greeting

Objective

Given an answering machine and a procedures manual, the learner will record a greeting into the machine so that when a call is received the recording plays in the allotted time.

Content

- Parts of an answering machine
- Length of a message
- Components of a message
- Steps to record a message

Instructor/Learner Activities

- Instructor shows overhead visual of answering machine and its parts.
- Instructor presents examples of recorded greetings.
- Learners write their greetings.
- Learners adjust greetings to fit allotted time.
- Instructor demonstrates how to record a greeting.
- Learners record greetings.

Case Study Scenarios

Read the case study scenarios. Outline the steps that you would take to respond to each scenario. Next, use the module design template to develop your training outline of a typical training module.

Case Study 1: The local print shop has just purchased a high-speed copier. The owners of this company want to train employees on how to use the copier. There are 15 people at two locations that need training.

Case Study 2: The local restaurant is going to sell box dinners to patrons at the outdoor theatre during the summer months. The owners of the restaurant want the daily pick-up and delivery of the box dinners to go smoothly, and they want their restaurant staff trained in a process for getting the boxes ready to be collected by the driver. They want a training program that will teach the staff to accomplish this task in the most efficient way possible.

Case Study 3: The CEO of Training System Group likes to bring the management staff from all nine locations to its headquarters at least twice a year for one day of management development and leadership seminars. This CEO believes in providing staff with an opportunity for training and development, and she makes it clear that she wants the upper-level managers to "get a lot" while they are at headquarters.

Module Design Template

Module Name: ______________________________

Objective	Content	Instructor/Learner Activities

Step 4: Report

Reporting your findings allows you to show management and other stakeholders what you have investigated, what needs to be changed, how the proposed changes will be made, and how the change fits.

You should use both a written report and an oral presentation. The written report summarizes your findings from the investigation and analysis, presents your recommendations, and suggests material the training manager should use for each stage of the project. The report should identify performance gaps and what needs to change, how changes will be made, and how the changes fit into the organization's goals. Think of this report as a sales pitch to management. It should state the needs and provide the business justification for using a training program.

You don't have to pick just one presentation method. Communicating the results both verbally and orally usually improves your chances of having management support the proposed program.

Step 4a: Prepare the Training Design Report

Be concise, and use clear language and short sentences when you prepare the training design report. Table 1-17 shows the eight components that constitute the training design report.

Step 4b: Complete the Final Report

The final report identifies performance gaps between the position in question and the function of the position as defined by the job description and job and task analysis. Again, this report is just like a sales presentation to management, in that it outlines the needs and provides the business justification for using a training program to address the needs.

There are eight components that make up this final report, as outlined in Table 1-18.

Table 1-17. Components of training design report.

Purpose	Describe the training need, the training format, and the history of the need in the organization. (This section should be one paragraph.)
Summary of Analyses	Briefly describe your training needs analysis. Clearly define the performance gaps that the proposed training program will address. Describe the audience, the job, the tasks that make up that job, and the key performance elements needed to fulfill the job requirements. (An extensive description is necessary because the performance gap is probably located in a task, in a performance element of the task, or in a lack of knowledge needed to perform the task.)
Scope	Establish the format for the course, and present an overview of the materials the trainer will use, the content (topics and subtopics) to be covered, and the instructional strategies to deliver the course.
Learning Objectives	Describe what the learner is to exhibit once the training is completed. Include three parts: *performance condition* (tools that the learner needs to accomplish the task), *performance statement* (action verb), and *performance criteria* (quality, quantity, time, or standard to be met). (The learning objective will guide the course material and the learning activities to ensure participants succeed.)
Test Item Strategy	Imagine a mirror image of the learning objective. Change the learning-objective verb to the past tense.[1] (This section describes how the learner will demonstrate mastery of the topic. It explains how and why you will conduct the test and what happens after the testing. For example, if the participants fail a test item, you should decide whether the test item should be rewritten or whether the training materials are a problem.)
Course and Module Design	Establish a blueprint (training outline), and include course and module title, learning objectives, content, and instructor/learner activities that are designed to teach the stated learning objectives.
Delivery Strategy	Describe the instructional methods, the length of the course, and the training format, timing, and location.
Evaluation and Measurement Tools	Explain how you are going to measure the learners' reactions to the training, their degree of learning (the results of the test items), and the learners' behavior (how the concepts mastered in the training will be translated back on the job).

Table 1-18. Components of the final report.

Executive Summary	Answer the question, "If readers are too busy to look at the entire report, what's the least amount of information they need to make an informed decision about supporting the proposed training?" (This section should be short. One page is ideal, and it should be no more than two pages.)
Training Needs Analysis Objective	Explain in detail the objectives of the training needs analysis, and answer the question, "What information did the training needs analysis hope to learn?"[1]
Brief Summary of Findings	Discuss optimal performance (what the organization hopes to achieve), actual performance (the organization's current level of performance), and how to bridge the gap between the two.
Proposed Change or Training Project	Explain the expected commitment required for this project, and answer the following questions, "How long before we see results?" "Who will be involved?" "How will the program be implemented?" "What resources are needed for the program to succeed?"
Data-Collection Method	Explain why the data are collected and the process used to analyze the information.
Expanded Discussion of Findings	Discuss the study results in detail. Use descriptive terms in your narrative and simple graphics or tables.
Recommendations for Future Action	Present specific recommendations, including at least the knowledge, skills, and attitude required for a particular position; a training strategy (what a training might look like—a module design in graphic form); and other problems you uncovered that management should resolve before proceeding.
Appendix	Include relevant supporting data, such as sample surveys and other data-collection methods, detailed analysis of the results, a cost breakdown, and a time line of the proposed change.

Step 4c: Make the Oral Presentation

When presenting your findings orally, it is critical that you know your audience. As much as possible, learn about their values, attitudes, needs, and work culture. The presentation should focus on answering the question, "What's in it for me?" from their perspective.

When making a presentation, it is a good idea to have visual aids. Below are a few tips about using PowerPoint slides and computer graphics for framing content:

- Limit the words per frame to seven words across and seven words down.
- Use pleasing and easy-to-see colors (e.g., use blue as a foreground or background and don't use yellow, which fades, or red, which is difficult to read).
- Use bulleted lists.
- Use readable graphics.
- Keep charts and graphs simple.

Remember, the oral presentation reinforces the material provided in the written reports. Even if you prepare the "perfect" presentation, it may not be accepted immediately. You may face opposition for any number of reasons. Or, perhaps the opposing staff member does not see the value in the proposed change.

The best way to overcome this situation is to diffuse it before it emerges. Be prepared for any objections that may come up by reviewing your proposal with a critical eye to identify soft spots ahead of time. Add some facts or responses to possible objections in the body of your presentation. That way the question never gets asked because you have already provided the answer.

How Do You Get Top Management Support?

To develop a training program or to introduce a comprehensive organizational change process, you will need management support. Management support is not just a memo or a speech; it's a philosophy. You know when you have it when you see consistent words and actions that reflect a strong personal commitment to support the individuals and the learning. In particular, you will know that management is serious about the training when you see them:

- Take an interest in thoughtfully completing, on time, performance appraisals that include individual training plans.
- Think about cross-training and identify and develop position backups.
- Endorse staff participation in seminars, university courses, in-house workshops, and other development activities.
- Promote staff participation in transfers, task forces, special projects, and on-loan assignments.

When creating your final presentation, consider integrating one or all of the following six points, which promote the audience's thinking of the many uses of your proposed training:

1. Promote the thinking that training and development are an integral part of the business enterprise and its operation. Obtain a copy of the organization's strategic plan. Review the plan for opportunities that might call for training or development. Meet with key managers, and find out their plans. Determine where the company will need training support, and begin with high-priority and high-impact work. Look for new technology, organizational changes, new product lines, and new organizational direction.

2. Learn the business. You've simply got to know what you are talking about. Do you know what the organization's earnings per share were last year? Do you know the net profit? Do you know the contribution of the major division? Get to know the financial people so you can be comfortable with financial objectives, return-on-investment (ROI) and sales figures, debt equity, and cash flow. Then, go back to those strategic plans to make sure you understand the "what" and "how" of the new business venture or organizational direction.

3. Develop programs and activities that line managers can get involved in. Start with departmental managers; you can worry about staff departments later. Use your study of the strategic plans and operating reports and your discussions with managers as a starting point. In your presentation of needs, you can and should give managers the guidance to recognize what training is necessary. Be sure that what you do reflects what the managers really want and need.

4. Involve top management. Ask them which needs are most important. After you've completed the survey at all levels of the organization, develop a master plan covering those levels or general types of training. Your plan should encompass all activities either in place or to be developed. Obtain top management's agreement, and get them involved in the training and development process by offering them an opportunity to train.

5. Develop practical how-to programs that give people tools they can use on the job immediately. Stay clear of fads. It's probably best to tackle these hot topics after job training is completed.

6. Get a handle on ROI. Becoming involved in ROI includes identifying existing programs or activities that have a direct measurable effect on performance. Design evaluations of these trainings, and carry them out. Use before-and-after results to compare groups and measure the effect of training and if savings occurred as a result of the training. Once you have accumulated some meaningful statistics, publish the results to illustrate a positive training effect.

These six steps are not easy to implement. They take time and a well-developed plan to establish and monitor the actions. However, following them is certainly possible, and the rewards are worth the investment. Organizational alignment and productive people in the right jobs are only a few of the outcomes.

Chapter Summary

Sometimes the opportunity to assess training needs is limited, or there is a lack of available data. Gathering information about the training need and the actual or potential participant need or expectation is the first step. Below is a list of information to gather each time you conduct an assessment; this will help define the training outcome and promote meaningful learning strategies:

- Nature of the role and tasks performed
- Skills needed for the role or task
- Number of participants
- How familiar the participants are with the subject
- Attitudes and beliefs about the topic
- Successes or problems participants have encountered
- The competence level of the participants
- How well do the participants know one another
- Whether the training is mandatory
- Expectations of management about the training

You can avoid misunderstandings of the expectations by assessing them before the beginning of the training because:

- It helps to determine the training content.
- It allows you to obtain case study material.
- It permits you to develop a dialogue early with the participants.

After your training program is completed, it's important to continually add data and information to the files that you started in Step 1. That way, you'll be prepared whenever a future training or performance issue comes up. By keeping an up-to-date master file system, with related data about your company and your industry, whenever a training or performance possibility arises, you will have the background information and a clear idea of how the issues have evolved.

Analysis is the most critical element when creating your training program. For a successful training program, ensure that you do the following:

- Include the six training design success strategies—management commitment, stated outcome for the training, training need/outcome questions that guided your analysis, identified factors that influenced the process both positive and negative, types of training, and performance standards and criteria.
- Identify the trainees' needs.
- Follow the four-step needs-analysis process: surveillance (scan the organization to determine if there is a need or performance gap); investigation (determine the type of data you need to guide your decision about the training and determine the data collection method); analysis (obtain a clear picture of the problem, the evidence, and the data sources to help determine type of problem and determine the best source for training—in-house personnel, hiring consultants, or purchasing a complete package); and reporting (present your findings to management).
- Consider time, need, and timeliness for addressing the identified training need.

In the next chapter, you will begin to write your instructional materials and learning activities by looking at the steps to design a training program and by discussing learning theory.

CHAPTER TWO

Design the Learning to Fit the Need

In this development step of the design and delivery model, you will begin to write your instructional materials and learning activities. Though the mechanics of project design are essential for a good program, they are based on an understanding of instructional systems. Therefore, the chapter has two parts: the first part gives you the specific steps to follow in designing the training program; the second part offers a general discussion of learning theory.

Beginning Your Program Design

The choice of appropriate instructional materials and methods is, at best, a guess if you have not been able to conduct a formal training needs assessment. One way to avoid mismatching an instructional method with a particular audience is to be sensitive to an organization's demographics and preferences.

In all cases, the word that guides your choice is *appropriate* use of instructional technologies. The instructional technology you use should be appropriate for the audience, the content, the organizational environment, and, most of all, the proposed learning objectives and methods. These preferences provide you with:

- A design template to assist in developing the content for your program material
- A checklist for making decisions about the learning activities

The output of the development stage is a training that is ready to be implemented. Figure 2-1 shows a sample lesson plan.

The development process consists of the following five phases:

Phase One: Develop the following:

- Training content
- Graphics
- Media needs
- Lesson plans
- Instructor guides
- Evaluation needs
- Software needs

Phase Two: Revise all items in Phase One.

Phase Three: Complete the following.

- Conduct the test.
- Revise the program on the basis of the test.
- Schedule a second test, if needed.

Figure 2-1. Sample lesson plan.

TITLE:	How to use the bundling machine
WRITTEN BY:	Author's Note DATE: Date Written
OBJECTIVES:	At the end of this session, the participants will be able to
	1. State one reason for using the bundling machine
	2. Demonstrate the correct use of the bundling machine located in the workshop
	3. State when the bundling machine is used
SESSION TIME:	15 minutes
NUMBER OF PARTICIPANTS:	6 (up to 10)
ENTRY LEVEL:	New employees
AIDS/EQUIPMENT:	Sample bundling machine
	6 bundling cards for each participant
	Whiteboard and markers
POTENTIAL FAULTS:	Session not to be conducted at start or finish time of workshop
METHOD:	Show and tell

Phase Four: Conduct the following.

- Pilot-test a prototype program.
- Evaluate the pilot test.
- Identify the required revisions.

- Revise the program as required (on the basis of the pilot test).
- Schedule another test, if needed.

Phase Five: Follow-through on the following.

- Finalize the training program content.
- Produce the training program in final form.

During the development phase, you will select, write, or otherwise obtain all training documentation and evaluation materials. These may include the following:

- Training materials
- Instructor guide (including lesson plans and a list of required supporting materials)
- Learners' guide or workbook
- Nonprint media (computer software, audiotapes and videotapes, equipment checklists)
- Program evaluation materials
- Procedures for evaluation
- Supervisors' form for evaluation of course participants' post-training job performance
- Training documentation
- Class attendance forms and other records for participants
- Course documentation (written objectives, authorship and responsibility for course material, lists of instructors and facilitators, and their qualifications)

What is meant by instruction and instructional methods? The purpose of any training is to promote learning. Instruction promotes learning through a set of developed activities that initiate, activate, and support learning. Use instructional methods to:

- Motivate learners
- Help learners prepare for learning
- Enable learners to apply and practice learning
- Assist learners to retain and transfer what they have learned
- Integrate your own performance with other skills and knowledge

The appropriate method to use depends on a variety of factors, including the following:

- Type of learning (verbal information, intellectual skills, cognitive strategy, attitude, or motor skill)
- Audience
- Demographics or profile (age, gender, level of education)
- Learning styles (kinesthetic-tactile, visual, auditory)
- Number of learners (individual, small groups, large groups)
- Media (selected by appropriateness, number of learners, and financial considerations)
- Budget (funds available for development and presentation)
- Instructor's skills and training style

Each factor influences the choice of method for presenting, reinforcing, and assessing retention of the material. A model depicting the relationships among these factors is shown in Figure 2-2.

Organizational Needs and Learning Possibilities

Everyone has an interpretation of what training success means. Also, there are so many variables to consider when you try to evaluate success. For example, the learners may see a particular course as a success because the training was fun and they learned a lot that clarified what they do on the job. Yet, suppose an immediate transfer of information to the job

Figure 2-2. Factors influencing instructional strategy.

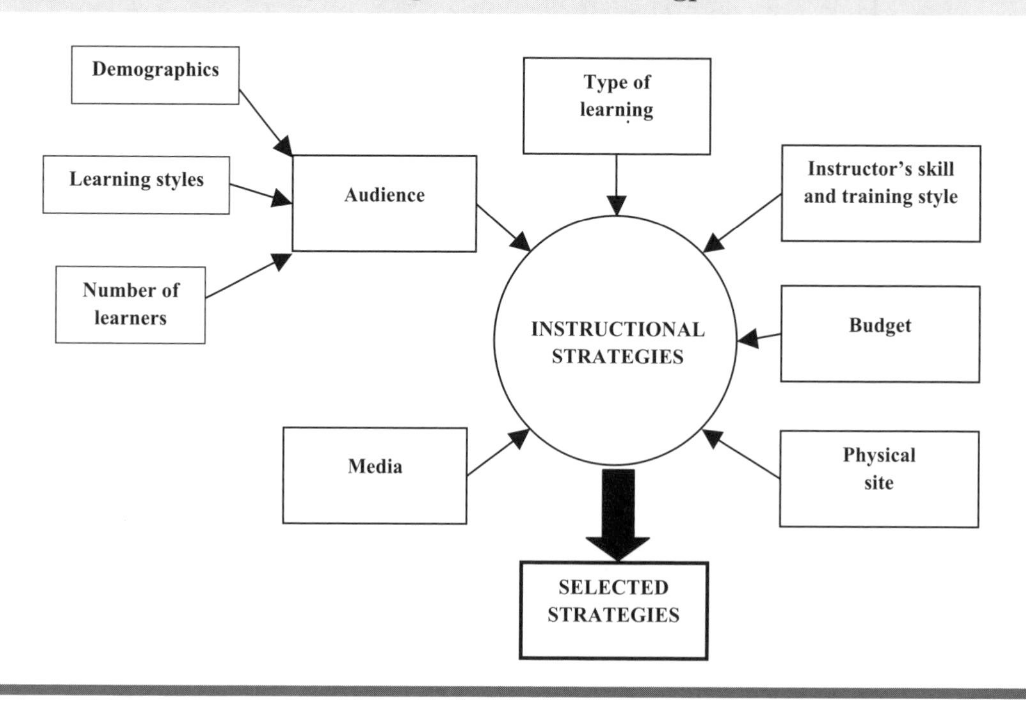

does not happen because the learners do not have to execute the task immediately. Does that mean that no training transfer occurred? No, what this brief scenario shows is that results deemed successful depend on the level of evaluation that the training designer has created for the program; for example, suppose the level of evaluation was to test whether the reaction to training is favorable, as shown in level 1 of Table 2-1. Planning your level of evaluation at the same time as you design your course and your instructional strategies is a success factor for your training.

As Table 2-1 shows, each level of the training model measures a different aspect of the training and affects a different level of the organization. As a trainer or course designer, you can manage to ensure success only at level 1 (Reaction) or level 2 (Learning). To measure success at

Table 2-1. Stages of successful transfer of learning back to the job.

Level	Evaluation	Description
1	Reaction	How did the learner react to the training?
2	Learning	How well did the learner apply the new skills or knowledge?
3	Training Transfer	What changes in job behavior resulted from the training?
4	Organizational Impact	What were the results of the training on the organization's bottom line?

level 3 (Training Transfer), you have to rely on feedback from the learners' supervisors/managers or the employees.

Each level of the Kirkpatrick model evaluates a different aspect of the training; therefore, the question that you must ask yourself when conducting the training is, "Was the training successful, and what level of training transfer am I evaluating?"

Principles of Learning

It's important to be familiar with the following principles of learning when you are deciding on the training methods to use. (The second part of this chapter gives a more detailed survey of learning theory, but for these purposes you need to know what the ten principles of learning are.)

➤ **Part-Learning or Whole-Learning Segments.** Part learning is more common than whole learning because trainees prefer to deal with a series of separate assignments. In part learning, the skill or knowledge is divided into parts or segments; in whole learning, the skill or knowledge is viewed as a large, unified block of material. When dividing material into segments, the trainer should follow two guidelines:

1. The segments should not be too large. Although the subject matter is familiar to you, the material will be new to the learners. Therefore, review the skill or knowledge from the learners' perspective, and then organize it into segments for training.
2. The segments should follow a logical sequence so that the learners can relate each part to the next. A logical flow of new material will enhance learners' ability to later recall new skills or information. Proceed from the known to the unknown, moving from one segment to the next after you know, by the learners' behavior, that the learners have understood and accepted the information. (Caution: Do not oversimplify. After separating the material into segments and developing a logical sequence, check to make sure the segments are not so small as to be boring.)

As an example of whole learning, consider teaching someone to ride a bicycle. This training could be divided into three parts: balancing, steering, and pedaling. But learning each part independently would be difficult because steering depends on balancing and on how hard the pedals are pushed, while balancing depends on steering and pedaling. Teaching someone to ride a bicycle requires whole learning. Whole learning is fairly uncommon, however; more training models are based on part learning.

► **Spaced Learning**. Spaced learning is learning over an extended period of time, in contrast to crammed learning, which is learning a lot of information in a short amount of time. Spaced learning is superior to crammed learning, particularly if learners are to undergo training for a long time. Spaced learning has its basis in what we know about the incubation of knowledge and thought. That is, the brain needs time to assimilate new facts before it can accept the next group of new facts. Spaced learning creates opportunities for regular review and revision of what has been learned, which also slows the rate at which learners forget new material.

➤ **Active Learning.** Actively involving learners in the training, rather than having them listen passively, encourages them to become self-motivated. Active learning is more effective than passive learning, and it is often described as "learning by doing." Provide learners with plenty of opportunities to practice the skills they learn and think about the information they are absorbing.

➤ **Feedback.** The feedback principle of learning has two aspects: constructive feedback to learners on their progress, and performance feedback to instructors on their effectiveness.

Feedback to learners can vary in complexity from simply explaining why an answer to a question is correct or incorrect, to commenting on learners' performance during an activity, to discussing the results of a test. Regardless of the complexity of the feedback, the best feedback is that which is given earliest. The more immediate the feedback, the greater its value, especially for preventing loss of self-confidence and, thus, loss of motivation.

Feedback given to trainers should answer the following questions:

- Are learners receiving and understanding the information? (Test them.)
- Do learners have doubts or questions? (Ask them.)
- Are learners paying attention? (Observe them.)
- Is the session boring? (Observe them.)
- Would learners benefit by using more techniques during this session? (Ask them.)

Two-way communication is critical for feedback's effectiveness.

➤ **Overlearning.** Overlearning means learning until the learners have near perfect recall, and then learning the material just a bit more, perhaps through practice. Overlearning decreases the rate of forgetting. In other words, forgetting is significantly reduced by frequency recall or by repeated use of the material. Two important facts to remember in this instance are as follows: (1) Repetition by trainers does not maximize retention; whereas (2) active involvement by trainers does maximize retention.

➤ **Reinforcement.** Positive reinforcement can improve learning because learning that is rewarded is much more likely to be retained. A simple, "Yes, that's right," can mean a great deal to a learner and can enhance retention considerably. Positive reinforcement confirms the value of responding and participating and encourages active learning. In contrast, negative reinforcement simply tells learners that their responses were wrong, without providing guidance for making correct responses. Negative reinforcement often discourages learners from further investigation.

➤ **Primacy and Recency.** When learners are presented a sequence of information, they tend to remember what they have heard first and what they have heard last, but they often forget what they have heard in the middle. To guard against this, emphasize and reinforce facts that are in the middle or else present the critical information at the beginning or end of the session.

➤ **Meaningful Material.** Unconsciously, learners ask two questions when they are presented with new information: (1) Is this information valid relative to my own experiences? and (2) Will this information be useful in the immediate future?

The first question emphasizes the notion of movement from the known to the unknown, as well as the fact that people tend to remember material that relates to what they already know. In designing your training, make sure to assess learners' current level of knowledge.

The second question emphasizes the fact that the learners want to know that what they are about to learn will be useful to them in the near future. Meaningful material links the past and the future and promotes two beneficial effects:

1. Security (when learners move from the known to the unknown)
2. Motivation (information will be useful in the near future)

➤ **Multiple-Sense Learning.** Research suggests that people will obtain approximately 80 percent of the information they absorb through sight, 11 percent through hearing, and 9 percent through the other senses combined. Therefore, to absorb as much as possible, trainers should design the sessions to use two or more of the senses.

Employing sight and hearing in the training is a straightforward task, but designing sessions to use the other senses, such as touch, might be just as crucial for successful learning. For most learning, however, sight is the means for providing the most information, so trainers should emphasize visual aids when designing their sessions.

➤ **Transfer of Learning.** The amount of knowledge and skills that learners transfer from the training room to the workplace depends mainly on two variables:

1. The degree of similarity between what they have learned in the training (including how it was presented) and what occurs in the workplace (e.g., can learners apply their new knowledge and skills directly to the job without modifying them?)
2. The degree to which learners can integrate the skills and knowledge gained in the training into their work environment (e.g., does the system at work or the supervisor allow or encourage use of the new skills?)

Be sure to consider these variables as you plan your training. Make three-by-five cards that define the lesson and the outcome objective. These cards then become tools that learners can take with them to use as references back on the job. Develop a checklist of the learning outcomes for the training, and then have learners check off each as they perform the task when they are back on the job. Also, either provide each learner with a journal to record progress after the training, or check with the learners approximately one month after the training to get feedback on the training transfer.

Learning Preferences

Motivated people learn. As you develop your training, assume that the audience is more likely to participate when the setting is conducive to interaction between the trainer and the learners. A learning environment that is relaxed but structured—with an agenda, stated learning objectives, established time frames, and defined tasks—is one in which learners will willingly participate and, therefore, one in which the learning will be successful.

There is a relationship between learners' demographics and their preferences for particular instructional methods. If you match the audience's learning preferences to your approach, your design will achieve increased attention and motivation, increased mastery, more successful transfer of information and skills, and enhanced retention and recall.

In most cases, you can collect information about the potential learners during your analysis and design process. The basic audience information you need to know is:

- Age (usually a range)
- Gender
- Occupation (current as well as previous on occasion)

- Race or ethnic group (known only occasionally, owing to Equal Employment Opportunity Commission restrictions)
- Years of work experience (usually a range)

The demographics alone do not reveal the learners' learning preferences, although this is a good starting place. In general, people like group discussions the most, followed by case studies, games, and skill practice. Lectures and telecommunication methods are least liked. Films, intrapersonal and interpersonal training, self-instruction, and computer-based instruction fall in the middle of the preference continuum.

By determining the preferred instructional method for the group you will work with, you are better able to develop and deliver training that appeals to their interests and motivation. Remember that today's learners want to be excited about the learning event, have fun, learn new things that can be transferred to the job, and not feel bored. By keeping in mind the various trainer styles, learning preferences, and learning environments, you will be able to meet learner expectations.

Course and Module Design

Course design and module design are linked to course development through a series of documents that include the problem analysis, job analysis, and audience profile sheet. From these documents you create your course outline and content map.

The blueprint you create should list the proposed learning objectives. Supportive information about the content is then linked to each learning objective. Training and content experts generally select the instructional content together. They define the course modules and describe how the instructional strategies will be used to introduce the content. In addition, they determine the appropriate learning techniques, develop opportunities for practice, and select the appropriate media. Remember, the media chosen should have a definite purpose—to amplify the learning event, not to entertain a bored audience.

The instructional specifications include the following:

- Module title
- Introduction (content summary, utility, importance)
- Sequence of topics and activities (flow, transitions, links)

Each lesson relates to a specific task in the task analysis. The purpose of a lesson is to provide the content and practice that allow the learners to perform the tasks at the end of the training.

The Learning Objective

A learning objective is a statement that tells what learners should be able to do when they have completed a segment of instruction. Learning is a cognitive process that leads to a capability that the learners did not possess prior to the instruction. To write learning objectives that are clear, specific, and focused on the learning outcome, begin with this suggested phrase: "At the end of this [course/module], you will be able to." This opening will help keep the statement outcome-oriented and measurable.

The Three Components of the Learning Objective

There are three components to a statement of learning objectives, as shown in Table 2-2, and these components are essential for each learning objective: (1) a statement of condition (resources needed); (2) a statement of performance (action desired); and (3) a statement of criteria (standards to be met). Each of these components, when rephrased as a question, reflects an action or behavioral intent.

Table 2-2. Three components of a learning objective.

Component	Definition	Example
Performance Condition	Describes the conditions under which the learner will be completing the activity.	"Given 10 lenses of unknown quality, a magnifying glass, and the lens defect detection tool . . ."
Performance Statement	Describes the observable action that the learner will complete.	"The learner will inspect the lenses for defects and separate acceptable lenses from unacceptable lenses . . ."
Performance Criterion	Describes the standard necessary to achieve in order to successfully complete the activity.	"With no more than two errors."

- **Condition.** Under what conditions do you want the learner to be able to perform the action? A learning objective always states the important conditions, if any, under which performance is to occur. This entails the resources that the learner needs to perform the learned task.
- **Performance.** What should the learner be able to do? A learning objective always states what a learner is expected to do as a result of the training. The performance statement is the action desired.
- **Criterion.** How well must the learner perform? Whenever possible, a learning objective describes how well the learner must perform the new task to be considered acceptable. Thus, all objectives must be specific, measurable, and observable.

A learning objective is a statement that describes what the learner will be able to do at the end of the training.

Usually, the statement of a learning objective begins with the performance condition, followed by the performance statement, and then the performance criterion. For example:

- Given 10 overdue credit scenarios and the credit agreements for each, the learner will calculate the interest to be paid by each, with no errors.
- Given three customer scenarios and the guidelines for overcoming customer objections, the learner will role-play overcoming customer objections according to guidelines given by the course instructor.

Use Table 2-3 to practice how to identify performance conditions and learning objectives.

Table 2-4 presents these three components of the learning objective, with questions to ask yourself and guidelines for creating the learning objective statement.

Table 2-3. Learning objectives quiz.

For each learning objective given below, circle the performance condition and mark "PC." Then circle and mark ("PS") the performance statement. And then circle and mark ("PCR") the performance criterion.

1. Given the guidelines for effective problem solving and three case studies containing performance problems, analyze the situations and write three alternative solutions for each according to the guidelines.
2. Given repair tools, maintenance procedures, and a broken laser printer, repair the printer until the printouts are aligned properly, in focus, and in two colors.
3. Given the company's mission statement, its guidelines for effective customer service, and five videotaped situations, view the video and respond to the customer according to the company's standards for customer service.
4. Given the guidelines for menu building around dietary requirements, plan a week of menus for the following patients on special diets.

Learning objectives are important because they provide learners with expectations of what they will accomplish during a course and how their learning will be measured. Learning objectives also provide course outcomes for the instructor and the learners' management. Robert Mager established the need and format for writing learning objectives in his book *Preparing Instructional Objectives.* There, he makes clear the purpose, methodology, and benefits of completing this critical component of the design phase.

Table 2-4. Guidelines for writing learning objectives.

Component	Question to Ask Yourself	Guidelines
Performance Condition	"What resources or tools does the learner need to use to perform the task?"	• Try to match job condition as closely as possible. • Include all resources needed because this becomes a checklist for the resources you will develop or gather for the training. • Include job aids, hardware, software, and checklists.
Performance Statement	"What should the learner be able to do at the end of the training?"	• Use action verbs that reflect observable behavior—e.g., *operate, calculate, fill, enter, restate.* • Avoid ambiguous verbs—e.g., *know how to, understand, feel*.
Performance Criteria	"What level of proficiency is required during performance?"	Criteria can include: • quality • quantity • accuracy • speed • ability to meet specific guidelines

The Levels of Learning Execution

Training generally attempts to meet two types of educational goals: knowledge and application. When you write a learning objective, keep in mind that there are six levels of execution, as shown in Table 2-5. For example, your training may present a new policy (knowledge) or procedure (comprehension) that learners must know how to use (application) to review a claim (analysis).

Review Table 2-5 to choose an appropriate verb for the objective statement you intend; for example, for the Knowledge level, choose a verb such as *identify*. Table 2-5 also lists verbs to avoid, like *understand* or *know,* because they describe a learner's internal state, which cannot be observed. The learning objective should always be a well-defined behavioral outcome statement.

Table 2-5. Levels of learning objectives and their corresponding vocabulary.

Level of Execution	Verbs to Use	Verbs to Avoid
Knowledge	Write, define, repeat, name, list, identify	Know, learn
Comprehension	Relate, discuss, describe, explain, review, translate, locate	Understand, appreciate
Application	Operate, illustrate, use, employ	Apply knowledge of, show
Analysis	Differentiate between, calculate, appraise, compare, contrast, solve, critique	Analyze, think
Synthesis	Compose, propose, design, collect, manage, construct, organize, prepare	Be creative, bring together
Evaluation	Evaluate, rate, select, estimate, measure	Show good judgment of, consider

Once the objective is defined, it serves as the blueprint for designing the course and modules, as well as the supporting facilitator and participant manuals.

Validating the Learning Objectives

Once the learning objective is stated, you can use the following questions to validate that objective, making sure that the statement is clearly written, doable, and measurable:

1. Who is to perform the task?
2. What type of learning is involved?
3. What is the terminal behavior?
4. Under what conditions will the task be demonstrated?

For each objective, there should be documentation elaborating the following:

- Special teaching points
- Instructional methods to be used
- Media requirements
- Testing requirements

The Course Outline

The training sequence is best developed in a logical order. The usual sequence is to use step-by-step, or simple-to-complex, or to give an overview of the training concepts and then drill down to each element. When it's appropriate for learners to know how a complex system or process works before you present the details, provide an overview so that the learners can create a mental model of the topic being presented before approaching its component concepts.

Once you decide on a design strategy, the first step is to make general decisions about the training methods. One simple way to choose an instructional method is to ask whether the course will include on-the-job training, classroom instruction, lab or workshop instruction, or self-instruction. Likewise, ask whether the course will use textbooks, consumable workbooks, computers, or interactive CDs or DVDs. The instructional method that you select must match the stated learning objectives for the course. For example, the strategies for a course to help learners master a computer skill should not rely heavily on pencil-and-paper activities.

Support requirements include materials, equipment, and administrative support, such as computers, chart paper, and wall charts. It is critical to identify the support requirements to ensure that they will be available when you need them. When you have the learning objectives well stated and your media requirements itemized, you can estimate the support resources you'll need and the number of days for the training by using the checklist in Table 2-6. The list identifies some typical items necessary for running a training program. Itemized lists like this can help you ensure that all of the support personnel and materials have been arranged for the programs.

The second step in developing your instructional map of the training is to design content test items to be used during the training as a way of checking on the learning process. Well-written learning objectives will specify that the learner demonstrate observable and measurable actions. The criterion test is another part of the blueprint that will help you develop the course. A criterion test allows you to translate the test score into a statement describing the behavior to be expected of a person with that score or his or her relationship to the specified subject matter. Most tests given by schoolteachers are criterion tests. The objective is simply to see whether or not the student has learned the material. Criterion-referenced assessments can be contrasted with norm-referenced assessments.

If the course is long enough to warrant intermediate mastery tests, you should specify the behaviors to be measured at each checkpoint, along with determining the format of the test. Place whatever format

Table 2-6. Support requirements checklist.

Item	Date Required	Date Ordered	Cost
Travel and lodging costs			
Travel and lodging arrangements			
Consultant fee			
Reproductions (notebooks, CDs, job aids)			
Documentation production schedule			
Materials (e.g., tabs, binders)			
Binders			
Gifts, prizes, mementos			
Temporary personnel			
Facility availability			
Equipment availability			
Media arrangements			
Evaluation forms			
Instructor scheduling			
Instructor training			
Software costs			
Software reproduction			
Software distribution			
Legal review			

you select for the blueprint in a reference binder for subsequent use by the following people:

- Course developer and suppliers in specialized media
- Instructor or facilitator to get an overview of the content of the course
- Training department staff to counsel employees on which course to add to their professional/career development plan
- Managers to determine if a course contains specific material

Test Items

Many times we think that, once the learning objectives are written, we can go right ahead and develop the training materials. Not so fast! There is one vital element that most instructional designers skip, yet it is a key factor in the process, and it's best done after creating the learning-objective statement. This next vital step is to create the test items that will ensure that the objective performance is the same as the performance to be assessed.

A *test item* is a test or assessment activity used to determine whether the training has been successful.

Well-designed test items are important because they indicate whether the learning objective has been reached. Think about the test item as a mirror image of the learning objective. The only difference is the verb: the learning objective is expressed in the future tense, while the test item is expressed in the present tense. So, write test items that correspond to the following learning objectives:

- Use the same resources and tools as stated in the condition component of the learning objective.
- Get the learner to complete the action stated in the performance component of the learning objective.
- Measure success as stated in the criterion component of the learning objective.

Here is an example of a test item that fits the learning objective:

OBJECTIVE: Given 10 lenses of unknown quality, a magnifying glass, and the lens defect-detection tool, the learner inspects the lenses for defects and separates acceptable lenses from unacceptable lenses, with no more than two errors.

TEST ITEM: Here are 10 lenses from molding machine number 4. Use your magnifying glass and the corporate lens-defect reference card to pick out the defective lenses. Put all acceptable lenses in pile A. Return defective lenses to Operations. You may not have more than two mistakes. In this case, the test item accurately measures the objective.

Here is an example of a test item that does not fit the learning objective:

OBJECTIVE: Given skills practice (role-plays) that deal with customer objections and guidelines for overcoming objections, the learner role-plays overcoming customer objections with the course instructor until the objections are taken care of according to class guidelines and the instructor's requirements.

TEST ITEM: In your participant packet, there are three skills practice (role-play) situations whereby you must close the sale with the customer. While your instructor plays the role of the customer, you assume the role of the salesperson and close the sale according to the guidelines and the instructor's feedback.

(Note: This test item doesn't measure whether the trainee has learned to overcome objections because the test item asks the trainee to close the sale.)

The Course Map and Structure

Having completed the task analysis, written the objectives, and designed the test items, you now have a good idea of what is going to be included in the training. The next step is to outline the information you plan to present and develop the course map. It is critical to keep your audience and the purpose of the course in mind. The course map, a sample of which is shown in Figure 2-3, lists in hierarchical order the modules within the units. Some trainers describe the hierarchy as modules within chapters or as units within lessons within modules. The terminology is not important.

The course map is paired with your media selections and support requirements, as shown below the course map in Figure 2-3. You should think about these resources as you design your course map and ensure that the design is consistent with the following:

- Course objectives
- Class size
- Training site
- Pre- and post-coursework

It is important to consider the big picture when you develop a course, especially keeping in mind the reasons for the course, as you develop a course sequence. Here are some guidelines for sequencing the course:

- Focus on what happens on the job.
- Use the job analysis to establish the sequence of chapters.
- Arrange the course from general to specific or simple to complex.

Figure 2-3. Sample course map.

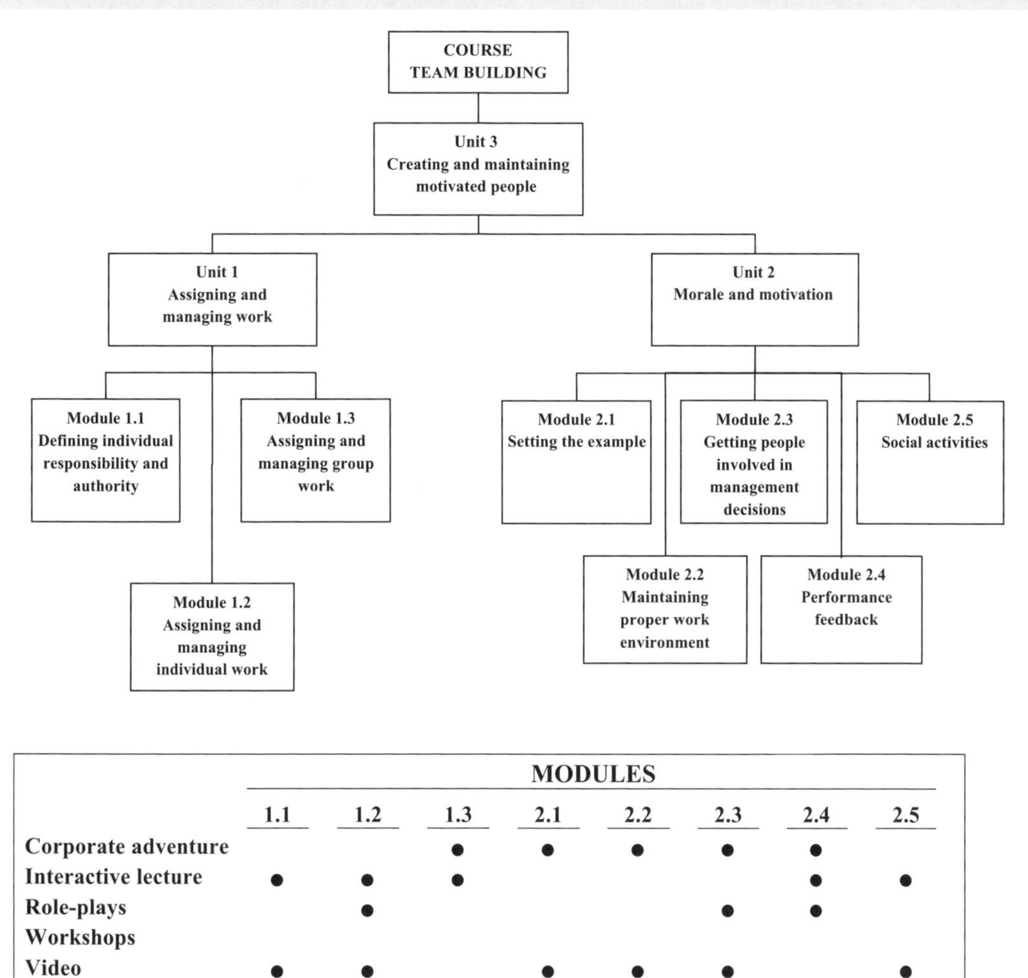

	MODULES							
	1.1	1.2	1.3	2.1	2.2	2.3	2.4	2.5
Corporate adventure			●	●	●	●	●	
Interactive lecture	●	●	●				●	●
Role-plays		●				●	●	
Workshops								
Video	●	●		●	●	●		●

- When there is no job-related basis for sequencing, arrange the course in the most logical fashion for the learner.
- If a performance model is available, use it as a guide for sequencing the content.

- Use the same training advisory group to test the content sequence as you did to validate other areas of your analysis and design process.

You have the objective statement and the test item, so you are ready to structure your training. Structuring your program is easy because it is just a matter of listing your course topics and subtopics and organizing the methods and activities. But let's begin with the lowest level of the course map: the lesson.

Lessons, to Modules, to Units

Designing and developing a training program is just like any other project you take on, and success comes with careful planning and preparation. You've come to the most crucial part of the design: structuring the series of lessons. In this top-down format, the lesson is the microcosm of information about the task and knowledge to be learned. It has a specific format and specific criteria.

Why start with the lesson? Because adult learners respond best to small, organized components of learning. Lessons become the building blocks of modules, which then become the building blocks of units. No matter what delivery method or medium you use, the lesson is your foundation.

> A lesson is the smallest unit of learning. It provides content and practice based on the learning objective.

What is the purpose of a lesson? Because each lesson relates to a specific task listed in the task analysis, the lesson provides the content and practice to allow the learner to perform that task at the end of the training.

Guidelines for Constructing Lessons

You can easily convert your task-analysis information into topical lessons. Table 2-7 shows the lesson structure as 10 percent introduction, 70 percent body of information, and 20 percent conclusion.

In addition to the *content* in a lesson, *learning methods* ensure that learners meet the learning objectives. You can use a variety of learning methods to stimulate learning and make training a learner-centered event. Ask yourself, "What is the purpose of this training, and how would I like to learn the topic, if I were the learner?" When you put yourself in the learner's shoes, you can build a training lesson that is probably more direct and employs more interactive training methods.

Table 2-7. Lesson structure worksheet

Section	Component	Instructor/Learner Activity
10% Introduction		
Importance		
Objective Statement		
70% Body		
Enabling Knowledge Content		
Task Content		
Practice Activities		
Content Review		
20% Conclusion		
Summary		
Conclusion		
Transition		

Likewise, there are many *formats* for a lesson plan; most lesson plans contain some or all of the following elements, typically in this order:

- Title of the lesson
- Time required to complete the lesson
- List of required materials
- List of objectives, which may be behavior-based (what the learner can do at lesson completion) or knowledge-based (what learners should know at lesson completion)
- The set (or lead-in, or bridge-in) that focuses the learner on the lesson's skills or concepts—these include showing pictures or models, asking leading questions, or reviewing previous lessons
- An instructional component that describes the sequence of events that make up the lesson, including the facilitator's instructional input and guided practice the learner uses to try new skills or work with new ideas
- Independent practice that allows learners to extend skills or knowledge on their own
- A summary, whereby the facilitator wraps up the discussion-and-answer questions
- An evaluation, or a test for mastery of the instructed skills or concepts, such as a set of questions to answer or an instruction to follow
- An analysis, which the facilitator uses to reflect on the lesson itself, such as what worked
- A continuity component, allowing learners to review and reflect on the content from the previous lesson

A well-written lesson plan reflects the interests and learning needs of the learners, as well as incorporates the best practices for the industry. The lesson reflects your teaching philosophy, which is your purpose in presenting this information. When you write the lesson plan, consider the elements of your initial design report and how you had divided the topics and subtopics to be covered. Eventually you will integrate the lesson plan into the instructor's guide that you will create after you have completed designing and developing the training components, learner materials, and instructional coursework.

> Courses are created out of units, which are composed of learning modules. Modules are developed by combining lessons. Lessons are the smallest units of learning.

The profile of the lesson design, shown in Table 2-8, is a blueprint to follow in laying out your materials for each lesson. As the table shows, you consider the development and flow, the content, and the delivery in terms of the stages in the lesson. Specifically, a lesson plan breaks down into several components, as listed in Table 2-9. For each component, you must know both the reason you include the component in the les-

Table 2-8. Profile of lesson design.

Development Goal	Content	Delivery
Prepares learners	Objectives	Introductory statement Transition statement Objectives
Presents information	Content	Enabling knowledge Task content
Practices skills	Training methods Learner activities	Learner practice activities
Provides feedback	Training methods Learner activities	Summary Test items Conclusion

Table 2-9. Components of a lesson.

Component	Reason for Inclusion	Procedure
Introductory statement	Gives an overview of the lesson	Write this after the entire lesson is written; it will be easier to see the big picture
Transition statement	Explains the relationship between previous information and new information	Tell learners where they have been and where they are going.
Objectives	Describes the lesson expectations and what learners will be doing during the training	Write job-based conditions, clear action statements, and achievable criteria.
Enabling knowledge	Provides the facts, content overview, rules, and new terms that learners need to know before doing the task	Place enabling knowledge before the task information to enable learners to do the task.
Task content	Delivers the actions or guidelines needed for learners to do the task	Write according to the type of tasks: • action-based • guideline-based
Practice	Gives learners the chance to practice the task or apply the knowledge in the training environment	Give application practice for all tasks. Give application practice only for critical knowledge elements.
Summary	Reviews the key points of the training	Create short summary lists; use graphics and checklists where appropriate.
Test items	Provides feedback and evaluation on learning progress	Match objectives' conditions, actions, and criteria.
Conclusion	Offers a lesson endpoint that directs learners to the next lesson	Let learners know what happens after their lesson.

son and the guidelines for developing that component, as shown in the table. Between the introductory and summary components of the lesson plan, three "content" components provide the bulk of the lesson, and they are the most time-consuming to develop.

Consider each of the following tips as you write the lessons for your training program:

1. **Timing.** List the time you will spend on each topic and subtopic of each lesson. A typical training day is six hours, and you have 55 minutes in an hour for training. You should allocate at least 10 percent of the time to introduce or make a transition to the topic, 70 percent of the time to deliver the content (which might include preparing the learners to learn, presenting the material, and practicing using the material with an exercise and feedback). The final 20 percent of the time should be devoted to summary, conclusion, and transition to the next lesson or module.

2. **Content.** List the topics and subtopics that you will cover during each lesson. Do not combine lessons. Develop and deliver each lesson topic independently, using transitional statements to bridge from one topic or subtopic to another. In the lesson plan, indicate your introductions, breaks, and sequences in one lesson. Don't have run-on sessions without using transition statements. (Run-on sessions are those that continue without using transition statements and might not be similar in content or practice.) Deliver the content in complete and inclusive parts. Illogical breaks that occur because you did not scope the content appropriately will leave the learning session in an awkward state and the learners will feel that the training is incomplete.

3. **Training Techniques.** Explain whether the session is to be a lecture, show and tell, or participant discovery.

4. **Learner Activity.** List the types of things that learners will be doing during the lesson (listening, looking, practicing). By documenting

this information, you'll have the opportunity to build a variety of activities into your training.

5. **Training Aids.** List the instructional aids and strategies or peripherals that you'll use and the order in which you'll use them.

Remember, too much information at one time creates confusion. *Chunking* is the term used to describe breaking down concepts into meaningful parts. Give learners a maximum of three large pieces of information. If you have three major components to a topic, deliver them within an hour. Once you deliver the three large chunks, summarize and break. Similarly, cluster the topics into organized sections, such as introduction, body, and activities. Grade the content presentation to target the correct amount of information to deliver.

A lesson plan gives you the advantage of determining in advance if your delivery sequence is correct, if the content is relevant, and if your instructional strategies are appropriate. The lesson plan also is a resource checklist, an aid for you in preparing the auxiliary materials required for the lesson, such as handouts, videotapes, DVDs, CDs, or wall charts.

Note: Do not make your lesson plan too complicated. It is a road map to help you organize your course and stay with your objectives.

Guidelines for Constructing Modules

Lessons get grouped into modules. The module design, a sample of which is shown in Figure 2-4, brings a series of lessons together into a major section of what ultimately is a unit. The module is your course blueprint for further developing the content and instructional strategies of the training program. Make sure that, for each module in your program, you state the objective and identify the content topic.

Think of modules as containers for your lessons. The task analysis

Figure 2-4. Sample module design.

Module Name: ______________________

Objective	Content	Instructor & Learner Activities

you did previously shows what tasks belong with each function. Now, you just decide in what order your lessons will fit into the modules and how the module relates to a specific task in the task analysis. There are several advantages to using a modular structure:

- Key modules can be developed first to speed up the training time.
- Participants can sign up to take specific modules, based on personal need.
- Sequence of training can be easily rearranged according to audience need.
- Each section of the training is organized the same way to ensure consistency.

Here are the major elements of a module:

- Objectives
- Knowledge content to enable the learners to complete the task
- Task content
- Practice activities to help reach the objectives
- Assessment mechanism, such as test items, to determine if the objectives were achieved

Other factors to take into account when creating a module include the best method for getting the objectives met, the timing and breaks, the amount of material to cover, the class or group size for activities, and any simulation of job conditions. Some tips for sequencing multiple lessons within a module are as follows:

- Use your task analysis to establish the sequence.
- Present enabling knowledge first to prepare for the task.
- Use the same advisors to test the sequence as you did to validate other areas of needs analysis and design steps.

Some Overall Considerations

Design principles can provide a framework for organizing your learning materials. This framework then directs the flow of material and determines the activities so that you can decide which learning methods to use. For example:

- **Learner Directed.** If the learners understand why they need the information you will give them, the lessons will be easier for them to learn; in this case, structure a lot of involvement and activities.
- **Experiential.** Learners gain more from experiencing the concepts being taught than from lectures or presentations. They want active

involvement and relevance to their job and organization. So include practice and applying the concepts rather than strictly lectures.

- **Able to be Evaluated.** When teaching a concept, define it. Specify as clearly as possible the result you want from the learners. Identify what changes in knowledge, skill, or attitude will take place as a result of the training.
- **Residual.** Adults learn more effectively if they build on known information, facts, or experiences rather than from independent, arbitrary facts. Provide information that builds on their experience and knowledge, and leads them into deeper knowledge.
- **Numerous Instructional Methods.** People vary in how they learn best. Incorporate various instructional methods into your lessons.

An Example: A Course for New Managers

Drew has to develop a problem-solving and decision-making course for new managers at this company. After completing a thorough task analysis, he uses the guidelines for course structure and the sample course map to develop a graphic representation of the job functions and tasks. He then translates those functions and tasks into a full-scale course with units and modules. Remember, the job function translates into a unit and the job tasks translate into lessons making up the modules. To begin, Drew organized his elements into a logical framework and then developed subtopics, as shown in Figure 2-5.

The Design Report

Earlier, in connection with writing the lesson plan, a "design report" was mentioned. The design report is a summary of the analysis and program design completed to date. It serves as a preliminary communiqué to inform management of your progress, and it provides an opportunity for receiving their suggestions and feedback on the plan. It is a way to

Figure 2-5. Drew's management training course.

Unit 1: Problem Analysis
Module 1: How to state the problem
Module 2: How to define the standard
Module 3: How to define the differences

Unit 2: Cause Identification
Module 1: How to determine training deficiencies
Module 2: How to determine other deficiencies

Unit 3: Data Collection
Module 1: How to create data-collection questions
Module 2: How to use data-collection sources
Module 3: How to manage data collection

Unit 4: Idea Generation
Module 1: How to use individual techniques
Module 2: How to use group techniques

Unit 5: Solution Selection
Module 1: How to evaluate ideas
Module 2: How to select best ideas

Unit 6: Solution Implementation
Module 1: How to manage resources
Module 2: How to complete a time and action plan

Unit 7: Solution Evaluation
Module 1: How to measure effect of solution
Module 2: How to document results

ensure that your training meets management's expectations, as management support for the course objectives is critical to your success, as well as the success of your program and the learners. The report serves to inform management of the proposed training. It also provides a road map for the instructional designer to use in developing the training. And it offers the instructor the necessary information on how and why the training was developed.

A design report contains seven narrative components:

1. Purpose of the course
2. Summary of the analyses
3. Scope of the course
4. Test item strategy
5. Course and module design
6. Delivery strategy
7. Level of evaluation to be tested

In the last section, the example of a management training course was introduced. Here, Figure 2-6 shows a sample design report for a similar problem-solving course for new managers. In the design report, the following elements are discussed: purpose, summary of analyses, scope, objectives, test items, delivery format, and evaluation.

Figure 2-6. Problem-solving course for new managers.

Purpose of Course

The course will introduce new managers to the established problem-solving strategies developed at our company. These problem-solving skills will be separated into several training sessions. The course will be designed to integrate current company problems, rather than use problems discussed when the course was last held five years ago.

Summary of Analyses

Needs analysis and problem analysis: When the course was last taught, these analyses led to the development of an internal problem-solving model for use during management sessions. That model was successful, but it needs updating.

Audience analysis: The company has 30 managers located in eight regions who need to learn the problem-solving model to participate more effectively in management meetings.

Job and task analysis: The problem-solving model already exists. We need to customize it to meet the new managers' needs and overcome questions about our new product line. Attached is our survey of their needs.

Scope of the Course

This course will use a seven-stage model of problem solving. The three-day course will be held at our corporate headquarters. All new managers will attend.

Task Learning Objectives

Objective 1: Given the problem-solving model and one case-study scenario, resolve the customer question to the level of satisfaction of the instruction.

Objective 2: Given the product features guidelines and the problem-solving model, resolve the customer product complaint to the satisfaction of the customer within acceptable guidelines of the company policy.

Objective 3: List and define the steps in the problem-solving model.

Test Item Strategy

The learners will have to demonstrate mastery of the problem-solving model by using all seven stages of the model in two case studies in the workshop. They will be assessed at the end of each chapter.

Delivery Strategy

This course will be an instructor-led, three-day classroom training. The instructor team will include a member of the training staff and an experienced company manager. The course will be held at corporate headquarters.

Evaluation Stages Measured

- Stage 1: Learner Reaction. Daily classroom reaction sheet.
- Stage 2: Learning. Test items will measure learning.
- Stage 3: Behavior. Surveys will go out to all management before and after training to assess changes in managerial problem solving.

The Enabling-Knowledge Bull's Eye

As stressed earlier, the "must know" information to be included in the training program is the *enabling knowledge* that gives the learner the ability to perform the task or job. The "need to know" information is the background knowledge in order for the learner to understand that "must know" information. The "nice to know" information includes what is not necessary for the learner to know but could be helpful in better grasping the points covered in the session.

It's reasonable to assume that if you aim your training program at the bull's eye—the "must know" area—you will also spend time hitting the "need to know" area as a review. If time permits, you can spread the aim wider yet, hitting the "nice to know" area. However, it is likely the time would probably be better spent reviewing the "need to know" and "must know" areas. It is better to deliver too little well rather than too much badly. Use the guidelines in Table 2-10 to focus your eye on delivering the enabling knowledge.

Action-Based and Guideline-Based Task Information

Action-based tasks are derived from the task analysis. Guideline-based tasks also originate from the task analysis, but the sequential format is not required, as it is for the action-based tasks. Use the guidelines in Table 2-11 to write your action-based and guideline-based task information and practices.

Teaching Methods

You have defined the learning objectives and organized the course as a series of units composed of modules, which are themselves composed of lessons. You have also submitted your design report and received feedback. Now you need to decide on your teaching methods.

Table 2-10. Guidelines for delivering enabling knowledge.

Category	Guidelines	Examples
Rules, policies, standards, cautions, warnings	Use strong, clear language. Place knowledge where learner will clearly see it.	"The purchase order must be signed by your manager."
Factual information	Include essential facts only.	"Brainstorming is one technique used to generate ideas in a large group."
Content overview	Give the big picture of what happens on the job. Show how the task to be learned relates to the other tasks and other employees' jobs.	"Before an instructional designer can develop a learning module, the training needs must have been defined and designed."
New terms	Define the term. Give examples that show how the term is used. Provide instances of how the new term differs from other terms.	"A projector is a machine that uses light and lenses to show an enlarged visual image on a broad surface." "An Acme LCD is an overhead projector. An Acme camera, model ABC, is not an overhead projector because it does not project visuals onto a surface but, rather, uses film to capture the image."

At this point, it would be worthwhile to compare your plans to the teaching methods template shown in Table 2-12. This template pairs the training objectives with the methods and setting, such as individual or group involvement. Following that, you can consider the various materials and methods available to you.

Table 2-11. Action-based and guideline-based tasks.

Type of Task	Guidelines for User	Practice Activity	Examples
Action-Based	1. Use performance elements from task analysis as source material to write steps. 2. Use clear action verbs. 3. Present sequence of actions in logical order. 4. Use consistent language. 5. Use second-person command (imperative) voice.	Give learners activities that ask them to apply the performance elements the same way each time.	"How to write a check": 1. Fill in date. 2. Write in payee name. 3. Fill in cash amount in box. 4. Write in cash amount in words. 5. Write in reason for check on memo line. 6. Sign check.
Guideline-Based	1. Use performance elements from task analysis as source material to write guidelines. 2. Use guideline-phrased language. 3. Sequence performance elements depending on situation presented.	Give learners different situations in which to apply guidelines.	"How to brainstorm": 1. Enlist ideas from the group. 2. Defer judgment. 3. Collect unlimited number of ideas. 4. Expand on ideas of others. "Here are three marketing problems. Your group will brainstorm ideas for solving these problems. Use the guidelines for brainstorming to develop your results."

Table 2-12. Teaching methods template.

Objective: What is to be accomplished?	Method: What is the instructional strategy?	Format: In what setting is it to be accomplished?
Introduction	Discussion, game, jigsaw learning, lecture, assessment, case study, job aid	Individual, pairs, small group, whole group, panel
Implement the new payroll policies	Case study	Small group
Identify the six qualities of adult learning	Lecture and quiz	Whole group followed by competing teams
Develop questions to use in a training needs assessment	Case scenario and response cards.	Individual activity and whole group debriefing
Discuss the seven principles to manage time, and apply each to your identified time-wasters	Self-inventory and match the inventory responses to the seven principles to manage time	Provide each participant with the self-inventory; allow 20 minutes to work alone, and then pair-up with partners to discuss their time-wasters and the principle to apply

Training Materials for the Learners

Training materials must support course objectives. Available resources may include ready-made materials chosen for a specific course, customized materials designed for a specific course or module, materials taken from a previous course developed in-house, or new materials purchased from outside vendors.

➤ **Off-the-Shelf Materials.** Commercially prepared training materials save you and the company development time; however, their topics or content are generic, which means they may not fit exactly with your specific situation. That is, you may need to make some adjustments. If you need the material to be client focused, then you'll have to spend time and resources customizing the off-the-shelf program.

► **Custom-Made Materials.** Creating materials in your company will take longer than if you simply purchase off-the-shelf products. Custom-made materials usually also are more expensive because they must be made from scratch. However, once created, custom-made materials can be repurposed because your company owns the copyright on them.

Matters of Copyright

Bear in mind when developing course materials that copyright laws protect intellectual rights and creative efforts. Trainers try to use the very latest materials, but they must guard against using anything done by someone else without obtaining permission. Copyright, as defined by SHRM guidelines, is "the exclusive right or privilege of the author or proprietor to print or otherwise multiply, distribute, and vend copies of his/her literary, article, or intellectual products when secured by compliance with the copyright statute."[1] The Copyright Act of 1976 stipulates that copyright begins with the creation of the work in a fixed form from which it can be perceived or communicated. SHRM points out that registration of the copyright with the Copyright Office of the Library of Congress is not a condition of copyright; the law does, however, provide inducement to register work. The exclusive rights of the author or proprietor are limited by the fair use of copyrighted works in certain circumstances, but whether a use is fair depends on several factors, including its purpose, nature, amount, and effect on potential market value.

"Fair use" standards may apply to training materials. As a trainer, you can make a single copy of copyrighted materials for your own use, but check with the copyright holder before you make multiple copies. As SHRM points out, "if a trainer violates copyright statutes, the penalties can be severe and may include injunction, actual damages, defendant's lot profits, statutory damages, and attorney's fees."

For anonymous works and works made for hire (such as those prepared by trainers or other employees at the request of employers), the period of protection lasts for 75 years, from the first year of publication, or 100 years from the year of creation, whichever expires first. Employers, rather than employees who did the writing, are considered the authors of the work and the owners of the copyright.

A work that has fallen into the public domain is available for use without permission from the copyright owner. A work is considered public domain if it meets one of the following characteristics:

- It was published prior to January 1, 1978, without notice of copyright.
- The period of copyright protection has expired.
- It was produced for the U.S. government by its officers or employees as part of their official duties.

Until recently, copyrights had very little to do with the daily work of trainers. Intellectual property was easy to protect. However, with the advent of the Internet, it is easy for any computer user to copy, distribute, or publish virtually anything, even that which was written and belongs to someone else. Bear in mind that messages or articles posted on a Usenet newsgroup or e-mail are automatically copyrighted by the authors.

Assembling Your Resource Library

Keep a library of all the course materials you use or develop. It just might be that, on occasion, you can use a module from a previous source or can customize an in-house program to fit a new course. It is okay to do this. The course material belongs to your company, unless you have borrowed it from another company. In general, it's better to have customized material in your library than the generic. You will have more control of the content and will understand the rationale behind the design of the training.

It is important to make sure that the teaching materials you use are accurate and will achieve the desired results. There is nothing worse for an instructor than to get to class and have the learners point out errors, find the material confusing, or be unable to follow the directions. Similarly, you need to validate older material you are using to be sure it is right for your new intended use.

Ways to validate the material include individual (one-on-one) tests conducted by the course designer; group tests (several learners in a segment of the course led by the course designer); or pilot tests (trial run by the course instructor). You should make any changes to the material after each validation. Conduct another validation after revisions have been made to ensure that your objectives will be achieved. Table 2-13 offers some guidelines for this type of validation.

Table 2-13. Guidelines for validating and revising training materials.

Participants to Watch	Data to Collect
Learners	• Timing • Ability to use the materials • Ability to complete instructor directions • Completion of individual and group activities • Questions or confusions • Difficult areas, terminology, sequence • How well objectives were achieved
Instructor	• Timing • Difficult content explanations • Use of interactive techniques • Ability to answer learner questions • Sequence • Ability to lead learner to achieve objectives

Evaluation Materials

Because evaluation is a natural consequence of training, you will need to produce feedback forms for your learners. These forms should be easy to understand and require minimum time to complete. Make certain that the forms are complete in what they are surveying, otherwise you'll get incomplete, possibly invalid, information. (Of course, once the evaluations are done, you will have to provide copies to the course developer, the course evaluator, and the course administrator.)

Each stakeholder reviews the evaluation differently and acts on the content. For example, the developer will look for remarks on topic treatment and instructional activities. The data then serve as the basis for course revisions. In the same manner, you'll be keeping data on the learners and the program results. Training records can be kept in paper files or on a computer database. (To maintain good training records, try the commercial registrar or similar record-management systems.) The course administrator can be responsible for maintaining this database.

Training Materials for the Instructors

Now that you have compiled the learner materials, moving on to the instructor materials is easy. In many corporate training structures, the course designer is responsible for producing an instructor guide that tells the instructor what must be accomplished in the class. The individual instructors are then responsible for developing their own training aids. So the extent of the materials you need to provide varies with the situation.

In conducting a training program, most instructors use specific materials so as to provide consistency, standardization, quality control, and visual effect. The guidelines in Table 2-14 should be helpful in assembling the instructor materials and include a variety of visual aids.

Table 2-14. Guidelines for preparing instructor materials.

Type of Material	Guidelines
Instructor guide	• Include expected outcomes/objectives • State course timing • Include topics covered • Add instructions for conducting class • Use visual aids
Overhead visuals	• Use simple content • Include simple graphics • Make easy to read • Insert one topic per visual • Use seven plus or minus two items of information
Charts	• Write legibly • Avoid light-colored markers (red too!) • Prepare ahead of time or build with learners • Use for small-group work
Learning charts	• Use multiple colors • Add graphics • Keep words and phrases simple • Place key topic in center of chart

The Legal Implications of Training

As you are developing a training program, you need to be aware of the legal ramifications of your situation. There are laws that require your ensuring that everyone involved has equal access to the training. Likewise, you need to be able to address any charges of discrimination.

Laws Against Job Discrimination

Since the 1960s, federal laws have required employers to provide equal opportunity in employment and career progression. All of these laws require employers to inform employees of their rights by posting copies of the laws themselves, related notices, and open positions in the company. You should be familiar with the following laws that affect training and professional development.

➤ **Title VII, Civil Rights Act.** Congress passed Title VII of the Civil Rights Act of 1964 to bring about equality in hiring, transfers, promotions, access to training, and other employment-related decisions. Title VII also stipulates that there must be equal opportunity to participate in trainings. If employees have nondiscriminatory access to the same training, everyone will have the opportunity to be better qualified for advancement.

➤ **Age Discrimination in Employment Act.** The Age Discrimination in Employment Act (ADEA) was enacted in 1967 to protect older workers. Generally, the ADEA protects workers over the age of 40 against employment discrimination on the basis of age. This protection includes giving qualified employees over 40 years of age equal access to training.

➤ **Americans with Disabilities Act.** The Americans with Disabilities Act (ADA) was modeled after the Vocational Rehabilitation Act of 1973 and the Rehabilitation Act of 1974. People with either mental or physical disabilities or limitations, or who are regarded as having such impairments, sometimes suffer from employment discrimination in that they are not considered for jobs that they are qualified for and are capable of doing. The ADA protects qualified individuals from unlawful discrimination in the workplace, including access to training and career development.

➤ **Labor Relations and Union Statutes.** Union activity between the 1930s and the mid-1950s provided the impetus for the development and passage of two acts that affect training and professional development:

The National Labor Relations Act of 1935 (NLRA) and the Labor-Management Relations Act of 1947. The NLRA, also referred to as the Wagner Act, prohibits discrimination against union members with respect to terms and conditions of employment, including apprenticeships and trainings. The National Labor Relations Board considers training to be a condition of employment and a mandatory subject for collective bargaining.

The Labor-Management Relations Act, also known as the Taft-Hartley Act, prevents unions from discriminating for any reason except for payment of dues and assessments. The act also permits noncoercive employer free speech. This may affect trainers; for example, if your company president supports a particular political party, it could be assumed that you support that party. In training, you should use no examples, case studies, or role plays that infringe upon a person's personal philosophy or belief system.

Defense Against Charges of Training Discrimination

It is not difficult to defend yourself against a charge of training discrimination if you can show that your programs are designed and delivered without bias. The following guidelines apply to all of the employment laws discussed so far:

- Register affirmative action training and apprenticeship programs with the U.S. Department of Labor.
- Keep records of all employees who apply for enrollment in training and the details of how they were selected.
- Document all management decisions and actions that relate to the administration of training policies.
- Monitor each trainee's progress, provide evaluations, and ensure that counseling is available.
- Continue to evaluate results even after training is completed.

Budget Matters

The goal of training and professional development in most organizations is to have a positive, cost-effective effect on the organization. Yet, the training department often appears as a departmental cost or organizational expense. Training provides a significant return on investment, and it can be viewed as such rather than as a line-item expense in the budget.

Using traditional cost-accounting principles, you can show a return when you cost out your training. To do this, you must calculate the total cost of the training. Next, you indicate the savings or benefit to the organization. Finally, you calculate the cost of the training per employee. Here's the basic formula:

Total cost of training = cost per trainee ÷ number of people trained

The Training Costs Involved

The information needed to justify the cost of training depends on a number of factors: project name, project number, staff costs, graphics, instructor binders and materials, technology costs, printing and reproduction, and participant materials. Actual costs will vary depending on the training site and whether the programs have been custom-designed, purchased off-the-shelf, or developed in-house. You should include both direct and indirect costs in your overall budget. *Direct costs* include regular operating costs, such as wages or salaries of participants and trainers, and costs for travel, lodging, supplies, and materials that relate to a particular program. *Indirect costs* include secretarial and clerical help, use of telephone and audiovisual equipment, and costs associated with lower productivity when a worker is attending a training session.

When you prepare a budget proposal, include the estimated savings or increased profits that might result from implementing the training. Also include supplemental details for each program, such as program length, space requirements, number of trainees per session, materials, equipment, instructors (both internal and external), and an estimate of the materials development and administrative costs.

A Closer Look at Training Costs

Most trainers look at cost figures to measure the effect of training success. Cost figures are taken directly from the budget and can be found in three general categories:

1. Costs: expense per unit of training delivered
2. Change: gain in skill or knowledge by the learner
3. Impact: results or outcomes from the learner's use of new skills or knowledge

No simple calculation can account for all possible training costs and benefits. However, the easiest calculation involves adding up all of the expenses (both direct and indirect) and dividing by the total number of people trained, as the following equation shows (SHRM, 1997):

$$\text{Cost of training} \div \text{cost of unwanted behavior} = \text{ROI}$$
$$\text{probability of occurrence}$$

For example, suppose the cost of targeted training was $10,000. The cost of unwanted behavior to the organization was estimated to be $190,000. Once the targeted training was delivered, the unwanted behavior would have a recurrence of only 10 percent of the time. The targeted training would immediately save the organization 53 percent of the projected $190,000 that would be lost if the unwanted behavior persisted.

Increasingly, trainers are being asked to demonstrate a return on skills trainings and professional development programs. Organizations are not willing to approve or continue to fund training and professional development programs unless they are aligned with the strategic and tactical plan and can be cost-justified. Providing actual savings and showing a return on investment can provide the tangible example that justifies the training budget. The key to your success is to design and deliver trainings that are appropriate for all employees so that the skills and knowledge they gain contribute to corporate knowledge and help gain its competitive edge in the marketplace.

The Project Plan

If you decide to create a custom-designed training program, and you have projected costs for the design and delivery of this project, you need a project plan to help you organize and keep track of the tasks required for designing and developing that program. A basic training project plan consists of three components, as shown in Table 2-15. Each component of the plan provides a task and a time schedule.

1. **Instruction.** This section defines how the instruction will be sequenced, the topical content, and how the topical content will be presented. The training outline starts with organizing a lesson, and

Table 2-15. Training project plan.

Task	Time Line (Days, Weeks, or Months)
Component A: Instruction	
Component B: Delivery	
Component C: Management	

the lesson pattern consists of the introduction, body, conclusion, and assessment.

2. **Delivery.** This section defines the instructional media to deliver the training and develop ways to organize and group the audience.
3. **Managing.** This section defines how to schedule the sessions, how to allocate the resources to implement the instruction, how to get the instructional resources to the learners, records management, budget oversight, and the evaluation process.

The field of instructional systems design (ISD) has come a long way since its beginnings in the 1950s. From its origins as a systematic way to apply behavioral psychology to programmed instruction and audiovisual media, instructional design now occupies a central place in both education and training organizations.

Since its earliest days, instructional design has been influenced by the view that learning is a complex system that can be facilitated by instructional theory. According to this view, instruction can be broken down into three basic parts: input, process, and output. Each must take into account the characteristics of the learner. The input to instruction includes such things as a learner's previous knowledge and experience, an organization's needs, and the resources available. The process includes development of courses and delivery of training tailored to the learner. The output includes learning outcomes and organizational outcomes.

The purpose of instructional design is to provide learners with the content and process they need, when they need it, and in a structured and standard format that they can readily use. The ISD model includes five steps: analysis, design, development, implementation, and evaluation.

LEARNING THEORY IN THE TRAINING ENVIRONMENT

How Learning Happens

As mentioned at the beginning of this chapter, the second part of Chapter 2 reports on the extensive educational research that has been done regarding how people learn new things. This research has accepted a model with three major learning categories:

1. **Knowledge:** Cognitive ability is what one knows to perform, such as the principles of accounting.
2. **Skills:** Psychomotor ability is the muscular actions needed to perform a job or task such as writing or operating equipment. Skills can be observed and, therefore, are easily quantifiable.
3. **Attitudes:** Affective ability is what one brings to the job in terms of feelings. How people feel about their job, workspace, and the organization affects their performance.

A learning objective written in the *psychomotor domain* will specify that learners will develop a skill. This type of objective requires that learners coordinate their brains with the physical activity. A learning objective written in the *cognitive domain* will state that the training is designed to enable learners to know or understand something. That is, after the session, learners will be able to point that something out, describe the something, recognize the something, or define the something. A learning objective written in the *affective domain* will use verbs that connote feelings and emotions, such as respect, cooperative, and hard working.

Sometime after delivering the training, you can evaluate the learners' performance by measuring it by referring to the original objectives, as stated in the course lesson or module. If the training fails to produce a measurable result in participant learning, you must ask yourself whether the objective statement might have been unclear or unrelated to the on-the-job performance, or perhaps the test item was not written to measure the learning objective. Therefore, after writing the learning objective, and before you develop the training, it is a good idea to consider what the learning process is and how this process interacts with learners' expectations and training experiences during the session.

Many popular definitions of learning emphasize a change in behavior that lasts a relatively long time. But what, for example, about new ways of thinking that open the possibility for new behaviors but take a long time before a person is able to exhibit those new behaviors? Or, you might ask, what about new ways of thinking and new emotional experiences that would lead to new ways of behaving, except that the organization or social system frowns on or punishes these new ways of behaving?

In such cases, learning is certainly stymied. Some would explain these situations by saying that thinking and emotion are themselves behaviors. But don't we all know that there is an undeniable difference in the experience of thinking, feeling, and behaving, and that grouping these three establishes the dynamic process of learning? Yet, we can't really determine which element in this learning process makes the learning outcome occur. So, consider this statement when you begin to design your training: *learning is more than a change in behavior.*

When people learn, they respond differently to their situations by thinking differently, feeling differently, and acting differently. When trainers conduct a training session, they are interested in how learning makes people think differently, and how they learn new ways of responding emotionally to support new behaviors that help individuals be more productive and fulfilled in their work.

Behavior is action in the world outside of us. Thinking is the synthesis of people's experiences to develop their own understanding of how the world works and how people can better act in it to achieve their goals. Thinking uses the complex set of symbols in language to develop understanding of the world by categorizing the things people encounter in their experiences. Thinking also makes connections between the many categories of behavioral responses. People learn when they have experiences that enlarge their behavioral categories and when they make new connections between categories. Thinking allows new ways of perceiving and responding to the world. Thinking often can prompt new behavior.

Emotions, likewise, involve people's understanding of the world and each person's place in it. Psychologists have identified several emotions: happiness, curiosity, surprise, desire, sadness, anger, disgust, fear, and shame. These emotions affect people's thoughts and behaviors all of the time. Also, emotions involve a physical sensation. You feel energy when you are curious or surprised. You feel your heart drop when you are sad or ashamed. You jump when you are frightened, and you pound when you are angry.

Feeling is an emotion, and you usually go beyond the initial sensation and think about how you should react. Emotions intertwined with thinking can develop into the most intricate and complex aspect of what it is to be human. Learners react to situations with different emotions, and learning to react to emotions with new ways of thinking *will* often prompt new behavior. Thus, learning involves all three—behavior, thinking, and emotion—as shown in Figure 2-7.

Figure 2-7. Learning pyramid.

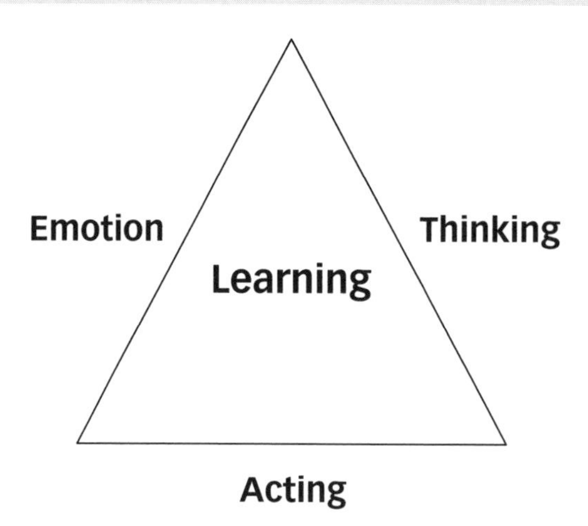

Learning Is Change

Learning is any change in a person's usual way of thinking, feeling, or behaving. All learning comes from experience. Read a book, attend a class, participate in a workshop, see a movie, attend a training, take part in an organizational change—all of these are experiences that can produce learning. There are two basic types of learning experienced during the learning process:

1. **Firsthand experience** is when people directly live through the situation. Most people readily acknowledge the powerful learning they have gained from their firsthand experience.
2. **Secondhand experience** is when people develop an understanding of a situation experienced by someone else. People are able to draw from someone else's firsthand experience. Secondhand experience can also be a powerful learning tool. Examples that you might use in the learning environment are books, workshops, or films.

Trainers are interested in how learning to think differently and learning new ways of responding emotionally can support new behaviors that help people become more productive and fulfilled in their work.

Stages of Learning

During the learning process, people go through a number of intellectual and behavioral responses. This learning process takes place when learners begin to internalize the content and learning processes that are presented during the training. The learning occurs in four stages. Think about these stages when you begin to design the various learning activities for your program:

1. **Retention.** Learners begin to analyze how much of the information is meaningful during the training. This phase directly relates to the overall feeling of the event being a positive or negative experience.

2. **Test.** Learners begin to question the information, its utility, and how they can transfer this information back on the job.
3. **Behavior.** Learners begin to internalize the information and seek ways to use the information immediately.
4. **Impact.** Learners think through ways of making adjustments to the job so that they can integrate this new knowledge and skill to increase job performance.

Researchers over the years have developed theories about this learning process and learning behavior. They concluded that there are two types of learner strategies. The first is the learner who is a *global processor*, meaning that the individual wants to understand the big picture first and then construct meaning. The second is the *linear processor,* who wants to understand the details first and then systematically work toward constructing the big picture.

The terms *global* and *linear* have also been described, respectively, as right-brain or left-brain oriented; sequential and simultaneous; inductive or deductive, according to Robert Dunn and Thomas DeBello (1999).[2] Further, Dunn stated that in the adult population, 55 percent are considered global thinkers and 28 percent are linear thinkers. The remaining are considered to have the ability to process information using both approaches. Robert Smith (1991) defined learning styles as "one's characteristic way of processing information, feeling, and behaving in learning situations,"[3] while Dunn and DeBello (1999) defined learning as "the characteristic of cognitive, affective, and psychological behaviors that serve as relatively stable indicators of how learners perceive, interact with, and respond to the learning environment."

Although there is no one comprehensive learning-style theory that all researchers agree on, they do agree that individuals learn differently and learners exhibit preferences for processing the information to be learned. The preferences most often identified have been classified, according to the above-cited researchers, as processing preferences, perceptual preferences, physiological preferences, and other learning preferences. This information is helpful when you decide on the instructional strategies for a program, determine the levels of the learners, and assign what roles the trainer will play.

Conceptualization of Learning and Training

Over the past 30 years, there has been extensive research done on the brain. Specifically, Dr. Paul McLean (2008) developed what is called the triune brain theory, which is an oversimplified yet useful metaphor for understanding aspects of the learning process.[4] According to McLean's theory, during the learning process the brain manages three roles: information reception, processing, and expression. The brain processes and organizes information using both spheres of the brain. So you ask, what are these left and right brains?

The left side of the brain is distinctly different from the right side, displaying differences in functioning: think left is linear, sequential, logical; right is global, imaginative, and creative. However, such a simplified approach moves us away from considering brain functioning as a whole, which is the optimal manner. The brain has many areas of specialization, which overlap and complement each other. Let's look at this information and see how we use it to facilitate and maximize learning.

Traditional Training

Do most traditional training programs tap into the variety of human information processing, such as focusing around language, logic, and numbers? No. The integration of the three, and the migrating of human interactions with the learning process, does not always take place as part of traditional learning. Thus, disconnects during the learning process happen when the creative brain processes are part of the training delivery process, making evaluation of the learning experience difficult. In fact, the brain achieves maximum efficiency and productivity when both hemispheres work together. To achieve this maximum interaction in your training, think about including the following:

- Global and linear presentations of material
- Words and symbols
- Color
- Music
- Wall charts

Training to Fully Engage the Brain

A critical part of your design, development, and delivery of a training program is knowing who the learners will be and what knowledge, skills, and attitudes they bring to the sessions. With this information, you can maximize their learning by linking their known information with what is to be learned. This, in turn, will nurture greater understanding of the information presented, retained, recalled, and used.

What is to be concluded from the brief overview of the brain's functioning and the learning process? It is that the training you design requires organization. Adult learners need a structured process during the learning event, so consider this suggested structure for your next learning event:

Step 1: Gain attention.
Step 2: Promote motivation to learning.
Step 3: Give an overview of the modules and lessons.
Step 4: Explain and demonstrate knowledge.
Step 5: Provide learner practice with supervision.
Step 6: Conduct an informal or formal evaluation.
Step 7: Provide a summary of the information.
Step 8: Remotivate the learners and close.

When you analyze this eight-step structure, you might think that it is limited and that the training is "done to the learner." But there is an alternative way to present training, and this alternative is at the heart of good training-program design: determining the locus of cognitive processing. That is, cognitive processing can be primarily generated by learners (low scaffolding), primarily supplied by instruction (high scaffolding), or at any place between the high and low scaffolding.

Scaffolding is the support system for cognitive processing that the instructor provides the learners, allowing them to absorb complex ideas that would otherwise be beyond their grasp if they depended solely on their own cognitive resources. Thus, instructors selectively aid the learners where needed, supplying the scaffolding. This is called the "expanded events of instruction."

Learning Styles

There are three types of learning styles: visual, auditory, and kinesthetic. You need to use a variety of delivery approaches to appeal to the three types of learning styles. For example, mini-lectures appeal to the *auditory* learners, and PowerPoint presentations appeal to the *visual* learners. Hands-on tasks are welcomed by the *kinesthetic* learners. If you can deliver training with all three learning styles in mind, the learners will engage in the learning and you will find that the training is fun to teach because everyone is interacting and benefiting.

Andragogy

For several decades, writers have been saying that adults learn differently from adolescents or children. Yet the only difference, based on years of educational research, is that adults bring greater quantities and different qualities of experience to the learning situation. Given these differences, adult learners require the following:

- Opportunities to use their experience as a resource for their learning. As a trainer, you use these adult experiences to foster more learning by involving the learners in discussions on how new information can be applied to their experience on the job.
- Learning bridges to ensure that their learning relates to their day-to-day experiences. Therefore, remember to include application exercises as part of most training.
- Communication with a facilitator who focuses on dialogue. A good facilitator gets a feel for how learners' experiences have prepared them to absorb the training topic. Using warm-up exercises, soliciting learners' expectations about the training, asking questions at the start of the training, and setting the training pace accordingly all contribute to a dialogue that reveals learners' experience and prior knowledge.
- Videos, readings, models, and theories based on learners' experiences. Learners must be given opportunities to apply these secondhand experiences to their firsthand, day-to-day lives.

Learning Strategies

Adult learners may enter their first training session with expectations similar to those they had when they were in school. But much more is expected from adult learners, in that the training will involve the learners actively and the learners will be responsible for their own learning process. Therefore, design the program with the following elements in mind:

- Focus on real-world problems.
- Emphasize how participants can apply what they are learning.
- Relate the learning to the participants' stated goals.
- Relate the participant materials and new knowledge presented to participants' experiences.
- Allow the participants to debate and challenge ideas.
- Listen to and respect participants' opinions.

- Focus on participants' expectations and what the training will do for the learners.

The final item on the list above may be the most important, one that you could use to provide a positive effect from your training and yield a successful outcome. For training to be effective, learners must believe that the training is for their self- and professional improvement, not simply to increase productivity or fulfill a manager's yearly obligation to provide training.

Remember, adult learners bring rich life experiences to the training. Adult learners will remember the information best when they do the following:

- Make their own decisions about which aspects of the training are important.
- Validate the information presented based on their specific beliefs and experiences.
- Have a lot of experiences and fixed viewpoints.
- Bring significant knowledge to the training.
- Expect what they learn to be immediately useful.

Categories of Learners

As mentioned earlier, there is no right or wrong ways to absorb new information. The process for learning is complex. Yet, there is a universal agreement that learners tend to fit in one of five categories: confident, affective, transitional, integrated, or risk taking.

Confident Learners

Tasks assigned to confident learners must have a clear purpose. If they are given the opportunity, confident learners will set their own goals and may even help set the direction for the training. Confident learners like to be involved and consulted, and they will happily respond to a request to identify a certain number of work-related issues, problems, or themes to which they would like the training to be focused. Trainers can use confident learners to help decide what content would be relevant and meaningful for the group.

Confident learners sometimes prepare in advance for the training and may be irritated by trainers who progress too slowly, have less than well-defined objectives, or do not seek input from the learners. Confident learners may be potential leaders and need opportunities for interactive learning experiences. Group discussions, team projects, and shared experiences appeal to confident learners as do learning from peers and helping peers learn. Confident learners prefer training that leads to specific goals. These learners may actually confront trainers whose programs or techniques appear inadequate, but they will not threaten well-prepared trainers.

Affective Learners

Affective learners are influenced by their feelings, and they like to know they are doing fine in the training. They want to feel an attachment to their trainer, and they expect the trainer to be an expert who is being paid to explain, synthesize, and decrease the complexity of a subject. Affective learners want to be invited to participate and can be counted on for their patience, endurance, and loyalty when the path to reaching a learning goal might seem long and circuitous to others.

To best reach affective learners, here are a couple of tips:

- Provide clearly written assignments or clearly defined exercises.
- Encourage enjoyable learning activities such as interaction with other adults who value training.
- Specify particular reference books for further information.
- Recognize that these learners will strive to fulfill the trainers' reasonable and well-defined expectations.

Transitional Learners

Transitional learners are promoted or moving horizontally to a new job. These learners tend to focus more than others on the particular type of information they are learning and on how that learning will apply to their new situations. Transitional learners may be apprehensive about making job changes and may want to tell trainers about their work experience, their work environment from which they are coming, or their work environment to which they are moving. Transitional learners need to be reassured that they are fully capable of learning and succeeding. Trainers can do so by inviting these learners to discuss training objectives and techniques.

Transitional learners tend to see everything as potentially new and highly relevant. Many of them may not yet be familiar with all aspects of their new work environment. To best appeal to these learners, challenge them to learn. Transitional learners may not expect everything that is covered in the training to have simple, obvious, and conclusive outcomes. They are happy taking one step at a time and putting pieces together when and where they seem to think the pieces fit in their world.

Integrated Learners

Integrated learners present a particularly interesting challenge to trainers because, more often than not, they establish peer-like relationships with trainers. Integrated learners are not satisfied merely to receive information. They want to do something with the information they receive. Integrated learners know where they want to go, enjoy being responsible for their own learning, and want freedom (within some structure) to accomplish specific tasks and assignments without much outside guidance.

Integrated learners are self-directed and demand quality from others as well as themselves. They want their work to be good and well integrated with the overall learning objectives of the training. Because integrated learners know what they want to learn and have used processes to learn on their own, trainers do not need to tell them precisely how to undertake specific learning tasks. They figure things out on their own.

Risk-Taking Learners

Risk-taking learners thrive on learning new skills and information. They like to deviate from traditional course content and techniques and to change their routines and schedules. In general, risk-taking learners are willing to work hard to meet goals, particularly if they will benefit from learning new concepts. Risk-taking learners will stray from course guidelines happily if straying presents an opportunity to gain new knowledge.

Trainers need not be concerned if they have sketchy materials because risk-taking learners will welcome the opportunity for interactive exercises.

Instructional Elements

Clarifying expectations, learning objectives, or learning goals is essential to designing the training program. From the beginning, learners must understand the desired outcome of the training and the relationship between those outcomes and their jobs. It is not sufficient to define the learning objectives as part of your introduction. Throughout the session, you must reiterate the objectives that you have integrated into the session design. By adhering to the following guidelines in your consideration of learner expectations, you will be well on your way to designing successful trainings:

- Write the learning objectives clearly and directly.
- Explain the reasons for the training.
- Relate the training to work performance.
- Clarify management's role.

- Negotiate and discuss with learners to gain their ownership of the training.
- Review the course materials regularly, and revise if necessary.

Measurement

Expectations are more likely to be met fully if the training design incorporates the means by which the trainers, learners, and management can measure progress toward accomplishing them. Incorporate the following elements into the design:

- Measurable training objectives
- Measurable performance requirements aligned with training requirements
- Methods that do not threaten learners
- Methods that allow for self- or peer measurement.

Capacity

Successful training can occur only if learners have the capacities to succeed. Trainers should take care to do the following:

- Identify capacity requirements for training and job performance.
- Screen prospective learners for physical, intellectual, or emotional capacity prior to their selection as part of the group.
- Provide opportunities for remedial training whenever possible and appropriate for learners who do not meet certain capacity requirements.

After taking the above steps to ensure that learners have the capacity to do the job for which the training is being designed, you might find that some learners lack certain skills and the requisite knowledge base. Failure to address these gaps when designing the session would not be fair either to the learners with the deficits or to those with the requisite skills and knowledge base. Consider doing the following:

- Specify clearly and in advance the prerequisites for the training.
- Study the learners' characteristics.
- Administer pretests whenever possible and appropriate.
- Ask questions randomly to determine the learners' general level of preparation.
- Design the training to meet the group's preparation level.
- Prepare alternative routes through the course of instruction on the basis of the group's preparation level.

Attitudes and Motivation

Learners must have positive attitudes and be motivated to benefit from training. As a trainer, you can increase the likelihood that learners will have positive attitudes in the following ways:

- Do what you can to ensure that learners are informed well in advance about the forthcoming training.
- Exclude threatening or competitive issues from your materials and content.
- Include input from the learners and union leadership (if relevant) in the design.
- Relate training to job requirements.
- Encourage prospective learners to volunteer to attend.
- Build adequate amenities, such as beverages, lunch, and food for breaks, into the program. (You don't have to provide amenities equal to those from a luxury spa, but learners should not feel as if they are in boot camp.)

Positive attitudes and motivation to learn are critical to effective training and individual performance. To a large extent, motivational climate determines whether attitudes are positive or negative during the session. Determine if any factors are adversely affecting learning and performance, and, if they are, correct the problem by doing the following:

- Remove constraints and barriers to the learning.
- Ensure that positive consequences follow positive performance.
- Ascertain that negative consequences do not follow; correct with care.
- Develop a supportive, trusting environment for learning and performance.
- Provide opportunities for participation.

Instruction

Although the design of instructional materials is extremely important to successful training, materials cannot substitute for high-quality instruction. By adhering to the following guidelines, trainers can ensure that their instruction will be topnotch:

- Involve the entire learner population in icebreakers and a discussion of their expectations.
- Demonstrate the skill or the learning that is to be trained.
- Provide brief and to-the-point content.
- Encourage feedback at every step.
- Build in several opportunities for learners to practice.
- Pace the training to the learners' level.
- Allow significant time for questions and answers.

Instructional Resources

Remember that you are training people to perform in their regular work settings. The training you provide must, therefore, be easy for them to transfer from your session and replicate on their jobs. Learners who lack appropriate resources when they return to their work settings will not be able to replicate what they have learned. Understanding that this may be the case, you need to know what resources trainees will have available to them before you design the training. Be sure to do the following:

- Request an inventory of resources.
- Conduct an inventory of resources if none is available.
- Incorporate the resources into the training design.
- Give access to follow-up information.
- Provide reference materials.
- Allocate time to practice what was taught.
- Assign individuals to help learners apply what they learned.
- Offer support materials, such as training videos.

Feedback Loops and Enforcing Learning

Feedback is critical to the success of any type of intervention. Learners need to receive clear, appropriate, and timely information about their performance both in the training and on the job. Feedback systems should be designed to provide learners with performance-based information that specifically takes into account what they have learned in training, especially during the first several weeks following the training. Three types of feedback are especially important:

1. Trainer's feedback, in staff and team meetings
2. Supervisor's positive feedback
3. Peer learners' corrective feedback, provided it is given with sensitivity

Remind all those involved feedback must be based on specific information that the person receiving the feedback understands and on performance that the person can apply.

Performance Support

Frequently, the link between training and on-the-job performance is tenuous or totally neglected. To support performance once learners have returned to work, suggest to management they consider implementing the following actions:

- Hold follow-up meetings.
- Provide learners opportunities to use their new skills and knowledge.
- Reinforce what learners mastered.
- Empower learners to explore new areas.
- Allow learners to fail at new endeavors without penalizing them.
- Integrate supervisors into the training process.

Training Designs

Two general types of designs are used that may be thought of as being on a continuum. At one end is a totally preplanned design, and at the other is an emerging design.

In a *preplanned design*, the trainer decides everything in advance for each of the sessions. Of course, you must be open to the reality that you may need to alter, rearrange, add, or drop your plans. However, understand that to design successful trainings, you must adhere to the program goals, use appropriate instructional techniques, and use evaluation criteria that target the program goals and dictated learning objectives for each lesson/module. The new or relatively inexperienced trainer should use this preplanning design.

Here are some guidelines to use to assist in the preplanning design:

- Avoid overplanning, especially minute-to-minute outlines.
- Allow for flexibility.

- Prepare for some resistance to change if feedback during the training indicates the need to make changes.

In an *emerging design*, little is decided in advance. By designing moment to moment, you could lose consistency of thought, action, and intent. The moment-to-moment design could maximize the learners' experiences and interactions on the training activity; it's an option. Sometimes an emerging design will have a plan only for the opening session, with the remainder of the plans emerging as the training proceeds. An emerging design requires minimal preplanning and maximizes the trainer's skills.

Following are some guidelines to use for creating emerging designs:

- Advertise the training activity accurately to the learners so they know a flexible training design will be used.
- Adhere to the design.
- Stop occasionally during the training to ask yourself, "Is this producing learning in accordance with the defined training goals?"

Whatever design you use, remember that adult learners absorb material best when it is given during presentations, demonstrations, readings, dramas, discussions, case studies, visual aids, role plays, games, and participant-directed inquiries.

Notes

1. SHRM, *Learning System Certification Guide* (Alexandria, Va.: Society for Human Resource Management, 1997).

2. Robert Dunn and Thomas C. DeBello, *Improved Test Scores, Attitudes, and Behaviors in America's Schools* (Santa Barbara, Calif.: Praeger, 1999).

3. Robert M. Smith, "How People Become Effective Learners," *Adult Learning,* April 1991, p. 11.

4. Paul McLean, "Brainblog: News About Our Knowledge of the Brain and Behavior," http://neuropsychological.blogspot.com (accessed January 10, 2008).

CHAPTER THREE

Prepare to Conduct the Training

You have defined the need for training and have designed a training program to fit that need. Now, as you prepare to conduct the training, you face many new decisions, mostly about how you will present the material so as to achieve the success your program deserves. This chapter presents, first, the mechanics of preparation for conducting a training program, including consideration of the leadership role, establishing credibility, choosing the best teaching methods, and controlling for behavioral factors. Then, I follow up with pointed discussions of topics behind these matters of preparation, including some more sophisticated group techniques, how to make your lectures engrossing, and what best ways there are to sequence your presentation of ideas to the learners.

Be Prepared to Train Others

The term *training* is used when instructional experiences focus on individuals' acquiring a skill. When training is to be designed and delivered, it requires leadership skills. Learners perceive at the start of a training program that the event is a structured setting, with an agenda and a set of learning objectives. The learners expect that the trainer will tell them when to begin, what to learn, how to proceed, and when the training session will end. The trainer automatically is identified as the group leader. However, if the trainer fails to fulfill the leadership role in the learners' eyes, that trainer will be alienated from the group, leaving a vacuum for someone else to fill, presumably from the group. Therefore, it is important for the trainer to establish credibility within the first five minutes of the first session.

There are three basic trainer styles: authoritarian, laissez-faire, and democratic. Each style affects the learning process, encouraging some adult learners and discouraging others. At one extreme is the *authoritarian* style, whereby the trainer tends to dominate the learning process and the information flows in one direction, from the trainer to the learner. This style leaves little room for learners to interact with the trainer, and generally it limits learning.

At the other extreme is the *laissez-faire* style, whereby learners may feel that there is little direction to the training and that the learning experience is disorganized. The trainer might establish the focus for the conversation or topic, for example, and then allow the learners to control the direction, content, and flow of the exchange of information. The laissez-faire style of training may confuse learners and also inhibit the acquisition of skills and knowledge.

The *democratic* style offers a balanced approach. The trainer establishes a dialogue with the learners, and both trainer and learners have responsibility for exploring the topic. This approach allows for an interplay of personalities, and the instructional foundation is solid, with collaborative learning.

To assess your training style, take the quiz in Table 3-1.

Table 3-1. Self-assessment quiz of trainer style.

1. Consider a trainer you have observed or worked with:
   a. What were the trainer's strengths?
   b. What were the trainer's development needs?
   c. What made this trainer successful?
   d. What were the trainer's unsuccessful situations?
2. Consider the trainer interactions with the class:
   a. What did you learn from the trainer?
   b. What method of learning did you most enjoy, and why?
   c. What does that tell you about developing your own style?
   d. If there was a training team, how did the trainers complement each other?
3. Consider three trainings you have been involved in:
   a. For each one, consider the roles played by the trainer.
   b. How did the trainer facilitate learning?
   c. What could have been done to improve learning?

The Leadership Role

There are a number of ways to assume leadership immediately when you open the beginning session:

1. Set the agenda, and stay on track.
2. Teach to the learning objectives.
3. Protect the rights of each learner.
4. Listen for understanding.
5. Summarize important topics and subtopics.
6. Review frequently to promote connections.

7. Focus the attention of the group on the subject at hand.
8. Manage any challenges to your authority.
9. Involve the silent members.
10. Provide opportunities for reflection.
11. Promote their asking questions.
12. Respect their silence.
13. Provide direction for the program.
14. Establish ground rules for the group meetings.
15. Develop a "parking lot" for handling off-the-topic questions.

There are numerous ways to assume the leadership role, but these 15 techniques are a good start. Let's look at common elements among these techniques to be sure you include them in your training procedures.

The Agenda

The *agenda* is the contract you establish with your learners. That is, when learners come to the training, they want to know what they are going to learn, how they are going to learn it, and what requirements they need in order to complete the session. Your first responsibility as leader is to set the agenda and follow through on it. Specifically, you need to present the learning objectives and sequence of lessons as listed on the agenda. Remember, stick to the agenda. Learners will tolerate some deviations, but such changes from the stated course must be negotiated and agreed upon. As part of the agenda, you need to establish the administrative parameters: breaks, lunch, and beginning and ending times for the sessions.

The Learning Objectives

A credible trainer keeps the course on track, and that track leads to meeting the learning objectives. This task can be easy to do if you design the course to meet those learning objectives, you teach to the objectives, and you evaluate success by comparing achievement to the objectives.

Environmental Distractions

Always be on guard for both internal and external distractions. Outside distractions are the main reason new training facilities are designed windowless. If your training room has windows, arrange the learning space so that the learners can't see anything going on outside, if possible. Internal discussions can be frustrating, too. Poor seating, inadequate lighting, uncomfortable room temperature, poor visibility of the media equipment, odd noises, and strong smells can contribute to learners' being unhappy and distracted. Consider the following when evaluating your training environment:

- Seating—Are there adequate desks, tables, and comfortable chairs?
- Lighting—Is it too light or too dim?
- Temperature—Is it too hot or too cold (keep learners from changing the thermostat)?
- Arrangement—Can everyone see, have a place to work, and have enough materials?
- Schedule—Have you scheduled at least one break in the morning and one in the afternoon (ideal would be one break after every 90 minutes of training)?
- Windows—Can you shut the windows and blinds to minimize glare and distractions?

The Trainer Role

The most important, most visible role of the trainer is to deliver the training. A trainer should be good at organizing and providing accurate information in a way that holds the attention of the audience.

Training is more than just standing up in front of people and presenting information. Individuals attend training sessions to acquire new job skills and knowledge. They want to learn about new resources and new technologies and to observe new ways of doing their job. They also want to network among fellow workers and meet new people. In all training situations, the facilitator has a diverse role that cuts across three distinct responsibilities: subject-matter expert, method expert, and group manager.

Subject-Matter Expert

The learners expect trainers to know something about the subject they are teaching, so the more you know and the better you communicate that knowledge, the greater your credibility increases. Keeping informed is an important part of your professional development, and being current in your training practice is essential.

Of course, nobody can be a complete book of knowledge. If you don't know something, admit it. Be truthful. Recognize any expertise in the group, and call upon it when appropriate. Also, if you are teaching a specialized subject, consider bringing in an expert for a group chat; the expert can offer particular knowledge, and learners will appreciate a change in teaching style, which is often beneficial. One cautionary note, though: do not create such an aura of expertise that you become unapproachable. Credible experts with the human touch are far more respected than aloof ones. The best way to acquire the human touch is to be natural.

Method Expert

There are numerous instructional methods available, and trainers should be familiar with most, and feel comfortable and competent with a few. Part of your responsibility is to exercise sound judgment, choosing the best and most appropriate method for meeting your learners' needs and accommodating the learning preferences of the group.

Becoming increasingly proficient with a variety of instructional methods should be a constant goal and part of your professional development. Watch other trainers, and learn from them. Take occasional risks, and be open to experimenting. As in all walks of life, it is only when we take a few risks that growth and development occur.

Group Manager

Facilitation skills are most obvious when the trainer is acting as group manager. Trainers require a high level of interpersonal skills to manage (not control) a group, for they are serving as motivators and counselors, according to the situation.

Be sensitive to the atmosphere in the group and people's moods; notice the individuals, too. Part of your role is to analyze individuals as well as the group, so you'll need some understanding of the concepts of group process and psychology.

The Trainer Characteristics

As a trainer, you need to have a sense of purpose and understanding of your role. As a facilitator, you realize you are not the center of the discussion; you manage the conversation, making sure that everyone stays on topic and that remains specific to the learning objectives. As a trainer, you are organized, know your material, and are respectful of time. You are fair, open-minded, and thoughtful, making sure that each learner has an opportunity to learn the material you provide. You listen, engage others, and ensure that the information is accurate, delivered in the most efficient and effective way for all the learners.

Being Fair

As leader, you treat all the learners equally, with respect. You establish yourself at the outset as honest, fair, and available to all. You don't accept abusive language or tolerate disrespect of your role or of others in the group, and you don't let one individual dominate. Finally, you do not let learners become scapegoats, for your own or others' failings.

Listening Well

Active listening is a difficult skill to master; it takes practice. Remember, you cannot hear what someone is saying while you are speaking. Listen more, and you will learn more from others. Listen to what they say, and respect their input.

To become a better listener, practice these three active-listening skills:

1. **Listen to summarize**. When learners are speaking to you, focus on the content and context of their message—what they are saying and how they are saying it. For example, determine what their feelings or intentions are by bringing up the subject.
2. **Check for understanding**. When you lose track of the message, ask for clarification. For example, summarize what you have heard or share your reflections on what you thought you understood.
3. **Offer feedback**. When responding in turn, determine if the person has heard what you said by soliciting a response.

Practicing the art of active listening provides an opportunity for you to "listen to hear." During every training session, focus on your communication pattern, be aware of the process, and use active-listening techniques to interact with the learners. Remember to mentally summarize what is being said, check for understanding, paraphrase to show your understanding, and provide appropriate feedback.

Answering Questions from Learners

Questions from learners can be used to facilitate learning, clarify points, and provide additional information. You can use these questions also to initiate a forum for discussion; and if you create a climate for the open exchange of ideas, you will be asked questions almost as often as you ask them of the learners. Here are five steps for handling questions from the learners.

1. Listen to the question being asked.
2. Acknowledge the question.
3. Ask for clarification, if necessary.
4. Answer the question.
5. Verify that your answer is acceptable.

When you follow this process for guiding the direction of learners' questions, you stay focused on the topic at hand and answer the question directly. If someone asks a question that puts you on the spot, remain neutral and say something like, "That's interesting." This response conveys your interest, yet keeps you from talking aimlessly. Once you have listened and clarified the question, you can answer it and then verify that you have addressed the matter sufficiently.

Using Questions to Facilitate

The ability to design a question that facilitates the training process is a talent that takes time to develop. Good questions are an opportunity to get the group moving and involved. They also help you determine where the learners stand on an issue and how much they already know. You can use questions to draw out reticent learners, as well.

Well-phrased questions can clarify points, focus a training session, and move a discussion along. By asking questions, you provide an opportunity for learners to take responsibility for their learning and a chance for them to help others in mastering the new tasks.

There are seven types of facilitation questions that you can use in your training. Table 3-2 shows each type and provides examples.

Table 3-2. Seven types of facilitation questions.

Type of Question	Application
1. Open question (asking for a lot more elaboration)	"Can you tell me more about that?" "How did you feel when that happened?" "Thanks for that input. Can you say more?"
2. Closed question (asking for a short answer, no elaboration)	"Have you ever experienced a group brainstorming session?" "Did you answer yes to number 1?"
3. Echo question (paraphrasing for clarity)	"In other words, you feel . . . ?" "Can I paraphrase your comment by saying . . . ?"
4. Direct question (attempting to get a specific answer)	"What did you like about the group activity?" "If you were to improve the skill practice, what would you do?"
5. Loaded question (forcibly seeking agreement through emphasis)	"This is the best process to take—right?" "We are moving forward—don't you agree?"
6. Interrupting questions (interruptions, diverting activities, or expanded discussions)	Parking lot approach: "Mark, you might want to post that question in long-term parking." Entire group approach: "I think it would be helpful if we could have only one conversation going at any one time."
7. Reply questions (processing questions, getting the group moving, putting energy into the discussion, or forcing group or individuals to take responsibility for their learning)	Facilitator to participant (single question directed at one participant): "Cheryl, you seem anxious to share what happened in your group. Can you tell us about it?" Facilitator to group (one question directed at the group in general, which helps stimulate thought and interaction): "How did the rest of you react to that?"

Participant to facilitator, then facilitator to different participant (turns over the discussion to another participant who may shed further light on the subject): Peter: "I was reluctant to start the exercise. Is that common?" Fran:"Let's find out. Cathy, were you reluctant to begin?"
Participant to group or participant to another participant (direct question that does not go through the facilitator). (Be careful of this strategy; this can get out of hand, and you may lose your leader control!): Peter: "Larry, what do you think?" Fran: "Did that happen to anyone else?"

Responding Appropriately

A critical task for the trainer is getting individuals to participate in the training. The learners expect that you will keep them engaged and teach them something they can apply on the job. They look to you to teach, manage the classroom, and take care of the administrative matters with ease and efficiency. If they recognize your leadership, they will buy into the learning experience.

Nevertheless, there may be occasional challenges to your leadership. If you get challenged, guard against getting defensive. Here are some guidelines for handling a difficult situation.

- Greet the challenge openly, with a smile. Walk toward the challenger (never walk away or stand behind something, which would signal that you want to hide).
- Ask for clarification, or state your understanding of the matter.
- If the issue is a genuine one, allow the person to provide specifics.
- Conclude with some resolution (even if it means that you say you will have an answer tomorrow, or when you check things out—just provide some deadline).

- When the challenger and others are relaxed, move on to the next sequence of the training.

Five-Star Credibility

The initial question learners will ask about you is, "Who are you?" They have signed up for the training, and they need to trust you and identify with your knowledge. When you begin your session, think about the three questions that learners probably have on their minds during the first 10 minutes of any training program:

1. Can I identify with her/him?
2. Is he/she knowledgeable?
3. Can I trust him/her to be right?

Given these three questions, you need to settle just who you are in this relationship.

Here's how to start. Use what they already know about you and the training from the brochure that describes the program and you. Acknowledge the value of what they will be learning and its importance to their professional and personal development. Ask them for their input about the learning objectives, and then conduct a brief, on-the-spot audience needs assessment. Write the responses on chart paper, identifying each topic with the learner's name. Review the list, and respond by organizing the topics into major categories. Explain how the course will be conducted to meet some of these needs. If there are topics on the list that are not going to be covered, talk about why that is. Don't ignore the issue.

Next, build a mental bridge for the learners by focusing on the topics that will be covered. Determine what is known and unknown among the group, and illustrate how the new information will fit with their existing knowledge.

Components of Credibility

An important aspect of effective training is your personal style—the "This is me!" element. One of the best ways to establish your identity and your credibility is to present yourself in a frame of "Five-Star Personal Credibility." This model (see Figure 3-1) consists of five points on a star, which represent parts of your persona that the learners will observe.

Below, I discuss each of these points and show their importance in establishing your credibility. It is important that you examine each and consider situations where you have successfully displayed all five at the same time. The model should become part of your natural human spirit, so that each time you conduct a training session, you convey this positive image.

Figure 3-1. Five-star credibility model.

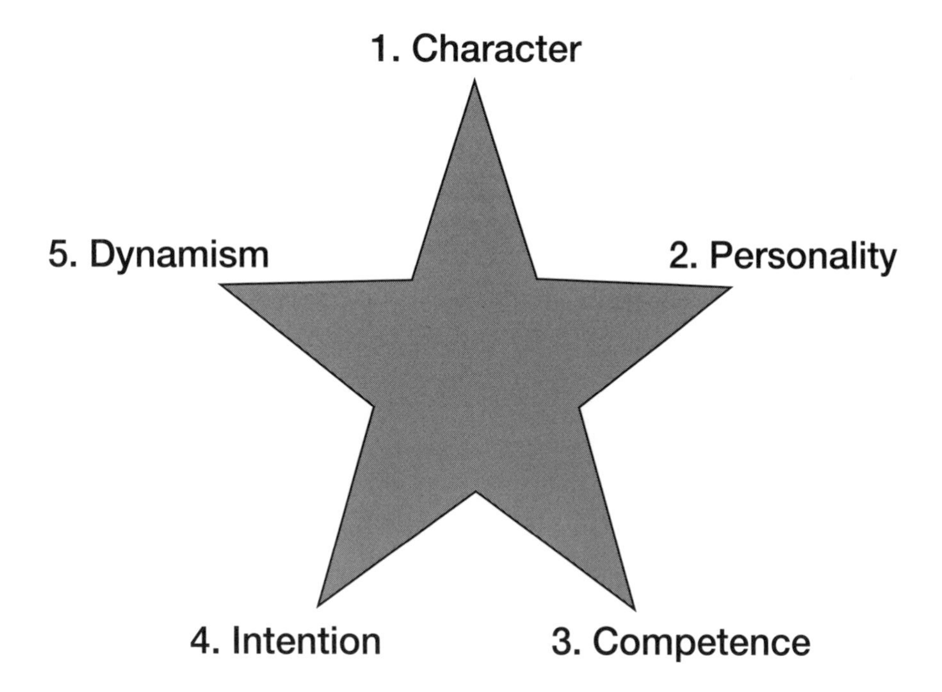

1. **Character.** You act as a role model. You are ethical, and you have integrity. You set the good example by avoiding gossip and negative discussions about the organization, its executives, managers, or trainees.

2. **Personality**. You know yourself, laugh at yourself, maintain a positive attitude, and display empathy for others.

3. **Competence.** You have the knowledge, expertise, and experience to offer the training. You have good presentation and facilitation skills.

4. **Intention.** You display motivation and make it obvious to others why you want to be there.

5. **Dynamism**. You show and have self-confidence; your charisma attracts others.

Phases of Credibility

A training program has specific points at which different aspects of credibility will emerge. These points can be viewed as three distinct phases in the program. Although they appear to be simple to manage, remember that training is a partnership, a process, so you make conscious attempts at certain points, such as the words you choose to use and the way you explain things. Remember at all times, however, to appear natural, and the instruction will also flow naturally. The three phases of training credibility are:

1. **Initial Credibility**. This occurs even before the training begins, and is based on the organization's reputation, the trainer's reputation, and anything else that learners have heard about the course or about you.

2. **Derived Credibility**. This occurs during the training. The learners continually evaluate you and the information you are providing. Your credibility can either increase or decrease during this training.

3. **Terminal Credibility**. This occurs after the training is completed, and it is based on what the learners have seen, heard, experienced, and taken away from the session.

Folk Wisdoms and Credibility

Trainers often exchange tips and pass along what some term "folk wisdom." The folk wisdom that I remember best is about credibility: learners evaluate their trainers in the first 60 seconds of the session.

So, how do you make a positive first impression? You provide a short welcome. In your welcome statement, you briefly state the topics to be covered, you explain why you are the trainer, and you offer something that might motivate them to learn from you—some "benefit" they may gain that suggests the journey you are taking together is worthwhile. One of my favorite opening statements is a *guarantee statement*. I say, "If you participate, you will be able to apply 80 percent of what you learn immediately."

The Recipe for Trainer Success: Preparation

The secret for successful training is good preparation, including how you plan, conduct, and manage the sessions. You can apply this recipe to any length training or any topic. Preparation provides the basic ingredients for establishing a well-balanced event that will ensure success.

Taking our metaphor of a recipe further, let's look at the ingredients list:

1 well-written program
2 parts subject-matter knowledge
3 parts program preparation
4 parts confidence
1 great opening
6 practice sessions with training aids
1 great summary and closing

Put all ingredients in a large bowl, and mix thoroughly. Repeat, practicing several times until the training begins. Review the recipe after the event, and make modifications, if necessary.

Preparing for your training is the best defense against the unmanageable. With careful preparation, you can reduce your down time and optimize the training time. There are four steps to organizing your training: plan the training, know the audience and venue, select the materials and format, and organize and present. Let's consider each in turn.

Step 1: Plan the Training

The first step is the most essential and the most time-consuming. Planning requires establishing the topic and subtopic areas, understanding the audience's needs, sequencing the topics for logical and easy learning, and building these into your training.

To begin, determine the *purpose* of the training. Trainers often confuse purpose with objective, so it is important to understand the difference. The purpose of the training is a single, broadly stated goal, the one result you want your delivery to achieve. In contrast, the objective is a description of specific steps you need to take or achieve in accomplishing a task.

Next, you think of your purpose in terms of the audience. Remember that your purpose is to effect a change; you want your audience to think and behave differently, or to have acquired new knowledge as a result of your training. So, you determine the purpose on the basis of your training needs assessment. The following are examples of training purposes:

- Teach newly promoted managers how to be effective in their new roles.
- Show technicians how to service the organization's computers.
- Illustrate how sales staff can improve customer relations.
- Demonstrate the computerized reservation system to new travel agents.

The training event begins when the first individuals register for the program, so when planning and organizing, keep in mind the prospective learners. A majority of them will suffer some fear of the unknown; they may be concerned about what is expected of them during the training, worry whether there will be tests involved, or if they will like the other learners. Likewise, they will wonder if the training material will be easy to use, if they will have fun learning, and if they will learn something to take back to the job.

One of your first tasks in your introduction to the training is to speak to those fears. You'll also keep these fears in mind when you plan the setup of the training room. You'll arrange the room so that it appears to be a comfortable, organized space that will energize the learners. (There's more about venue later in this chapter.)

There are instructional strategies and techniques that can make your training exciting, so don't be afraid to use them, and don't reserve them for a special day. (That opportunity to train on the topic might not come again, and you can always create new, exciting things if it does.) Your planning at this early stage should include fun for you and the learners. Get some props or wear a costume!

Delivery is important to successful training, so think about how you can show your "stuff." Plan opportunities to make your training more interesting—and thereby make the information stick!

Step 2: Know the Audience and Venue

As part of your preparation, you need information about two essential elements: the audience and the physical setting.

The Audience Personality

Every audience, even a training group, has a single definite personality, even though the group is made up of individual personalities. You will need to sense both the individual and the group characteristics of your learners. Listed below are many questions you can ask to learn about your audience:

The Audience's Makeup

- What are their job titles and functions?
- Are they managers, teachers, or physicians?
- Are they parents, young adults, men, women, or older adults?

Their Knowledge of the Topic

- What do they know?
- Have they undergone similar trainings?
- Is this topic new to them?
- What is important for them to learn?
- What do they need to know?
- Are they coming for general knowledge or for specific skills?
- If they are coming to learn specific skills, what kind of skills (e.g., job, personal, career, coping)?
- What is not important for them to learn?
- What do they not need to know?
- How much do they already know about the subject?
- What will they consider superfluous or boring?

Their Sensitivities

- What should you risk talking about?
- What kinds of backgrounds do they have?
- Is there anything in your background that you could share?
- What topics might insult their beliefs or their intelligence?
- What are their feelings about coming to this training?
- How can you build credibility with them?

External Issues

- Is the time of day convenient for them?
- What kind of atmosphere are they used to?

- Will the attendees be in a rush to leave at the end?
- Will they be drifting in and out during the training?
- Will they be eager to learn, or will they be skeptical about the training?
- What will they be interested in learning?
- Who is paying for them to attend, and how does that impact their motivation?

As you take the steps of preparing the training, always keep your audience in mind. Primary, here, is determining the audience's level of knowledge. Some learners may know more than you do about particular points, whereas others may not know enough to follow the training.

An audience's knowledge falls into the following five categories:

1. No knowledge
2. Below average knowledge
3. Average knowledge
4. Above average knowledge
5. Expert

Once you have a grasp of the audience's level of knowledge, you can make informed decisions about your delivery strategy. You have two choices: (1) For an informal or general presentation, you can aim for the average level of knowledge. (2) For specific skills training, you should ask the sponsor of the training, "In which of the five categories does the discerning mind sit?" If you miss by more than one category, you will not accomplish your training objectives.

If you are unsure about the audience's level of knowledge, be careful not to underestimate the audience's intelligence. Likewise, do not overestimate the audience's knowledge and experience. Remember, part of knowing your audience is understanding that the audience members want you to succeed.

Gathering information about an audience is a critical step in the design and delivery of an effective training program. To determine how the audience will learn best, you should consider a broad range of factors when assessing the audience's learning preferences. There is no one assessment of learning styles that all educators, researchers, or trainers agree is most effective; however, most agree that individuals learn differently. So, to create a training program that will appeal to all learners, consider how learning occurs.

Stated simply, learners initially observe that something is happening, then they reflect on what they have just observed, and they then apply their own meaning to that observation. Individual preferences come in when the learner tries to give that meaning to the observation. Expressed intellectually, we say that the learners are building a theory—their own theory of how this new information might work with something they already know, or fit what they perceive as new information with something that they already know. How well that application is made is determined largely by how easy people find the process. Learning differences owing to different learning styles and levels of learning maturity exist all of the time during training. Be sensitive to individual needs and aware of the audience's various levels and abilities.

The Venue Challenges

The configuration of the room in which you will be training affects your training success. Therefore, part of your preparation is to see your classroom, its size, and its shape. This will allow you to determine how to arrange the room and set up the seating. If you fail to check the training room arrangements before starting the event, you will quickly learn that you have left yourself open for trouble. Ideally, you should check to see that everything is in place before the first participant arrives. It is always a little troubling when early arrivals find you rushing around to put things in order. Use a checklist to make sure that you have everything ready.

Step 3: Select Materials and Format

Once you know your audience and the physical surroundings, you are in a position to select the most appropriate materials and format for your training. Again, consider the participants in relation to the content.

Participant Overview

When determining the format for your training, you need to address the following four critical elements:

1. **Learning is content based**. One of the principles of adult learning theory is that adults learn nothing new. They merely sort and fit the concepts presented in the training into their existing knowledge base.

2. **Motivation can be encouraged.** You do not have the power to motivate anyone to learn. However, you can create environments and opportunities for people to learn by making the training immediately applicable to the job or by ensuring that the training contributes to their personal and professional growth.

3. **Responsibility is shared.** It is your job to help participants share the responsibility for what they are about to learn.

4. **Learning needs structure.** In general, people learn by seeing, listening, or doing. Regardless of your learners' learning preferences, all of them learn best when there is a structured lesson plan.

Content Overview

The content of your training program is the information, knowledge, or skills you will impart. When deciding how to develop that content, consider whether the presentation should focus on the trainer (known as a trainer-centered presentation) or on those being trained (trainee-centered presentation). In making this decision, consider the learning outcome, the simplicity or complexity of the content, your skill level as a trainer, and the participants' level of learning.

Table 3-3 displays formats for trainings, according to the focus of the presentation. The left-hand column shows trainer-centered formats, in which the trainer is responsible for the presentation of information or is the lecturer. The right-hand column shows trainee-centered formats, which include contract learning, computer-based learning, and programmed instruction. These formats provide the opportunity for learners to assert their control over the content they are to master, and these formats let them decide the parameters for learning, including the time, place, and pace that suit their needs. The middle column shows formats that provide blended learning experiences, in which learners and trainer take equal roles and assume equal responsibility for the learning process.

Table 3-3. Training formats to match presentations.

Trainer Centered	In Between	Trainee Centered
Theory	Case study	Contract learning
Skills	Role-play	Computer-based
Lecture	Simulation	Programmed instruction

How do you "collect" content? One easy way to begin is by jotting down ideas as soon as you know you are going to give a training program. To generate more ideas, use brainstorming techniques, in which you write down anything that comes to mind, regardless of its practicality. Remember that, at this point, you are simply collecting content; you will not need to use every note but merely the best of the ridiculous or possible you have generated.

Trust yourself to know what content is best. That way you'll get out of your own way as you gather ideas by not judging those ideas prematurely. You are the authority on your subject, even if others don't recognize you as such. By virtue of your own experience, you are qualified to speak about experiences and events in your personal and professional life. Weave these experiences and events into your delivery in order to make points, expand on issues, or use as examples. In doing so, you will put yourself and your audience at ease. In fact, as you collect and select ideas, remember that this is merely a conversation with your equals—which is what training is.

If, after reviewing your notes, you believe your idea generation is a bit weaker than you would like, you can gather additional ideas through literature searches, personal observations, experiments, surveys, and interviews. Unless your subject matter is scholarly or extremely technical, you can probably find all of the content you need in books, magazines, and technical manuals.

Step 4: Organize the Presentation

There are numerous ways to organize the content and ideas you have collected and selected. One of the easiest is to write the purpose of the training (see "Step 1: Plan the Presentation" at the beginning of this chapter) in large letters on a piece of paper and tape it to the wall in front of you. Then, you can create a mental picture of the audience you have identified. You proceed to select the type of training and the method of delivery.

Select the Training Type

Most training programs have one of two basic purposes: to present information or to develop a skill. Therefore, there are two types of training sessions: information oriented (theory) and skill related. The information-oriented presentation, or theory session, stresses ideas, whereas the skill-related presentation stresses mastery of a particular skill. Often, the training topic will dictate which model applies. However, sometimes the training topic is ambiguous, so the trainer needs to consider applying either or both models.

Assume that you were asked to train employees on how to fill out a new form. By reviewing the form, you can obtain a clearer understanding of which model to use. For instance, do the participants need to learn only how to complete the form? Or must the participants also understand the reason that the new form is required and how that form relates to work processes or communication? If the objective is for them to fill out the form correctly *and* understand the form's role in the work processes, then you might need to combine a *theory session*, in which you explain the role of the form, with a *skill session*, in which you show how to complete the form.

Assume you will begin with a theory session, because trainers often precede a skill session with a theory session, during which they present background information about the skill. The theory session model, as Figure 3-2 shows, usually consists of three segments: introduction, body, and conclusion. First, divide your presentation into these segments, each of which may be relatively independent of one another or may build sequentially upon the others. Either way, each segment needs its own objective.

Figure 3-2. Theory session model.

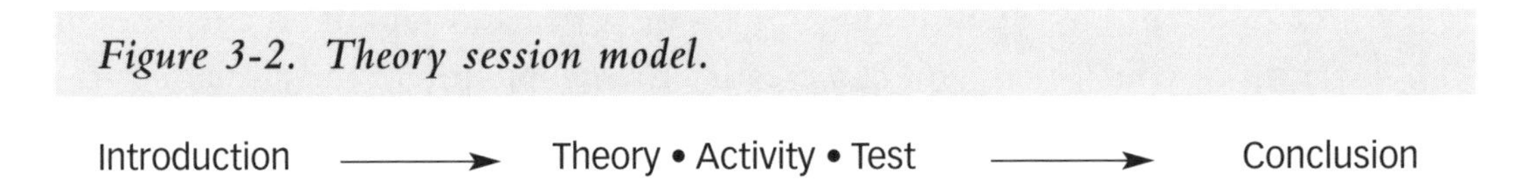

If you are creating a skill session, it will consist of the same three segments as for the theory session. However, the body will not include theory (only activity and test) because it is more important for participants to understand how to perform an activity than to know the theory behind why it is done. (This will be discussed in more detail in Chapter 5.)

Select Method of Delivery

When thinking about how you will deliver your training, remember, again, that you are holding a conversation with your audience. Although at first you might think it would be easier—or at least less frightening—

to read or memorize your presentation, if you do you will not be engaged in conversation. Imagine the times you have interrupted a direct telephone marketer to ask a question, and the person on the other end does not know what to do. Imagine yourself as that person in the audience if you were to deliver your training by reading or memorizing it.

Read or memorized presentations often sound artificial, and they create an unwanted distance between the presenter and the audience. Because you want to effect a change in behavior, you do not want to run the risk of losing your audience. Of course, it can be helpful to memorize certain sections—for example, the introduction and the conclusion. But remember that a read or memorized presentation leaves little room for spontaneity, or for responding to your audience. In fact, by reading or delivering a memorized presentation, you may be insulting your audience. If that weren't enough to discourage you from reading or memorizing, then think about this: You need to practice long and hard to read well—much longer than practicing presenting material as a conversation.

If you are most comfortable reading a presentation, however, use colored pens to indicate some of the following in your script:

- Slash marks to represent places to pause
- Underlined statements for emphasis
- Enlarged punctuation marks for exclamation or questions

Also, box in the passages that you plan to memorize, so that you can look up at your audience when you deliver them. In fact, think of memorization as another form of reading—reading from within. Rather than looking at notes, you search your brain for the content you have prepared. That's why memorization suffers from the same disadvantages as reading, especially the inability to maintain eye contact with the participants—your eyes are looking inward, not out to the audience.

By far, extemporaneous delivery is best, with the following advantages:

- It allows you to adapt to a variety of circumstances.
- It encourages audience involvement and interaction.
- It projects spontaneity and enthusiasm, regardless of how often you have delivered the same training.
- It injects interest and enthusiasm into your presentation.

For good extemporaneous delivery, you must plan and rehearse, as well as write the presentation. Though you do not bring your script, you do bring your notes to serve as a reminder of the introduction and conclusion, your key statistics, and any catch words and phrases that will help you make your points.

Use Visual Aids

Incorporate visual aids into your training. They have several benefits. They:

- Arouse interest
- Encourage participation
- Prevent misunderstanding
- Persuade
- Focus attention
- Save time
- Reinforce ideas
- Add humor
- Enhance credibility
- Explain the inaccessible

Visual materials supplement your presentation. Do not use visual materials as a script; rather, use them as a checklist of key ideas that you will explain, expand upon, and emphasize. The following are key types of visual aids:

Charts. Charts can be configured as words, as an organizational structure, as a pie, or as a series of sheets of paper. *Word* charts are lists and tables that you can prepare quickly. When creating word charts, use the seven-seven rule: limit lines of type to seven; limit words per line to seven. *Organization* charts are useful to explain processes and operations. *Pie* charts show percentage distribution, with the circle or pie presenting the whole and the segments. When using pie charts, make sure everyone in the audience can see the smallest part. Also, consider different colors for the segments you want to emphasize. *Flip* charts are large blank pads of paper, bound at the top. Use these charts with the adhesive on the back to stick to the wall—no more looking for tape to hang charts!

Cutaways. Cutaways are pictures that show the interior composition of an object, in three dimensions; these help clarify spatial relationships.

Maps. Maps should be simple enough to include only the specific features of land or sea that serve the purpose of the presentation.

Graphs. Several types of graphs are used commonly. *Line* graphs show how related sets of facts change according to a common measure of reference, usually time. *Profile* graphs present the same sort of information using shading or coloring. *Bar* graphs compare two facts, but do not show how they change over time.

Projected Visual Aids. Computer-generated slides projected from laptop computers are fast becoming the norm for presentations. Here are some rules to follow: Illustrate one idea only per slide, use only 15 words per slide, make sure the letters are legible, keep the content simple, use color whenever possible, and use several consecutive slides to explain complex information.

With regard to projected visual aids, you'll find that most facilities have overhead projectors on hand. Consider using overhead projection when you want to show texts and photos (your daily newspaper often contains the very item that will enhance your presentation; also, check books and magazines) or cartoons (use cartoons carefully to make sure they do not offend any member of the audience; you can turn an ordinary photograph into a cartoon by adding an incongruous caption).

Models, Mockups, and Props. These types of visual aids have high-impact value, but often can be expensive and time-consuming to prepare. The biggest advantage to using models, mockups, and props is that they add realism to your presentation because of their three dimensions.

For the most effective use of any visual aid, keep in mind the following points:

- **Size and Visibility**. The visual aid must be large enough so everyone in the audience can see it clearly and read it easily. Audiences find visual aids that they cannot see annoying and distracting. Instead of paying attention to what the visual aid is communicating, audience members are desperately contorting themselves so as to see the image. To make your visual aids large enough so everyone can see them, you need to know the physical setting in which the training will take place. If you can, experiment with the visual aids in the actual room in which you will be delivering your presentation.
- **Details**. Details that are not essential to your point can detract from your presentation, cluttering the visual aid. Unless decoration is the point you are trying to make, do not be decorative.
- **Precision**. Make sure your visual aids are neat and precise. Sloppy or careless visual aids reflect poorly on you as a trainer.
- **Focus**. Remember to keep your eyes on the audience, not on the visual aids, as you speak. The trainees' eyes will be on the visual aids.
- **Introduction**. Every visual aid needs to be put into context. First state what the visual aid is intended to show and then point out its main features.

- **Planning**. Incorporate your visual aids into your script, and rehearse your discussion of them exactly as you plan to present them. Do not show a visual aid until you are ready to talk about it, and as soon as you are finished talking about it, remove it from sight.

Perhaps the most important reason to use visual materials is that people learn more easily through sight than through any other sense. Visual materials help people retain what they learn, as well. As Table 3-4 shows, people retain information longer when the presentation is both show and tell. You can help your audience retain what you present by adhering to the KISS and KILL principles:

- KISS: Keep It Simple and Succinct
- KILL: Keep It Legible and Large

Table 3-4. Information retention.

Presentation Method	Percentage of Information Retained After 3 Hours	Percentage of Information Retained After 3 Days
Tell only	70	10
Show only	72	20
Show and tell	85	65

Use Quotations, Tell Unique Tales, and Incorporate Exciting Resources

Quotations from reliable sources can add credibility to your presentation. You can use business-related quotations, quote information from company publications, or incorporate statements from subject-matter experts. Likewise, telling some unique tales based on your own experience adds value—they say that you have "been there and done that!" Lastly, inserting some resources that learners will find exciting enhances your credibility, telling your audience that you are widely versed on the topic.

Below are some tips for using these presentation resources:

- Try to put yourself in your participants' shoes. What do they know about you? What do they want to know? Incorporate resources that will make them admire your skill and abilities.
- Remember that you know as much or more about the material than anyone else in the group, but if there are experts out there, make them your friends and include their expertise in your presentation.
- Develop your own presentation style, using extra materials as you see them fitting in. Don't try to copy another trainer's style.

Particularly when your presentation will be using visuals, you'll need to double-check that the equipment you'll need is on hand, in working condition, and ready for use. Table 3-5 is a checklist that you should review prior to beginning any sessions. In fact, bring the checklist with you on the first day of the event, and go down the list, checking off items as secured and ready. The more prepared you feel to use the auxiliary equipment, the more energy you'll have for being a great trainer.

Table 3-5. Classroom preparation checklist.

	Yes	No
• Is the room set up correctly—classroom style, team style, etc.?	☐	☐
• Are all of the materials correctly positioned for each learner?	☐	☐
• Have the refreshments been ordered? Are they set up?	☐	☐
• Is the technology in place—computer, projector, screen, etc.?	☐	☐
• Are the certificates printed?		
• Do I have the following supplies readily available: masking tape, chart markers, note paper, and pencil?	☐	☐

Effective Management of the Training Process

So far, this chapter has offered preparation tips regarding your role as leader and trainer, tips for establishing your credibility, and four steps to trainer success. Now, let's take a closer look.

Open with Energy

Opening exercises should accomplish three goals: (1) build teams—helping participants become acquainted with each other and creating a spirit of cooperation and interdependence; (2) provide on-the-spot assessment—learning about the attitudes, knowledge, and experiences of the participants; and (3) offer immediate learning involvement—creating initial interest in the training topic. According to Mel Silberman, author of *Active Training*, all three of these goals can be accomplished in combination or one at a time.

The opening of a training program is not a social event. It is a time to organize the participants, align their goals with the goals of the planned instruction, and provide an opportunity for participants to meet one another. The most popular opener strategy is the icebreaker, but there are many more creative ways to introduce the topics and the participants. Here are five ideas that are easy to design and fun to facilitate:

1. **Opening Activities**. Design activities that build interest in the entire course and introduce some of the major ideas of the first part of the program. For example, bingo games, 30-second TV "self" commercials, go-arounds (group provides short responses to questions), self-assessments, and pop quizzes.

2. **Headlines**. Reduce the major points in the lecture to newspaper headlines that will then act as verbal cues to aid memory. For example, tell and sell, tell and listen, or listen and tell.

3. **Use an active-listening mnemonic**. Give your participants ways to remember key information. For example, the word *trainer* is a good device for you to remember the characteristics of a successful trainer:

T = trust

R = respect

A = authentic

I = informed

N = natural or neutral

E = enthusiastic

R = resourceful

4. **Analogies**. Create a comparison between your material and the knowledge and experience that trainees bring with them. For example, suppose a trainer is discussing adult learning needs. Using the computer as a metaphor for the brain, the trainer says the adult can (a) turn off the computer; (b) doesn't have the right application on the desktop; (c) is not allowed to process the information; or (d) doesn't have a chance to save the information.

5. **Visual Backup**. Charts, brief handouts, and desktop presentation tools allow the learners to see as well as hear what you are saying.

Conducting a successful training requires organization, planning, and focus. If you know your material and have an appropriate portfolio of instructional methods and strategies, along with a good understanding of the audience, you are prepared and will do well. If you are in control, you can then focus your energy on providing a successful training. Here is a list of self-management techniques that you should think about to ensure a successful beginning of your training. It's all about engaging your audience:

- Prepare yourself to train.
- Arrange the physical environment.

- Greet the participants and establish rapport.
- Get the best from the first 20 minutes.
- Review the agenda.
- Invite feedback to the agenda.

Vary the Instructional Methods

If you use the same method of instruction all the time, it can build a barrier to learning. For example, a trainer who uses role-plays all of the time might have little success with that method when instructing a group learning how to use the computer. Or, the trainer who uses the lecture method might find that it is an inappropriate learning method when hands-on practice would work better.

Following are several methods of instruction and a brief description of when or where they can be used effectively. It's important to remember that these methods are not all limited to the classroom.

Traditional Methods

The most popular methods are usually the traditional ones. Most trainers know how to use these and do so most of the time. These standard methods are great, but they have their limitations. Make sure that your methods are best suited for the situation and the audience.

1. **Lecture**. The lecture is often referred to as "talking to" or "talking at" the group; it is simply addressing a passive audience. To be effective, lecturers need to be on top of things at all times and to be interesting or amusing to the audience. You also need to use an appropriate number of analogies, the correct level of language for the audience, and a logical sequence of ideas. For a lecture to be effective, the presenter needs to be aware of the participants at all times. The presenter's voice is particularly important, in both level and tone. Also, the material must be made meaningful to the group so that the members will

want to listen. It is also possible, and advisable, to use training aids in a lecture. Unfortunately, the lecture does not generally allow for any immediate evaluation or for two-way communication.

2. **Modified Lecture.** The modified lecture is similar to a lecture, except that the lecturer encourages some group participation. The modified lecture is now common in adult training; in fact, the lecturer often relies on the participants' experiences to generate some discussion. However, the lecturer/presenter needs to make it clear from the beginning that the session is not a straight lecture and that group discussion or participation is welcome. Questions should be encouraged. This form of presentation should allow for some form of evaluation at the end, as well. The modified lecture is an extremely efficient method of instruction and is commonly used in private trainings. When preparing for this type of presentation, allow sufficient time for group participation.

3. **Demonstration**. The demonstration allows participants to observe what the presentation is about. Most demonstrations are limited to situations requiring motor skills, but this need not be the case. Demonstrations could also be used to show participants some of the interpersonal skills, such as interviewing and coaching. A demonstration should follow a planned sequence: a verbal explanation showing the item or skill, participant questions, and practice. Among the things to remember when using demonstrations is that you should break the task into bite-size pieces so that the learner can progress through mini-goals rather than trying to achieve everything at once. When demonstrating, ensure that all members of the group can see the demonstration. It is also a good idea to check ahead of time that all equipment is in working order. Above all, make sure that there is ample time for participants to practice the skill.

4. **Learner Practice**. The learner practice should occur after every type of instruction. It is pointless to teach a new skill and not encourage learners to use and perfect that skill. It is the trainer's responsibility to encourage trainees to apply the skill. Under supervised practice, participants find out whether they can use the new skill effectively. The trainer also

finds out whether the final objective has been reached whereby the participant is able to perform the skill away from the controlled atmosphere of the training room. Learner practice on the job occurs when trainers observe behavioral changes. This is the most effective form of practice and ultimately the most important evaluation of the training. Positive feedback to the participants is also likely to encourage them to want to know more, and may encourage them to undertake further instruction because they will have learned the effectiveness of training.

5. **Learner Reading**. Reading can be used effectively, or it may be a total waste of everyone's time and effort. Learner reading before or during a course can be extremely relevant to group discussions and exercises; however, if there are one or two learners who do not do the reading, they won't know what's happening. Additionally, the group may have to mark time while the trainer brings these people up to speed with a quick overview. Therefore, learners must be given an incentive to spend their own time reading course material. The trainer could perhaps tell them that there will be a quiz. Also, they should know that if they don't do the required reading they will be wasting not only their time but also the time of the group. A recent idea is to give the learners note pads that have structured exercises for them to perform while reading. An example of such exercises could be a series of statements with missing words or phrases that the participants must fill in. If the trainer uses a structured note pad, many other forms of assignment can be designed for the learners to undertake while reading.

6. **Problem-Based Learning**. Problem-based learning is an instructional method that challenges participants to learn by working together in groups to seek solutions to real-world problems. Use problem-based learning to prepare learners to think critically and analytically, and to find and use appropriate learning sources. When trainers use the problem-based learning strategy, they can transform a traditional lecture into a group-centered, problem-solving experience. To prepare for a problem-based learning session, pay close attention to

detail, organization, and design of your program, and provide some built-in structure to introduce the problem, manage group dynamics, and provide a summary. Table 3-6 is a template for designing problem-based learning.

Table 3.6. Problem-based learning design template.

Introduction and Overview

Each person will have an opportunity to describe a problem for the group to solve. The exercise provides an opportunity for learners to work together to solve a real workplace problem.

1. Give the learners guidelines.
2. Instruct each group to elect a group leader. The group leader then has the responsibility to collect the problem statements from each member and read each proposed problem scenario to the group; the group adopts one problem statement to use throughout the training problem exercise.
3. Allow ample time each day for groups to work on the chosen cases and report progress to the group.
4. Provide each participant with a sheet of printed questions to help the groups arrive at a problem solution. Typically questions can be:
   - What is the problem?
   - Who is involved?
   - What would you like to see happen?
   - What is the worst-case scenario if your desired solution doesn't work?
   - What would the situation look like if the problem were resolved the way you consider appropriate?

In-Session Check-In

Assess the progress of group problem solving at regular intervals. If necessary, interrupt group work to correct misconceptions or to make sure that the groups are all in sync with respect to the task and time allotted.

Discussion Time

Allow time for combined group discussion of the problem at the end of the problem-based learning session or at the beginning of the next session of your training program.

Experiential Methods

Experiential learning means an emphasis on active and participatory learning. You use the experiential learning approach to enhance the understanding of concepts as well as a gateway to skill development. Experiential learning means that the learners must do the tests themselves, thus promoting self-learning. The trainer helps participants become aware of their feelings and reactions to certain issues and new ideas. In addition, they allow participants to practice and refine new skills and procedures. The experiential learning approaches are particularly suited for affective and behavioral training goals.

1. **Fishbowl**. This method can be used for analysis of group process or as a monitor of the effectiveness of group discussion. The participants need to be seated in two concentric circles—a small inner circle with a larger circle around it. The trainer usually selects an important, or controversial, topic and formulates several discussion-provoking questions. These questions are given to one person in the inner circle. It is the responsibility of those in the inner circle to keep the discussion going on the set topic. A number of observers are appointed to sit in the outer circle, and they are asked to note things such as who is doing the talking, who is interrupting, whether the discussion gets sidetracked very often, whether there are many disagreements, whether there are any signs of nonverbal communication, and any other points the facilitator wants to include in the debriefing of the exercise. The group members should be shuffled around so that all have at least one turn in the inner circle as a participant and a turn in the outer circle as an observer. This is obviously a fairly complicated method, and it would be advisable for new trainers to avoid a fishbowl until they feel comfortable with simpler group work methods.

2. **Role-Plays**. Role-plays, or skill practices, are situational examples. A role-playing exercise normally involves the trainer, or someone in the group, in designing a simple script involving a situation the

participant may be placed in. It is then a matter of getting some of the group members to act out the situation in identified positions, using previous experience, new knowledge or skills given to them, or other methods they would like to try under controlled conditions. Try to let the participants do most of the work because this will give them the commitment to follow the role-play through to the end. Don't use too many props, as they may be distracting; let the group members use their imagination in setting the scene. Hold a debriefing as soon as the role-play is finished; this gives everyone feedback on the process and highlights the important points or issues raised by the group.

3. **Simulations.** A simulation is sometimes used for team-building exercises. It is not unlike role-plays or skills practice as we know them, but is more complex in structure and requires more participant input. For a simulation, the group has to act in a team role, such as a team of consultants or a board of directors. With large groups, it is advisable to break the group into smaller teams with different exercises so that all team members can have input. The groups are normally placed in a situation in which they must get together and solve problems or build empires. It is normally a very descriptive exercise and may run for months. When the simulations have been completed, the groups present their findings to all of the participants. Not only may someone pick up good ideas, but it is also a fitting conclusion to the exercise. In some simulations, a lot of team effort is used, and this presentation period is the group's opportunity to show how successful it was. Simulations are also used for individual training, such as on flight simulators. Such exercises tend to be complex and generally expensive to set up, however.

4. **Games**. These can be simple (such as joining the dots in the shortest time) or very complex (such as who can show a million-dollar profit first). Games are normally competitive and usually related directly to the task involved. If games are made to be competitive, there should not be winners and losers, but should yield a variety of thoughts and ideas, and show how others may use them. When games are used to develop or

improve skills, they can be offered at any stage during training. Experienced trainers tend to keep their games for use after breaks. If you find a lively game that gets everyone involved and moving around, it may be worth designing your session so that this game can be used immediately after lunch. There are many books now available that contain hundreds of proven games for different topics. If you design your own games and they are successful, share them with other trainers.

5. **Observations.** Observation is watching others without directly participating. This can be an effective way to experience learning. Although it is worthwhile for participants to practice something, observation by itself can play an important part in training. The key is for the observation experience to be active rather than passive. There are several ways to design observation activities so that participants are actively involved. Provide aids to help participants attend to and retain pertinent aspects of demonstrations. When participants are observing a role-play or group exercise, provide easy-to-use observation forms containing suggestions, questions, and checklists. Expect observers to give constructive feedback so as to challenge them to observe carefully and apply what they have learned. Finally, be aware that observers can have strong vicarious experiences if what they are observing has personal impact; use simple forms to record observations.

6. **Mental Imagery**. Mental imagery is the ability to visualize an object, person, place, or action that is not actually present. Trainers can design five kinds of imagery experiences: visual, tactile, olfactory, kinesthetic, and auditory. There are simple guidelines to use when conducting a mental imagery exercise:

- Help participants to clear their minds by encouraging them to relax.
- Conduct warm-up exercises to open the mind's eye.
- Assure participants that it's okay if they experience difficulty visualizing what you describe.

- Give imagery instructions slowly and with enough pauses to allow images to develop.
- Invite participants to share their imagery.

Methods for Groups

There are a number of group or meeting activities to consider. Here are several types most frequently used in training.

1. **Group Discussions**. Group discussions are normally held with groups of 5 to 20 people, with common interests in a subject area. It is a conversational style of discussion whereby all have equal rights and equal access to the subject. A group discussion must be under the control of a trained facilitator or group leader. This group leader remains impartial in the discussion but ensures that the group stays on the topic and that all participants do, in fact, have equal input. There are at least three types of discussions. The *structured* discussion is a conversation among the learners to meet set objectives. It is usually better for the group to have input on the topics to be covered to meet the objective, as this gives them more motivation. (The motivation comes from the fact that they were responsible for setting the agenda.) The *open-form* discussion is an unstructured conversation and is a free-for-all with the facilitator as a referee. This type can be used to voice opinions or vent frustrations. One problem here is that one or two dominant people may do all of the talking. The facilitator should set the ground rules before the discussion starts (or during it, if necessary). One solution is to nominate an object in the room as the "microphone"; only the person holding the microphone may speak, and when the microphone is passed to someone else, the new holder takes a turn. *Panel* discussions are almost like a lecture, in that they generally do not allow for a great deal of participant input. The panel is usually made up of topic experts, each with a subtopic. The facilitator starts at a logical point, and each expert builds on what the previous expert has said, with all of the topics related. To

be effective, this instruction method needs to be mixed with a question-and-answer method, or perhaps the requirement for the participants to do some preliminary work on the subject matter.

2. **Conferences.** Conferences are usually larger groups. The numbers may vary from five to one hundred or more. The participants normally represent different departments or organizations, but all have a common interest or background. The activity of a conference is usually to look at problems within the specified subject area, and to endeavor to arrive at solutions by the end of the conference. Some conferences are simply venues for participants to exchange ideas or information or to find out about new technology in the industry.

3. **Seminars.** The seminar is a group of any size, from five to five hundred, conducted for a group of people who have a common need. Seminars are normally led by an expert in the topic area. A problem may be defined and then given to the participants to rectify under the supervision of the seminar leader. The seminar leader may also present relevant research findings so that the participants can discover the correct solutions based on those findings. Seminars usually follow more of a lecture format.

4. **Workshops**. The workshop may be a group of any size, but the members have a common interest or share a common background. A workshop is generally conducted so that the participants can improve their ability or understanding by combining study and discussion. Workshops tend to be user-driven; that is, the participants may influence the direction of the program from its very beginning.

5. **Clinics**. The clinic is a meeting at which a small group of people with common interests examine a real-life problem. The group members diagnose and analyze the problem and then offer solutions. Clinics may be used to establish procedures, as they are based on real-life situations, and the participants generally offer working solutions based on their past experiences.

Other Methods

Other methods have gained use with the advent of digital technology; likewise there are other teaching methods that tap participants' creative expression.

1. **Computer-Assisted Learning.** This is largely a refinement of programmed learning, in which individuals work through written material that is organized in a static, sequential format. Learners proceed in a step-by-step fashion, only after they received feedback on their previous responses. Such programmed learning has become more sophisticated in recent years with the advantage of DVDs, learning video discs, and the Internet. One of the great advantages of such training is flexibility; the learners can progress at their own pace and wherever and whenever they want. The disadvantage is isolation, which can result in low motivation and reduced commitment.

2. **Self-Discovery**. Learners discover the content of the course on their own by using a variety of techniques, such as research and guided exercises.

3. **Self-Paced/Programmed Instruction**. Learners read or perform course-related activities, progressing through the program at their own pace.

4. **Case Studies**. Learners analyze situations and draw conclusions or recommend solutions on the basis of the content presented in the course.

5. **Movies.** Content comes primarily from movies. Develop a set of questions to use as a guide so that learners focus their attention on the content and the purpose of the media.

6. **Individual Projects**. Learners work individually to apply the concepts presented in the course.

7. **Group Projects**. Learners work in teams to apply the concepts presented in the course.

Many trainers wish they were more creative in their presentations. However, creative trainers are not a special breed. Creative trainers work at being creative and use several tricks to help them do their best work. Remember, one design can accomplish two things at once. The same design can often be used for different purposes. And published designs can often be modified to suit your own needs. You have learned the vital elements required to put a training activity together. Now, take those elements and organize them into a training activity worksheet, as shown in Figure 3-3. The worksheet is a way of organizing a picture of the training activity that becomes an important part of your module and lesson design.

Figure 3-3. Training activity worksheet.

Course title:
Module:
Lesson:
Date/Time:
Objectives:
Methods:
Format: Individual Pairs Small-group Full-group Intergroup
Outline:

Supporting Factors for Successful Training

Most training sessions occur inside a building. Buildings can be dark and confining. Be conscious that the environment set for your training does not negatively affect that training. However, there are other factors besides the physical environment that come into play—for example, the time of year or time of day. Consider both your own and your participants' energy levels. Ask yourself: "Do I have more people registering for classes in the fall or during the summer months?" "Do I have more energy in the spring, feel more like getting things done, and being adventuresome?" "How happy are learners about coming to class first thing in the morning?" "Do they seem sharper later in the day?" and "What is too late in the day for them to concentrate?"

The learners coming to your training sessions have lives of their own, with individual daily rhythms. In short, some people are morning types and others can't really get clicking until afternoon. Consider the easiest and most effective path to reaching your learners, and adjust your teaching behavior accordingly.

Time of Day

Do you ever think about the effect of time of day on your training? When are you most focused and energetic? Is your most productive period in the morning or in the afternoon? This factor is always a personal characteristic that learners will experience. Similarly, your learners will have individual reactions to the time of day. Consider some time frames that you can use as a guide for designing and delivering your training.

Early Morning (7:00 to 10:00 AM)

This is wake-up time for most people. You have the task during this period to alert the learners that they are requested to be physically and cognitively present! Try interesting and useful wake-up exercises. Here are some techniques that you can use:

- Include introductions that use not only the typical biographic questions but also an interesting question that will yield something about learners' reasons for attending. For example, their wish for the training.
- Use team exercises before the introductions. Design this event as a 10-minute fun exercise that relates to the course content—discuss a case study that exemplifies the training goal. For example, learners assigned to a department in a hotel could design the façade of the hotel; they hang up the façade and tell the larger group how they developed it and a little about their department. Although drawing the façade is not a meaningful task, it does get people working together on a common goal and using their skill sets (or discovering new skills that they were not aware of). Also, the drawing becomes a team wall hanging that they can use when working on their assigned task. (This is a great time for you to assess how the groups work individually and collectively, which is invaluable information when you decide to have learners rotate to different groups or to have partners.)
- Write questions on chart paper for the groups to answer.
- Present the overview of the course—goals, objectives, and learning outcomes. By doing this exercise, you will invite more learners to interact and ask questions early in the training.
- Review the most cognitively challenging information during the morning session.
- Be more movement-oriented and energetic during the morning session.
- Review frequently using games and quizzes.

Late Morning (10:00 AM to noon)

This is usually people's most highly interactive and energetic time of the day. It is a time when the learners are most physically and mentally ready to accept a challenge and usually absorb new ideas and techniques quickly. They have settled in, and they are no longer feeling the fear of the unknown. Things that you can do to keep the energy going are as follows:

- Deliver as much content and detail as possible during the session. Remain focused on your delivery. Wrap your content around models, outlines, and metaphors so that learners understand not only the content but also the task. You have explained the skeleton of the body during the early morning session. From now on, in each session you are going to put meat on the bones.
- Blast away on the content. The learners are eager to learn the new content, work on projects, meet other new participants, network, and share.
- Conduct timed and focused discussions and interactive exercises or activities.
- Continually summarize the content that you have delivered and make the connections of where this information fits in and why and how this fit happens or should happen.

Midday (noon to 1:00 PM)

This is when learners always think about lunch. Do not try to stretch this time to 12:45 PM. They will hate you. There is something different about 11:30 and 12:30 as lunch time. This is considered a time for a break.

Early Afternoon (1:00 to 3:00 PM)

This is when learners are digesting lunch and their energy is sapped. Many will feel tired and lazy. Use games, projects, small groups, and other activities to review the morning work, and then give them the opportunity to try out the new skills. Make sure the activities review and use the newly acquired information and that this information is added to the knowledge foundation they have built and continue to build with your training.

- Use break-outs, discussions, information exchanges, and clarifying points as re-energizers.
- Try a small-group exercise after lunch instead of a lecture, and never show a video or movie.

- Illustrate a quick physical activity that they can use back home as energizers, such as "We are now going to make like airplanes. Stand up, arms spread out wide like airplane wings. Turn left and turn right. Move circles with your arms."
- Develop an exercise whereby they have to talk with one another. Interactions and sharing will keep them awake; the more people they know in the event, the more interactive and personal exchanges that they foster can enrich their experience in class and when they go back home.

Late Afternoon (3:00 to 5:00 PM)

This is time for involvement, clarification, exchange, and application. The physical and cognitive energy is at the moderate level. Your task is to keep it consistent and engaged. The primary concern is the duration, especially if the learners have been involved in earlier sessions. You need to monitor carefully to determine when it is time to call it quits.

When learners are cycling down for the day, they become weary fast. You have to keep them engaged in discovery and group mode for just the right time. Then, start a quick shutdown exercise and invite discussion and sharing; don't push them beyond their limit. If you do, they will gain nothing, and you will feel disappointed. Organize your material in well-designed chunks of time. Teaching less is sometimes more.

Evening (5:00 to 10:00 PM)

This time can be a mixed bag. You can develop an interactive lecture, a humorous talk, a self-help session, an exchange, or a retreat. To make this time successful, determine the need, the audience preferences and learning style, the time allotted, and the expected outcome. Call a few folks, and find out what they are expecting from the training. Physical and cognitive energy is not so high; however, learners are relaxed and not anxious. Here are some ways to capitalize on this relaxed energy:

- Use three to five teaching techniques to keep their attention and interest; assist in their learning by making sure you review many times; have them keep a journal of the evening outcomes.
- Keep things interesting and focused on the topic. Bring in props. Have things for them to do; they learn best by doing. Have fun. Bring rewards. Have work groups that learners can hang out with each day or during the week of the training, for example, interest groups during lunch. Have the group report back some of the things they discussed, and make sure to have take-aways.

Day of the Week

Unlike the time of the day, the day or night of the week does not directly influence a learner's capacity to learn or retain the information. Most learners prefer day classes on Mondays, Tuesdays, or Wednesdays, never Fridays! For night classes, the preferred days are Tuesday, Wednesday, and Thursday. For the weekend, Saturday is fine, but Saturday night is terrible. Some of the best weekend time is Sunday afternoon. The preference of day really does make a difference with respect to participants' learning.

SOME PRINCIPLES AND THEORIES THAT SUPPORT TRAINING

We conclude this chapter with a discussion of several disparate topics that both underlie the training approaches and techniques described so far and elaborate on those techniques in ways that can enhance learning, such as group involvement, reinforcement, and sequencing of information.

Additional Group Techniques

To supplement the suggestions for group activities given in this chapter, consider the following group activities, shown in Table 3-7.

Table 3-7. Advantages and disadvantages of group techniques.

Technique	Advantages	Disadvantages
Nominal group	Can create group motivation Everyone participates Incorporates brainstorming Generates ideas Opportunity for discussion	Can easily become boring Cost of not having experts at work Effect on productivity with experts gone Threatening if not enough ideas to list Embarrassment by lack of ideas
DACUM	No room for error Incorporates brainstorming Cost-effective Good representation of staff Generates specific information	Time-consuming Tense to tiring Needs competent leader Can get bogged down in detail May miss attitudinal changes needed
Critical incident	Directly task-related Input from participants Not always negative incidents Establishes correct procedures Looks at the entire situation	Time-consuming and cumbersome Defines what is and isn't critical Only critical incidents are recorded Input restricted to memories Needs competent leader
Delphi	Selective participation Geographically unrestricted Respondents are isolated Groups can be large Confidentiality	Long duration Lack of ongoing interest No personal contact Unpredictable response rate Data can be lost

1. The **nominal group** process is a decision-making method for use among groups of many sizes who want to make their decision quickly, as by a vote, but want everyone's opinions taken into account (as opposed to traditional voting, where only the largest group is considered). The method of tallying is the difference. First, every member of the group gives their view of the solution with a short explanation.

Then, duplicate solutions are eliminated from the list of all solutions, and the members proceed to rank the solutions. The numbers each solution receives are totaled, and the solution with the lowest (i.e., most favored) total ranking is selected as the final decision. There are variations on how this technique is used. For example, it can identify strengths versus areas in need of development, rather than be used as a decision-making voting alternative. Also, options do not always have to be ranked, but may be evaluated more subjectively. Though the goal is to break down a problem into manageable steps, the technique doesn't draw completely on facts. This drawback may be offset, however, by the time efficiency in the whole process.

2. The **Develop A Curriculum** (*DACUM*) program, as shown in Figure 3-4, is a model normally used by training staff to build a curriculum by dissecting a position into its jobs and tasks. A group of 10 to 15 experts (usually supervisors or skilled workers) meets and conducts a performance analysis and then creates a topical outline according to the task analysis results or topics and subtopic. The DACUM is usually a competency-based instructional/training design model. The DACUM technique may also be used to establish varying levels of competency for certain positions (that is, basic, intermediate, and advanced levels of knowledge or skill proficiency).

3. **Critical incident** is a training technique by which individuals in a group identify the critical incidents that led to a problem. When all of the incidents have been collected, they are collated and then discussed by the group. Obviously, the individuals in this group must have a common interest or background in the subject at hand. This technique is sometimes used in management training to get participants to identify the critical incidents in their career.

4. **Delphi** is a training and problem-solving technique whereby the group members don't get together; it could be called "the group you have when you're not having a group." A problem or situation is identi-

Figure 3-4. Develop A Curriculum (DACUM) program.

DIRECTIONS: Break down each position that is the subject of a training program into its component jobs and tasks, filling in the boxes below. Then use these levels of specific work details to develop the curriculum for the training program.

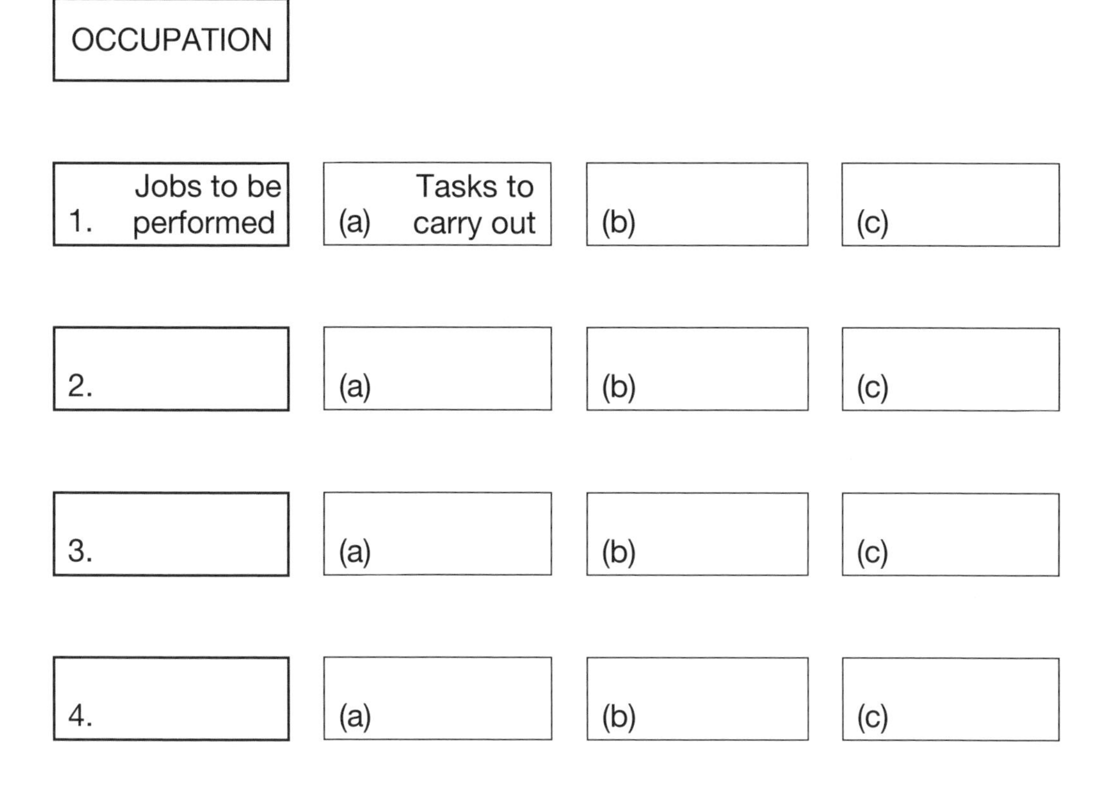

fied by management or a decision-making team. A group leader identifies the experts, then develops and distributes a questionnaire. When the responses have been collated, the group develops and distributes a second questionnaire, modified to suit the previous responses. Subsequent questionnaires ask respondents to reconsider their ideas, based on composite opinions. This process continues until the experts reach consensus. It is then up to the group leader to report the findings back to the management team. This technique may be modified for use with an assembled group as long as sufficient study is done.

All of the above group techniques (with the exception of nominal group technique) stipulate that the participants have a common interest or shared background in the subject matter. However, in the nominal group process it isn't necessary for individuals to have that common interest or background because the aim is to find new ideas or solutions. Someone without that insider viewpoint may offer the best solution. Here are some tips for starting and maintaining group discussions:

- Select a topic that everyone can become involved in.
- Let the group set ground rules for everyone to follow.
- Acknowledge all input from the participants.
- Select as your first speaker the one who will give a model answer.
- Go around the circle to begin with.
- Don't leave the expected worst responses to last.
- Ensure that everyone gets a chance to participate.
- Always get clarification if needed.
- Look for nonverbal responses.
- Use first names, and direct eye contact with the group.
- Don't always give the answers; let the group do it.
- Move from the foreground to the background as the discussion proceeds.
- Intervene if necessary, and keep the group on track.
- Be aware of your nonverbal communication.
- Be honest and enthusiastic with the group at all times. If you're not, you can bet they won't be.

Brain-Friendly Lectures

Lectures are the most efficient and cost-effective way to communicate information in a classroom setting, and they are useful for reaching a large group, especially when you need to get across general knowledge.

If you are committed to using accelerated learning principles in training, lectures can hold an important place. Remember, involving the learner in the learning maximizes understanding and retention through participative techniques. Even in lectures you can get learners involved.

There are five ways to involve participants during a lecture:

1. **Listening Role**. Assign participants the responsibility to actively listen to the lecture. At the end of the lecture, they should produce a list of points they agree or disagree with and have questions to be answered. Provide a summary of the contents and quiz questions. Listening assignments can be given to individuals or to the group.
2. **Guided Note Taking**. Provide instructions or a form indicating how participants should take notes. Stop at intervals for the participants to write reactions or ideas that go beyond what you have presented.
3. **Spot Challenge**. Interrupt the lecture periodically, and challenge the participants to give examples of the concepts presented so far or to answer spot-quiz questions. For example, give a lecture on disability and stop at a reasonable interval to give a multiple-choice quiz testing participants' understanding of the material.
4. **Synergetic Learning**. Provide different information to different participants. Allow them to compare notes and briefly teach each other.
5. **Illuminating Exercise**. During the presentation, intersperse a brief activity. This action calls notice and illuminates the information, ideas, and skills being presented.

Here are five ways to reinforce the learning that takes place in lectures:

1. **Press Conference**. Invite participants to prepare questions to be submitted to the trainer for response. Or provide a list of questions from which participants can select.
2. **Participant Review**. Ask participants to review the content of the lecture with each other (in any group configuration) and commit the major points to memory, or give them a self-scoring review test.
3. **Group Processing**. Ask participants to reflect on the lecture's implications for them. Use any group format you feel will maximize the quality of the processing.
4. **Post-Lecture Case Problem**. Pose a case problem for participants to solve based on the information given in the lecture.
5. **Experiential Activity**. Design an activity that dramatically summarizes or illustrates the lecture you have given. Use any of the experiential learning approaches presented in this chapter—role-plays, games, simulations, observations, mental imagery, or writing tasks.

Holding the Audience's Interest

To gain and hold the audience's interest, start the program with an introductory game. Here are five suggested formats:

1. **Scavenger Hunt**. This is similar to bingo. Create a card with familiar facts either about the audience or the information that you will be teaching (e.g., terms and definitions).
2. **Paper-Tearing Exercise**. Ask the learners to fold sheets of paper in half, tear the upper right side, fold and tear upper left, fold and tear lower right. Open them up to reveal snowflakes—not one is alike.
3. **Case Study**. Use one of these scenarios, or make up your own: (a) Your boss just came in and asked for a training outline for a one-hour course in professional development. What do you do?

(b) Sarah goes to the post office each morning and each afternoon. She has an accident one afternoon while leaving the post office. Is this compensable?

4. **Test Questions**. Introduce the presentation with true-or-false questions.
5. **Leadoff Story**. Tell a short story that makes the point that you will be presenting.

The Training Sequence

Sequencing your presentation of information is partly an art; some trainers just know where to place different pieces in the program and how to obtain a good mix and flow. Most trainers, however, learn to master sequencing through experience and trial and error. Here are six points that can guide your sequencing choices:

1. Build interest in new content before you delve more deeply. Set the stage for learning by using an activity that provides participants with the big picture of the training topic.
2. Place easy activities before demanding activities. Get participants settled in and warmed up before you put them through some hard work! Thinking takes energy.
3. Maintain a good mix of activities. Vary your training methods, the lengths of activities, intensity of activities, the physical setting, and the format.
4. Group together concepts and skills that build on each other. Generally, we learn more easily when one idea is an outgrowth of another.
5. Provide subskills before practicing complex skills. It's better to learn parts before the whole.
6. Close training sequences with discussions of "so what" and "now what."

Trainers have a number of sequence choices. Avoid always using the same sequences. You want to design action-oriented trainings that contain a variety of sequences designed to keep participants interested and also provide time for reflection.

- Go from the general to the specific.
- When teaching procedures, start with the first step or the last step.
- Place an experiential activity before a content presentation, or follow a content presentation with an experiential activity.
- Teach from theory to practice or from practice to theory.

The Zoom Principle

The success of a program, according to educator Ruth Clark, is all in the flow of events. She calls this process the Zoom Principle. It works like this. When you are introducing new information, provide an overview; this process is called an "advanced organizer." The advanced organizer sets up "data files" in the minds of the learners for each of the topics you will cover. Then, when the topic is mentioned the learners can "file" the information in the appropriate mental organizer. Later, the trainer "zooms in" on the detail, returning to it periodically to show learners how each detail relates to the whole.

Clark also points out that the training sequence looks more like a spiral than a straight line. That is, you reintroduce skills and ideas taught earlier, but in greater detail each time. She cautions that trainers avoid the urge to plunge into an important element without providing that transition from old to new material. Consider adding a brief activity, short presentation, demonstration, or team project to get the group warmed up and focused on the topic.

She suggests that a training sequence be built around a critical incident, a problem to be solved, or a task to be accomplished, rather than a set of concepts or skills to use. Lastly, she says that closing a training sequence can be either climactic or reflective. Sometimes a sequence ends with a bang to emphasize the accomplishment; for example, a dramatic finish could be a scintillating lecture, an intergroup competition, a role-play that serves as a dress rehearsal for later application, or a challenging case study.

CHAPTER FOUR

Set the Scene for Learning

You have defined the training need, designed the program, and chosen your methods and approach. Now, creating an environment that will encourage learners to challenge, experiment, and have fun is your goal. If learners become truly engaged in the task, and you present the information using accelerated learning principles designed for adults, the learners will begin to use this new knowledge with ease. Learning principles help you make the content more three-dimensional and move the class from the theory behind the training to the information the class will use in practice.

To create the setting that will work best to make this transition, you need to consider meeting both the physical and the emotional needs of the learners. The physical considerations are easiest, so let's begin with those.

The Physical Environment: Training Rooms

Unless you are an extremely lucky person, almost all of the rooms that you will use to conduct your training sessions were built for another purpose. The rooms you'll be given will range from traditional classrooms to hotel meeting suites, to conference rooms, boardrooms, and cafeterias, to living rooms, workshop floors, ballrooms, and even rooms in casinos. Make the best of your situation, and turn the environment into your workspace. Use anything you can find—be creative.

To begin, you need to establish the right space between you and the learners so you can maintain eye contact and manage the learning discussions while also establishing rapport. Beyond that, you need to determine how to configure the seating (unless it is fixed). To help you decide which configuration to use, consider the following from both your perspective and that of the learners:

- Visibility. Can you see them, and can they see you?
- Volume. Can you hear them, and can they hear you?
- Nature of the session. Is it formal or informal? This depends on the purpose, content, and audience.
- Degree of interaction. How much learner involvement will there be? Will there be discussion or just listening?
- Extent of audience relationship. How much rapport will there be between you and the learners?
- Potential for group dynamics. Does your program include audience/group participation?

Room Styles and Arrangements

There are six well-known configurations for a training room: classroom u-shape, round-table conference, chairs in a circle, small group cluster, and theater. Knowing ahead of time the configuration of the room, especially if it is fixed, is important because you can use that information to tailor your presentation. The size and shape of the room, the seating arrangement, and your location relative to the audience are critical factors to consider in the preparation phase (Chapter 3).

The right room setup can contribute to the success of your training; likewise, a poor setup can lead to devastating results. Yet, all it might take to change a nonconductive training room into an inviting setting is your shifting things around. Table 4-1 lists four typical room designs and gives tips on improvements.

Each room design has its pluses and minuses. Here are the characteristics of each style, to help you choose the best room setup.

Table 4-1. Possible room designs.

Designs	Tips for Use
Traditional Classroom	Design a fun, safe, and inviting environment. Use props to shift the mind; the traditional classroom brings back experiences with formal schooling. Put up posters, use a welcome sign on the door, create a welcome letter with bright color on the table, or give them an interesting article (can also send this out via e-mail) to read before the learning event begins. Or, design a fun welcome note and place it on your chart paper with your name, date, and course number. Other: put candy out along with colorful supplies such as colored paper, sticky notes, or paper tabs for marking places in the participant notebook. The intent for the props is to communicate to the participants that this is a fun, safe, and engaging event.
Corporate Meeting Room	Integrate the furniture that exists to create a multipurpose learning environment. Use the corporate round meeting table as the teaching section of the room. Use these four corners as the mini-event spaces; put up a welcome sign. Design a creative poster that promotes the topic of the course, and hang it on the door or strategically place on a wall that participants will see when they enter. Dress up in a costume, if appropriate; have a "learning stick" or a magic wand placed on the table to break the traditional feeling that this meeting room is noninviting. The intent of the props and shifting of the furniture is to establish the philosophy that the group is attending to learn, have fun, and transfer the learning back home. So, turn up the lights, if possible, take advantage of the high-tech equipment.

Hotel	Convert the image-neutral space into a learning activity. Set up a main event area; this is usually in the front of the room. Around the room, place learning spaces with wall charts, computers, and in out-box exercises—given the topic, this room could be transformed into a learning labor or a learning emporium. For example, write final exams on various posters and hang the posters around the room; place learners in learning groups, and each learning group is instructed to go around the room as a cooperative learning group (starting and ending in the order of the posters), recording their group answers for each of the posters. Once the group completes the task, their individual scores and the group score is used in the final group. The hotel space can serve as a serious learning environment, yet feel safe. The intent is to use what you have and think about how you, as a learner, would like to feel in this space.
Multipurpose Room	These rooms come in various sizes and shapes: churches, community centers, city halls, courthouses, hospitals, museums, art galleries, and public buildings. They are accessible and that's good. So, here's how to use the space. First, make the room fit the group. If it's a large one, section the room and create event areas and bring things into the event area like tables and chairs. Add tablecloths, coffee urns, and theater scenery (if appropriate). Set up extra tables as a library, break table, and chat table; put up banners! The intent here is that one or two outside items can make a big difference.

Traditional Classroom

The standard classroom arrangement provides a lot of chairs and tables, easy access to the seats. The learning environment is hardwired into us, designed to meet learning objectives and desired outcomes. The role of the trainer in this arrangement is as an instructor. Some points to consider about this arrangement:

- Takes up more space than theater style.
- Good for note taking.
- Fosters good presentations and delivery of information.

- Not conducive for discussions and group participation.
- Has an academic atmosphere.

U-Shape Style

A less traditional seating arrangement, this works well when participants will get up and form small groups. The role of the trainer in this arrangement is as a coach. Some points to consider about this arrangement:

- Takes up more space than theater or classroom.
- Good for groups of 10 to 30 people.
- Combines the ability to make presentations and hold discussions.
- Good for note taking.
- Has a business atmosphere.

Conference Style

This arrangement promotes interactive activities because participants can look and listen to each other while seated around a table. The role of the trainer in this arrangement is as a facilitator. Some points to consider about this arrangement:

- Good for groups of 4 to 20 people.
- Encourages discussion.
- Good for note taking.
- Good for presentation.
- Has a business atmosphere.

Chairs in a Circle

This arrangement promotes group work and interactions. The role of the trainer in this arrangement is as a consultant. Some points to consider about this arrangement:

- Best for informal and participatory groups.
- Allows presenter to serve as group member and less of an authority figure.
- Good for groups of 4 to 30 people.
- Suitable for interactive group games.
- Not good for note taking.
- Not good for presentations using notes or technical aids.

Small Group Settings

Similar to the U-shaped arrangement, the small-group style enables the trainer to walk among the learners or for the group to break into smaller groups for discussion. A small-group arrangement is good for presentations, especially those using visual aids.

Theater Setting

This arrangement permits the greater number of seats in the smallest amount of space. Theater style is good, and often necessary, for groups of more than 50, especially if the room size is limited. Theater style limits discussion and requires a more formal presentation. Also, make sure that all members of the audience can see you and your visuals.

Comfort Factors

Similar to the series of questions you might ask to get to know your audience, you will want to ask some questions to get to know the conditions in the room.

- Is the room properly lighted?
- Does the room have cool fresh air or sufficient heat? A room that is too warm and stale will put your audience to sleep, especially after a meal. A room that isn't adequately heated when needed is likewise too uncomfortable for people to learn.

- Can the lights be appropriately dimmed for the projection screen? A room that is too bright will make it difficult to see the image on the screen, but a room that is too dark will make it difficult to take notes.
- Are there outlets where you need them for your projector or laptop? If not, remember to bring an extension cord and tape it down so no one falls over it.

Your Training Space

The room setup is not complete without thinking about your own training space. Is the area where you will speak neat and looking professional? The lectern or stage is your personal space, and your audience will judge your effectiveness by how comfortable you are in it.

It has been discovered that the distance between you and the learners affects the degree of warmth, sense of closeness, and interaction that will occur. For example, if you stand too far from your participants, your presentation will appear formal. If you stand too close, participants may feel uncomfortable. The usual suggestion is to choose a moderate position, a comfortable interaction parameter, which means you can walk around, displace the furniture and equipment serving as barriers, and keep the space open between you and the audience. (For more discussion on training space, see Chapter 5.)

William Draves, in his book *Energizing the Learning Environment*, recommends that trainers be mindful of the "presenter zone." Table 4-2 presents some tips on managing that distance.

The Learning Environment

Not only will you be setting the physical scene for the training but you'll also be establishing the emotional and intellectual atmosphere. The learning environment is just as important as the physical environment. Without them both, learners will not maximize their learning.

Table 4-2. Presenter's Zone

Tip	Application
Line is drawn	Stand in front of the room; draw an imaginary line from the learner on your left to the learner on your right; you should be no more than three feet behind the line.
Chair trick	Move all of the comfortable chairs to the front row, thus, a reward for sitting up front.
Make chairs disappear	Take all chairs around the wall and in the back of the room, stack and ship them somewhere so that they cannot be used and distract from the room setup.
Move toward learners	If learners have migrated to the back of the room, remove the chairs in the front row and go to them. (Maybe have the class move the chairs with you, and make it a game.)

Learning Curves and Patterns of Instruction

Every training event has a rhythm that reflects the content and instructional activities of the program. Figure 4-1 shows the learning curves for a three-day course. Notice that each day starts off slowly and builds. Gains are modest on Day 1; Day 2 shows a large increase in learning, as mastery of the subject is constructed atop a foundation of prior learning. By Day 3, the learning is fully integrated, and concludes with a higher level of topic mastery.

Encourage a Relaxed Atmosphere

Each person has a preferred way of learning. When people recognize which techniques match their preferred learning styles, they will view learning as natural and comfortable. Their relaxed state of mind will promote the most effective and efficient learning. There are six strategies to promote a comfortable and enjoyable learning environment:

Figure 4-1. The overlap of learning curves.

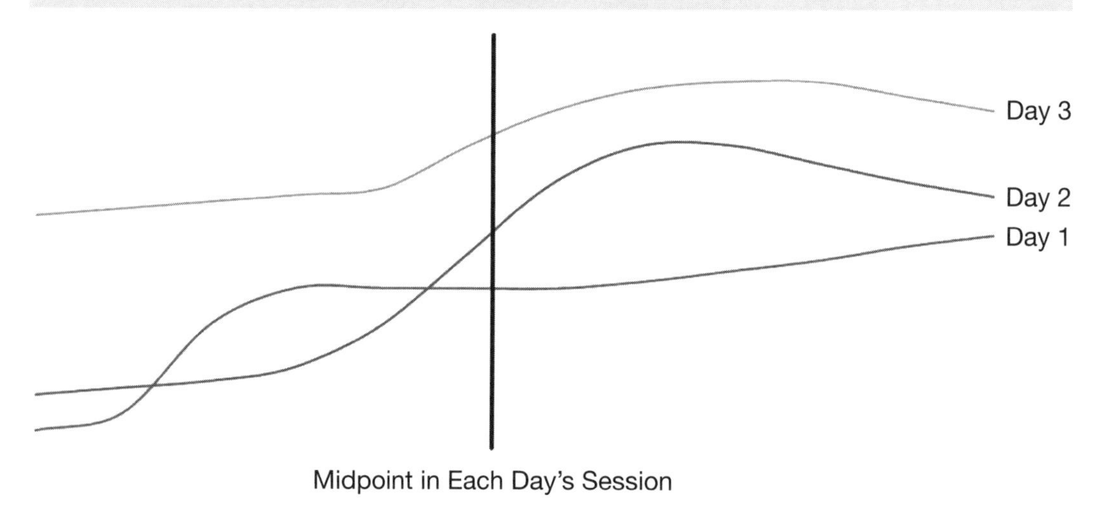

1. Create a low-stressed environment where it is safe to make mistakes, yet the expectation of success is high.
2. Ensure that the subject is relevant. Learners need to see the point of the training for them to learn.
3. Make sure that the learning is emotionally positive. Use humor and offer encouragement, provide regular breaks, and show enthusiastic support for their efforts.
4. Consciously involve all of the learners' senses, as well as engaging their left- and right-brain thinking modes.
5. Challenge them to think through and explore what is being taught and to make personal sense of the subject matter.
6. Consolidate what is learned as you go along. Promote consistent review, and provide quiet periods of relaxed alertness.

Twelve Accelerated Learning Techniques

The accelerated learning method is based on research about ways of learning. Each person has a preferred learning style. If you know and use the techniques that match a person's preferred way of learning, that individual will learn more naturally. And because it is more natural, the learning becomes easier. And because it is easier, it is quicker. By also incorporating well-researched memory techniques, you can use accelerated learning to make the training an enjoyable, successful, and satisfying experience that leads to behavior change and better performance. Static, one-way lectures are out; active, dynamic training is in. Accelerated learning, which recognizes the differences in how people absorb new information, is fast, effective, and efficient, but it only works when analytical skills are taught with a high level of participation.

Here are twelve accelerated learning strategies that you can use immediately in your training presentation:

1. Back-Home Exercise
2. Brainwriting and Brainstorming
3. Case Study
4. Collaborative Activity
5. Concert Review
6. Peripheral Materials
7. Demonstration in Class
8. Prework
9. Reading Assignment
10. Structured Note Taking
11. Skills and Knowledge Test
12. Self-Assessment

Such varied techniques provide opportunities to plan, organize, and create training sessions that are efficient because they make the training stick in a short amount of time. In essence, the content for your training program also is the process for instruction. Build into your training sessions the four basic steps for structuring the accelerated learning method:

1. Motivate the mind.
2. Acquire and absorb information.
3. Search out meaning (what is the implication and significance of the information?).
4. Trigger the memory by using accelerated learning techniques, including association, categorization, storytelling, acronyms, flash cards, learning maps, music, and review.

But let's take a closer look at each of these techniques.

Back-Home Exercise

DEFINITION. Participants are given an in-class opportunity to practice what they have learned by applying the learned concepts to an existing back-home problem.

DIRECTIONS. Each participant writes a short synopsis of a back-home problem. Next, each participant presents the issue to the group. By group consensus, one problem is selected to be used as a model problem to apply the new techniques that were presented during the class. The group works as consultants to the participant who has the issue, thus helping that person apply the concepts and skills from the group to use back home.

Tools and Tips. Here are suggestions to consider when managing this learning process:

- Use the steps in sequence.
- Use examples to reinforce learning with direct application to the learners' situations.
- Ask the class to share back-home plans.
- Make frequent referrals to back home during other activities.

Brainwriting and Brainstorming

DEFINITION. Participants record ideas, advancing previous ideas (brainwriting) or listing ideas (brainstorming).

DIRECTIONS. For brainwriting, write two questions on chart paper. Each question should be put on a separate piece of chart paper and put on separate walls on opposite sides of the room so that participants can line up in two lines and then switch lines; the two lines save time. (Note: Have participants silently write their answers for each question; you can use more than two questions, just make sure that each question chart is located far away from each other.) Give a time limit. Participants are to work in silence. After the participants have recorded their answers, process the responses or have two participants process the questions and answers. An example of a question to construct is "Training is successful when . . . ," and the opposing question would be "Training is unsuccessful when. . . ."

Use the mindmapping as a device for problem solving or decision making. The technique is based on the idea that many people find it helpful to dump a lot of ideas in a very short period of time and then organize the ideas. Have participants draw a circle in the middle of a paper. Put the key concept in the center, and branch out from the middle of the circle.

The brainstorming process allows participants to generate a list of responses to the question or activity in a given timeframe. This process gives the participants the opportunity to provide quick responses without being hindered by prejudgment. The point of brainstorming is to generate a lot of responses. Once the list of responses is produced, the participants review the list and delete responses that are not considered feasible.

Tools and Tips. Here are suggestions to consider when managing differences of opinion:

- Ensure that groups follow rules; monitor the groups closely; remember silence!

- Don't allow oral criticism (brainstorming).
- Keep groups and papers moving. Keep them on track (brainwriting).
- Point out that both brainwriting and brainstorming allow one person's idea to trigger another person's related idea.
- Point out that brainwriting allows participants to build on ideas without the threat of criticism.
- Use colored markers, and post charts.
- Try using mindmapping in brainwriting as a recording or processing strategy.

Case Study

DEFINITION. Participants work to solve a problem similar to ones they face back home. A case study usually has multiple parts (plot, characters, issue, and setting) and various solutions and is processed as the parts are completed.

DIRECTIONS. Write a narrative—one or two paragraphs. Include detail about the situation, the characters involved, and the rationale for why this is an issue. Do not write suggested solutions; the point of the case study is to invite others to discuss the various options.

Tools and Tips. Here are suggestions to consider when completing case studies:

- Monitor groups, and answer questions.
- Don't let the groups go too long without intervening.
- Don't use cases that are not related to the businesses of the participants.
- Point out that case studies encourage creative problem solving.
- Help participants learn from one another.
- Post charts from all groups around the room so all groups can learn from one another.

Collaborative Activity

DEFINITION. Participants work together to teach one another concepts, solve problems, or advance the learning objectives for the training.

DIRECTIONS. Create application exercises in the participant manual. The aim of the exercises is to invite learners to review the important points in the lesson. These exercises can include quizzes, scenarios, matching terms, or essays. The important point for this activity is that the group members can work independently and can then work together to pool their answers. This activity provides an opportunity for participants to ask for clarification and learn from others in the group; thus, each participant is becoming self-reliant while functioning as a team player.

Tools and Tips. This activity is a good way to review material and introduce the concept of the learning group, which means everyone helps one another. Here are some additional tips:

- Collaboration should pervade the entire training.
- Learning is more effective in small groups with supportive and helpful members.
- Individual learning focuses on only the individual and does not provide for effective feedback.
- Individuals tend to emphasize their own mistakes, faults, and weaknesses, sometimes blowing them out of proportion because they have no comparisons.
- Remember, there's strength in numbers.

Concert Review

DEFINITION. Trainers can review materials, periodically using music, presentations, wall charts, chart paper, movements, or oral reviews.

DIRECTIONS. This is a review activity. Tell participants that they are going to review the material covered thus far in the training and the number of concepts that have been presented. Have participants number their papers, assigning a number for each concept covered. Explain that the trainer is going to play music and at set intervals the trainer will put up an image that represents a concept that was presented during the training. Tell the participants that when they see the image, they are to write everything they know about the image until it disappears and another image appears.

After the presentation is complete, the learners should collaborate with their groups to clarify and check the entries on their recording sheets. This process is a great way to have the group work together, as well as to promote the collaborative learning processes.

Tools and Tips. The concert review approach to reviewing materials refers to the use of background music during review. The technique works for the three learning styles (visual, auditory, and kinesthetic) and the two ways people process information (linear and global). Some examples include the following:

- Visual. The facilitator silently goes through PowerPoint slides or wall charts. Background music is an enhancer.
- Auditory. The facilitator reads specific review materials while background music plays.
- Kinesthetic. The group follows the facilitator around the room from item to item (wall charts, demonstration models, learning aids, or displays) while music plays.
- Linear. The facilitator uses outlines of what's first, second, third, and so on.
- Global. The facilitator gives an overview.

Peripheral Materials

DEFINITION. The term *environing* refers to treatment of the learning environment. Trainers can ease the anxiety of adult learners by using themes for training and decorating the training space according to the theme. Prewritten wall charts are an example of environing materials, also known as peripheral materials.

DIRECTIONS. Decorating the learning room with interesting posters or wall charts that depict the major concepts being presented in the training can be a bonus for the learners and the facilitator. The topic for each of the wall charts could contain icons or words, display a manufacturing process, or summarize an important topic. Trainers should dress their training rooms to invite learners to be creative, holistic, or interactive with one another and the training material. Using attention-grabbers is the key to making these concepts blend with the training process and content delivery.

Tools and Tips. Environing materials are materials that make the learning environment more conducive to learning the concepts of the course. They include the following:

- Wall charts and newsprint
- Table decorations to fulfill a theme
- Mobiles and puzzles
- Candles and scents
- Anything that adds color, stimulation, and fun
- Funny bags to hold all of the supplies for each table team
- Basket for the trainer table with more supplies, candy, and surprises.

Demonstration in Class

DEFINITION. Participants observe or take part in a demonstration of the course concepts, techniques, skills, or tools.

DIRECTIONS. Adults learn best by doing. Therefore, an opportunity to demonstrate something involves the participants learning the concept and preparing to teach the concept. One suggestion for managing this concept is to take a section of the course material, form learning groups, and have each group prepare a 10-minute presentation. To accomplish this task economically, the instructor should pre-assign the material to be reviewed and prepare an instruction sheet for each group to follow to be ready to present the assignment to the large group.

Tools and Tips. The demonstration process serves as a teach-back tool and can serve as a mechanism to encourage collaborative group work. Here are some tips:

- Use actual equipment and resources as much as possible.
- Make demonstrations easy for everyone to see, hear, observe, and practice.
- Show trainees that you are an expert. This means that trainers may not be perfect at the skill, but, at the very least, they completely understand it.
- Don't cut the process short. Teach all of the steps.
- Point out that demonstration allows hands-on learning.
- Show participants how this technique reinforces auditory and visual learning. If time and situation permit, let participants demonstrate.

Prework

DEFINITION. Participants complete assignments prior to coming to the training session—it's part of the prepare step in the accelerated learning process (prepare, present, practice, gain feedback).

DIRECTIONS. Learners really like to receive an agenda so that they can get a sense of what they are going to do, how to do it, and what the expected results are. The prework provides the opportunity for learners to prepare for the session. It serves as a map of the learning adventure they will experience when they arrive at the training.

Tools and Tips. Adult learners like to know where they are, where they are going, and how they will get there. The prework can serve as a mechanism to provide that direction. Here are some tips:

- Fun packages can include toys used in class, t-shirts, course logo stuff (pens, pencils, and notebooks), and video of skits or cartoons.
- Serious work packages can include questionnaires, reassessment instruments, prereading material, audiotapes, or videotapes.
- Incentive-to-get-there packages can include course goals, course outline, testimonials from previous attendees, and statements of outcomes.
- If the course has a theme, theme the prework!
- Mix media and color, action, and fun.

Reading Assignment

DEFINITION. Participants are given evening or out-of-class assignments to supplement classroom materials and experiences.

DIRECTIONS. Reviewing and reflecting on the information gathered in class is something that you should encourage all participants to practice. Give them time to make connections between the new content and information that they already know. Look over the goals and objectives of the course, and develop summary handouts or search for expert sources of materials, articles, or case studies to expand the learners' knowledge of the topics discussed.

Tools and Tips. The art of reading should be a skill that people continually practice. The reading assignments and report backs are vehicles to ensure that all of the participants have read required materials. Remember that participants have lives outside of the training. Try to keep the assignments quick (short reviews previewing the next day's materials). Here are some additional tips:

- Make it memorable. Some people can learn a great deal by reading and homework; others hate it.
- Ask participants to record their learning creatively.
- Try memory maps or mindmaps.

- Create a mobile or three-dimensional object.
- Ask participants to make videotapes.

Structured Note-Taking

DEFINITION. Text materials and rough outlines show participants what's important and where to take notes. White space is provided for participants to add their own notes.

DIRECTIONS. Review the materials that you are to present in a lecture, and decide which sections are highlights of the training. Develop a note sheet for the participants to use to record the important points during your content delivery process. This teaching process can be a video, demonstration, discussion, or presentation.

Tools and Tips. The structured note process is something that people do all of the time in the form of recording thoughts or points in a meeting or developing a cheat sheet to remember points for a speech or presentation. The structured note process will assist the participants in remembering the important points of the presentation. Here are some tips:

- Design the courses to make everyone take notes once in a while.
- Remember that it's kinesthetic.
- Go slowly enough so everyone can get something on paper.
- Don't put too much on the PowerPoint slides.
- Don't use jargon that learners don't understand or can't spell.
- Remember that note taking reinforces learning.
- Have participants record in the participant guide, not on separate sheets of paper.

Skills and Knowledge Test

DEFINITION. Tests are used to determine how much participants have learned while they were attending the training.

DIRECTIONS. The importance of testing is to have participants reflect and recall information and to make the connections to their existing knowledge portfolio. The tests that trainers use should not be threatening but serve as a review. Prepare the tests, and put them in the participant manual in sections after the initial lesson or module. Trainers should use any test form they think appropriate. For example, fill in the blank, written response to a scenario or case study, or match the terms. Try to introduce the concept that tests can be fun and useful.

Tools and Tips. The tests are assessments, an opportunity to determine how well participants are grasping the information; therefore, make the tests collaborative and fun. Give prizes. Here are some suggestions:

- Daily review assessments work very well.
- Make sure all material is relevant, and use tests for different learning styles.
- Allow learners to retake tests that are important to success.
- Use testing creatively as a recall. For example, group quizzes with prizes.
- Don't publish everyone's score or make passing scores too high.
- If you have never written a test, get help!
- Participant-generated review questions add fun and show how much they are learning.

Self-Assessment

DEFINITION. Participants use profiles, tests, or inventories of their current skill levels to check their progress and learning during the class.

DIRECTIONS. Do not test for test's sake. Participants love opportunities to find out more about what they are doing well and not so well. If trainers are going to use the assessment technique, they should make sure that it is valid and meaningful. Trainers can buy assessment instruments or develop their own, using the content that they are delivering in the session. For example, if trainers are teaching the learners the instructional system design model, they can write a scenario about a training department that receives a request for training and ask the learners to develop a response to the client that provides the steps they will take to fulfill the stated need. This scenario provides real-world experience and also serves to review the material.

Tools and Tips. Either purchase or develop assessment instruments that correspond to or highlight the concepts you are teaching. Here are some suggestions:

- Provide opportunities for learners to discover more about themselves.
- Suggest learners use similar assessments in their own classrooms.
- Give learners fast and frequent successes.
- Try pre- and post-tests. This technique allows the learners to demonstrate to themselves what they have learned.
- Back-home quizzes let the learners know that there are some positive things going on they may not be aware of.

Using the above 12 techniques, you will add energy and excitement to every training session and ensure faster, more effective, and greater efficient transfer of learner skills to the workplace.

Management of the Learning Process

Learning is not directly observable, yet it is something that almost everyone can experience. For example, learners will say, "I feel I know that now." Or, "I saw how that formula works," and "I know it now because I hear the different sounds and letter accents." But what exactly is "learning"?

There are diverse definitions of learning. Most would agree that learning involves the process of change, and that learning is about acquiring new knowledge, skills, or attitude and comes from study or life experiences. Many popular definitions emphasize a change in behavior that lasts a relatively long time. When learning is defined this way, it is easy to measure. But what about new ways of thinking that open the possibility for new behaviors, but take a long time before they spark new ways of behaving? In such cases, learning is stymied, but can we really say that no learning has occurred? Learning is more than change in behavior. Learning involves three dynamic processes: thinking, feeling, and behaving.

Thinking is the analysis of our experience. It's about developing understandings of how the world works and how we can better act in this world to achieve our goals. Thinking allows us new ways of perceiving and responding to the world. Thinking often can prompt new behavior.

When people learn, they respond differently to their situation by thinking differently, feeling differently, and acting differently. When trainers conduct trainings, they are interested in how learning to think differently and learning new ways of responding emotionally can support new behaviors that help individuals be more productive and feel more fulfillment from their work.

During the learning process, participants go through a number of intellectual and behavioral responses. This learning process takes place when learners begin to internalize the content and learning processes that are present during the training. Adult learners have the ability to be intellectually flexible, like learning while doing, can organize and synthesize pieces of data to create an understanding for themselves, and can make the information their own to use when they think best. Motivation to learn is a big factor of any learner, and you can't motivate the learner—they motivate themselves to learn. What you can do is to establish the environment for the learner to feel motivated.

Motivate the Adult Learner

Participants attend trainings because they want to be there and to take away information and skills that will help them become more effective in their jobs. Providing opportunities for learners to interact with other participants during the classes is important. Developing opportunities for participants to share during group sessions is one way of providing the opportunity for sharing and exchanging. Sharing and interacting with and among groups during classes allows participants to hear and see a variety of ways to learn. Another way of providing sharing opportunities is to ask thought-provoking questions.

You've drawn up your plans and set the stage for training; in the next chapter, we discuss how you will implement the training program.

CHAPTER FIVE

Implement the Training

Implementing the training program is, in its simplest term, training delivery. It's the process of holding a conversation with your audience that is centered on specific topics. A successful conversation is one in which each participant hears the same message. And to be successful, that conversation must have audience interest, be well organized, and have a method for checking the listeners' understanding. This chapter provides the tools for delivering a training program; these tools will become part of your skills portfolio.

We begin with an overview of training implementation, first examining the role and responsibilities of the program designer, who often turns to others for the delivery phase. We then focus the light on the facilitators and speakers who deliver the training to the learners. Of course, many times the program designer is also the presenter, so all will benefit from this discussion of delivery techniques. The chapter concludes with some special tips on presentation.

The Role of Designer: Managing the Implementation

With completion of the design phase (see Chapter 2) and its subsequent validation and revision, your work as course designer enters a new phase: turning over the training program to your implementation team. Sometimes these teams include curriculum planners, training administrators, instructors, and follow-up personnel; other times the teams consist of one person: the designer is also the instructor. Whether your implementation team is just you or includes others, there is much planning and preparation ahead.

Managing the implementation phase requires overseeing three basic areas, as shown in Table 5-1: instructors/facilitators, learners, and administration. These three areas represent the usual arena for training implementation. A fourth area, management, is often overlooked or left out of the process, however.

Only with management's help can the training be transferred from the classroom to the job. Ultimately, the way management supports the learner and the instructor will affect the training. If management does not encourage course participation and follow-through, then the training effort will not succeed. On the other hand, if management acts as a visible and vocal sponsor for the course, the training that is offered will be practiced and in due time will be adopted on the job.

Check the Timing and Sequencing of the Presentation

Your design presents a coherent outline of the training program. It provides the basics: the necessary content, the sequence of subjects and activities, the instructional techniques to be used, and the length of the program and its subunits. As you well know, the program should be long enough time for participants to acquire the knowledge and skills, but within that time frame, the content should be sequenced in a logical manner. For example, a training program on presentation skills might

Table 5-1. Areas of training implementation.

Areas to Implement	What to Cover
Instructors/Facilitators	• Require a train-the-trainer program • Instructor guide • Certification process • Methods to measure consistency, instructor readiness, and ongoing performance • Accountability of instructor to meet objectives
Learners	• Learner expectations • Accountability to perform in training • Feedback systems • Training transfer systems
Administration	• Pre-course materials • Classroom materials —Practices —Test items —Evaluations —Hands-on materials —Hardware, software —Simulations, job-related materials —Post-course materials • Location/facilities —Training sites, rooms, break-out rooms —Technical/audiovisual needs —Hotel/restaurant facilities —Multisite locations —Course registration/confirmation procedures

begin by focusing on use of voice and gestures, proceed to a demonstration of how to organize a presentation, then focus on ways to be persuasive, ending with a discussion of the use of visual aids. Practice sessions might allow participants to try out these skills. The important point is to ensure that the design builds new skills upon a foundation of established skills. That's why you would cover the more fundamental skills earlier in the program. However, with some programs, flexibility in sequencing may be more viable. Let's review a hypothetical instance.

In a project-management training program, the designer might rightly decide to start with some exercises that demonstrate the benefits of teamwork over individual work. Then, the program would move to show the productive use of personality differences. The designer may decide that the program should end with developing action plans for how the teams could bring more products to market. In this instance, the designer may be correct, in that using a standard sequence is less important than building to a much-needed conclusion.

In another example, depending on the issues critical to a particular team, the designer may decide to conduct a module on conflict management before the module on typical problems with matrix management. At other times, the designer may feel it is better to do the opposite. Your experience with designing training programs and your sense of logic must work together to match the different training situations. Where you can, experiment with different sequences to uncover new approaches.

A sample training sequence is presented in Figure 5-1. At the top of the sequence are the program's objectives. Then, the time is broken down into different training exercises, with the time frames for each.

Check the Program Using the Training Plan Matrix

Using a training plan matrix helps you to see at a glance the overall nature and structure of the course you have designed and the degree to which participative rather than one-way communication methods have been planned. A training plan matrix has the hours of instruction on the left side of the paper in a vertical column. The other related columns, also vertical, show objectives, content, instruction methods and materials, and post-session handouts.

As an example of how this works, use the training plan matrix shown in Figure 5-2, write a training plan to develop a lesson on work-

Figure 5-1. Sample training sequence.

Teambuilding: A Two-Day Workshop on Improving a Team's Effectiveness

Program Objectives: By the completion of this program, participants will be able to:

- Make the most of their style and other members' styles
- Enhance group problem solving
- Help group members gain a deeper appreciation of each other
- Identify key issues for celebration to increase team spirit
- Improve communication and address communication problems
- Improve team interactions by providing feedback on group behavior

Day 1

9:00–9:45 Individual/Group Exercise: My Four Greatest Accomplishments
Group members draw pictures to represent the four accomplishments they are most proud of. Each team member presents and explains his/her pictures to the team.

9:45–10:45 Individual/Group Exercise: Individual vs. Team Decision Making
Team members take part in an exercise illustrating the effectiveness of group and individual decision making.

10:45–11:00 Break

11:00–11:30 Class/Team Exercise

11:30 –12:30 Competition and Cooperation Between Teams
Groups take part in an exercise illustrating the dynamics of cooperation and competition between groups.

12:30–1:30 Lunch

1:30–2:15 Lecture/Group Exercise: Communication in Teams
Class reviews a basic communication model. Teams then identify the fundamental communication problems they have within and between teams and discuss how the communication model might help to identify the problems and suggest some possible solutions.

2:15–3:15 Lecture/Group Exercise: Personality Types and Teams
Teams complete personality indicator and review Jung's theories of personality. Teams analyze their distribution of team personalities. Teams suggest the implications for greater communication within their team and with other teams.

(continues)

Figure 5-1. (continued.)

3:15–3:30	Break
3:30–4:30	Lecture/Group Exercise: Organizational Culture and Teams *Team members discuss organizational culture and diagnose both the actual and the ideal cultures for their teams, departments, and organization. Teams also share ideas on how they might help their teams, departments, and organization move closer to ideal culture.*
Day 2	
9:00–10:00	Lecture/Group Exercise: Organizational Influence *Class reviews some fundamental findings on influence and discusses the implications of these findings for the teams and the organization. The teams plan how these findings might be used to enhance team influence.*
10:00–10:45	Group Exercise: Identification of Team Issues *Groups complete a form that helps them analyze, as individuals and as teams, the problems that they see in their organization, departments, or teams.*
10:45–11:00	Break
11:00 –12:30	Lecture/Group Exercise: Problem Solving in Teams *Instructor reviews with the group the classical problem-solving model and the irrational influences on problem solving in organizations. Group selects a problem they want to work to improve (possibly one of those identified in the Identification of Team Issues exercise). They work through the stages of the model to devise an action plan.*
12:30–1:30	Lunch
1:30–3:00	Group Activities: Team Exercises and Feedback *Teams take part in a variety of exercises, competing among themselves to win points. After the exercise, team members provide feedback on how well they worked as a team and suggest strengths and areas of improvement for the teams.*
3:00–4:00	Individual/Group Exercise: Action Planning to Improve Team Effectiveness *Based on feedback for the team activities and what was learned in the course, individuals identify to their teammates ways in which their teams can improve. The teams agree on three problems to work on solving. Next, the teams discuss specific actions they might take to improve their effectiveness. If time permits, more problems may be selected and action plans devised.*
4:00–4:15	Discussion: Review of Workshop *Instructor and participants review what was learned and the commitments the teams have made to improve their effectiveness.*

Figure 5-2. Training plan matrix.

Time	Behavioral Objective	Content	Method	Aid

force diversity. Remember to write a job breakdown and use your SMART (Specific, Measurable, Achievable, Relevant, and Time based) objectives. Figure 5-3 then shows a sample training plan.

The Role of Instructor or Facilitator

The role of a trainer is similar to a teacher—to deliver the training program. As stated above, sometimes the designer also is the instructor or facilitator; other times, a different individual or several individuals serve in this capacity. In either case, the principles of instruction and facilitation are the same.

Figure 5-3. Sample training plan on workforce diversity.

Time (A.M.)	Behavioral Objective	Content	Method	Aid
9:00–9:30	Demonstrate the impact of perceptions on stereotyping	Participants' cultural perceptions	Discussion	Chart paper
9:30–10:30	Recognize existing diversity issues in the organization	Implications for manager and employee effectiveness on business	Text reading Discussion Exercise	Notebook
10:30–10:45	Break			
10:45–10:50	Examine how demographic shifts have and will affect the organization	Demographic shift data	Lecture	Chart paper

Facilitate, Don't Just Teach

Adult learners are usually a diverse group of people. Each comes to the training session with individual life experiences and individual expectations about his or her work and career. These life experiences include previous learning opportunities that reflect the person's age, gender, culture, values, and interests. The learning climate for your training should be sensitive to these differences, as reflected in the physical surroundings and intangible elements such as trust.

A relaxed, comfortable atmosphere permits learners to feel they have a degree of control over their learning, that they can ask questions freely, can influence the pace of the presentation, and can learn from others in the group. As the instructor, you will facilitate their learning, encouraging everyone to work together to solve problems and to share information. Especially, you will use good questioning techniques to explore the subject matter and you will encourage learners to ask questions to open up even more learning opportunities. Good questions stimulate insight and understanding, and encourage reflection. Also, remember that when learners ask questions, you can discover what points may be giving them difficulty.

Stay Within the Allotted Training Time

The time period designated for the training represents a contract between you and the learners. The two most important clauses of that contract are the starting time and the ending time. Pay attention to time. If, as instructor, you are establishing the times for each segment of the training, be realistic about how much you can accomplish in a set period. Break the session down into segments: five minutes for the learners to settle in, fifty minutes of instruction, five minutes to close, for example. During the delivery, if time is running out, make adjustments accordingly so you touch all the important points. Figure that eight hours designated means six hours of training, not eight. And there are breaks! Research on learning and the brain reveals that learners need to take mental breaks every twenty minutes and physical breaks every fifty minutes. Allocate your time accordingly.

Breaks are something you rarely get as a presenter, but don't forget to give them to your learners. Define the official break time, and then get back to work. If you leave the room for your own break, be back on time. And when you are on your break, do not solve problems, give advice, or hang out with the group. This is your time. If you don't take that break, you will never get an opportunity to rest.

Do Some Advance Preparation

A couple of days before the training begins, prepare your cheat notes and put them everywhere. Use the borders of your PowerPoint slides, add pencil comments on the newsprint, and use sticky notes. Also, make a list of where to go for technology help, and tape this list to something important so you don't lose it. Place the agenda and outline in front of you so that you can keep yourself on track.

Next, set up your training room the day before the event. Practice several times with every piece of technology you are going to use. Check on the lighting, room temperature, and location of the break rooms and bathrooms. Make arrangements for the coffee breaks. Be sure that you have enough copies of materials for every learner. Also, check each package to make sure that no pages are missing. Finally, decorate the room and make everything ready for the big event.

Find a quiet place, and practice your narrative, using a natural, conversational style as if you were talking to a colleague. Give yourself more than one day to prepare, if possible. The longer the training session, the more time you need to practice delivering the message. And, remember that successful presentations are clear and concise. Although they are conversational in style, the language you use is more formal than casual conversation between friends. Choose your words carefully; don't say anything that you wouldn't want to read in the newspaper!

Prepare Your Notes

Even though you have prepared your presentation in every respect, you will probably want to use notes to keep you close to your planned delivery. Also, should something distract you, those notes can easily help you find your way back to the topic. But the notes won't be helpful unless you can read them easily, under classroom conditions. You must be able to see your notes in bright or dim lights, and also when you change position to accommodate visual aids. The following is a checklist to make sure your presentation notes are ready:

- Use a large typeface.
- Double- or triple-space between lines, and double-space between paragraphs.

- Use hanging indents for paragraphs so the first line will be easy to spot.
- Put several spaces at the end of each sentence, so you do not run them together accidentally.
- Type the words the way you will say them (for example, one-and-a-half million dollars, not $1,500,000).
- Use only one side of the paper, and do not fasten the sheets in any way.
- Number the sheets of paper.
- Mark the page where visual aids should occur—put a symbol in the margin to indicate the aid.

Choose Your Attire and Prepare Psychologically

Getting yourself ready to make a presentation means choosing the most comfortable shoes and clothing that's appropriate to make you look great. Lay out your clothes the night before. Go to bed early, and get as much rest as possible. Then, get up early, dress, and look your best. Your confidence is up when you look good.

Just before the training begins, do a morning stretch—a couple of times, if necessary—because you don't want knots in your muscles. Talk to yourself to loosen up your throat. Remind yourself out loud that you are prepared. Next, double-check to see that nothing in the room was disturbed during the night. Stand up straight—it aids breathing and relaxation.

Try putting yourself in your learners' shoes; consider how uncomfortable they may feel at the beginning of the training, not knowing what to expect. Be there to greet each of them as they arrive; it puts them at ease. Visualize the day ahead; close your eyes and see yourself being successful.

Check the Presenter Zone

Chapter 4 discussed the importance of establishing the "presenter zone." This is the physical space between you and the learners. Table 4-2 listed ways to apply this principle in several different seating configurations. The presenter zone is all about how you handle your teaching space. In Western cultures, leaders assume and are awarded more space, both physical and psychological. But space is not important just to leaders. All people construct invisible boundaries around their bodies that become evident under certain circumstances. For instance, many people regard space, or "proximities," of up to one-and-one-half feet as intimate, and in normal interactions they allow only the people they care about to come so close.

When this space is violated, as sometimes happens in a crowded situation, people feel intense discomfort. But the space from one-and-one-half feet to four feet around most people is regarded as casual space, the proximity they accord friends and acquaintances who want to talk. All cultures have unwritten rules of behavior, and the personal boundaries and responses therein to violations of those boundaries vary considerably.

The distance that concerns most trainers, however, is 12 feet. Generally speaking, this is the space allocated for formal interactions. Most important for us in the training context, this is this distance that trainers maintain between the nearest learners and themselves. When you are closer, learners feel discomfort; they interpret this as either an invitation for greater intimacy or an authoritative encroachment on their personal space. You must use your space wisely, depending on what you are hoping to achieve. Figure 5-4 shows the degrees of personal space, aligned with training techniques. As you can see, formal presentations fall in the outer circle; discussions and close interactions come within the center of the circle.

So, how is this system of zones realized? If you wish to give the impression of strong leadership, walk around the room, check among the learners how they are doing, sit with the work groups, and lend a hand. In essence, invade the 12 feet to get closer to your group. Most people are consciously aware of personal space, so use these rules to affect the training environment without creating friction or discomfort.

Figure 5-4. Presenter zone.

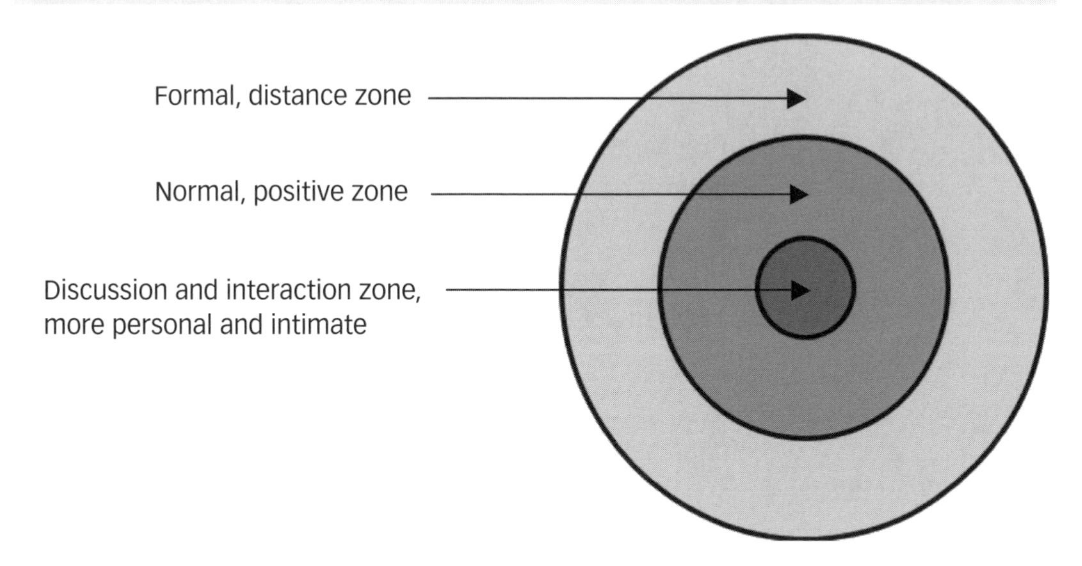

The Successful Delivery

If there is an opportunity before you begin your delivery, mingle with your audience, projecting a friendly, confident attitude. If there is no such opportunity, see if you can rework the schedule ever so slightly so as to create an opportunity to gather with the audience first. Once you are introduced as the presenter, walk briskly with purpose and confidence to the speaking position. Immediately connect with your audience, glancing at people with whom you have just mingled. Smile and limit your movements and gestures during the first few minutes of your presentation.

Begin speaking at a low volume, yet loud enough so as to be heard. Stand about six to eight inches away from the microphone, if you are using one. Even if you are shaking in your shoes and your hands are trembling, keep going and do not pay attention to your feet or your hands. After a few minutes, you will relax and be on your way to a successful delivery.

Watch Your Words

Simple words are the direct route to good communication. Use specific words to help your audience see, hear, feel, smell, or taste what you mean. Avoid words that are overly complex and that have more than one meaning or are misleading, or are only an approximation of what you want to say. The following tips may help you choose your words more carefully:

- Use familiar words. In general, familiar words are easier to understand than fancy words. Familiar words tend to be shorter, specific, and vivid.
- Avoid technical terms and business jargon. Stick with words that match your audience's level. Even if you believe your audience will understand esoteric words, do not use them (it is best not to assume anything). Use technical terms and business jargon only when you know every person in the audience will understand them.
- Use concrete, specific words. Pick up on the words that listeners say, rather than the canned speech you fall back on.
- Use action words. Incorporate words that suggest movement or meaning by how they sound or the images they convey. Consider dynamic words such as *slash* rather than *cut*, and *shred* rather than *crumble.*
- Use figures of speech, such as similes and metaphors. Similes are introduced by the words *as* or *like,* as in "My love is like a red, red rose." A metaphor is a direct comparison, without *like* or *as,* as in "business is war."

Use Dynamic Entrances and Openings

You have probably heard that you get only one chance to make a first impression. This adage holds for your training sessions, too. With your first few sentences, you will win or lose your audience. The purpose of your introduction, therefore, is to open up the participants' minds so they will be receptive to your delivery. You want to get them involved immediately.

To begin, tell the audience what the training is about and explain the overall purpose. You can use one or more of the following methods:

- Ask a question.
- Make a dramatic statement.
- Appeal to a special interest of your audience.
- Use visual aids.
- Tell a story, anecdote, or personal experience.
- Use a quotation.

Another way to begin your session is to introduce a team project that can serve as a "mixer." Use a puzzle, game, question-and-answer sheet, or a quick quiz. The key to success here is to use a theme and a prop that is coordinated with your topics.

The introduction is an essential step in setting the tone and direction of the training program. Although this is the first part of your session, prepare it last. Remember, you must accomplish the following in the introduction:

- Gain trainees' interest.
- Check the trainees' current knowledge.
- Orient the participants.
- Preview your material.
- Offer motivation.

Immediately, you must build respect and rapport. You do this by what you say, but also by how you act. Below are some techniques:

- Walk to the front of the room with poise, confidence, and authority.
- Take a deep breath.
- Step in front of any barriers.

- Think about the fun that you're going to have.
- Begin by greeting participants enthusiastically!

Then, go on to accomplish these tasks:

- Introduce the seminar.
- Introduce yourself, and let the participants know something about you. Tell them about yourself and your experience (and that experience should relate to your credibility of why you are presenting this class—keep it short).
- Set up your expectations for the course.
- Establish how you will deal with issues that are relevant but not priorities.
- Determine participants' expectations for the course.
- Use motivation and participation techniques.
- Get participants working on a project or in groups.

Provide a Solid Presentation of Information

In the body of your lesson, you present the major points to the trainees, in logical order and supported by evidence and reinforced with practice. For each new piece of information, you build on prior experience, give examples to illustrate, provide practice, and judge the comprehension.

Keep in mind that the body of the presentation is the development of a statement, which represents the theory or skill you want to teach. A statement can express an idea, make a judgment, offer an opinion, provide a fact, or present a matter of inquiry. You can develop a statement in any of these forms through illustration, interpretation, or reinforcement. For example, you can use the following to support your development of each statement:

- **Facts**: Statistics, data, something that can be proved, such as a typical circumstance or characteristic case to make the statement clear, vivid, and credible.
- **Comparison and Contrast**: A likeness or difference that associates the new with the familiar.
- **Testimony**: The say-so of someone other than you, preferably a well-known authority.
- **Quotation:** An opinion that is short and to the point.
- **Digression**: Built-in element that allows you to act as if you were departing from your script to tell a secret or to relate something that just popped into your head.
- **Demonstration:** Something you show how to do while the audience watches.
- **Visual Aid**: Laptop computer projected on a screen, wall charts, learning maps, 3-D models, or drawings add some pizzazz and interest to your presentation, make your point vivid, and help your audience remember the material.

Remember as you deliver the body of the lesson that each major point is a mini-presentation, with its own introduction, body, and conclusion.

Effective Use of Time

Total time allotment and schedule are important considerations, especially during the presentation. As discussed earlier in the chapter, you have a specific amount of time to present a specific amount of information. You must maximize learning per unit of time. Assume 60 minutes have been allocated for theory presentation. You don't actually have 60 minutes because 5 minutes will be spent on your introduction. Then 5 minutes will be spent introducing and bridging your lesson, and 5 minutes will go to concluding and summarizing.

The remaining 45 minutes is usually broken up unequally between theory and activity. Usually you spend less time on theory and more on the activity. For example, in a 45-minute presentation in which you present two concepts, allocate 5 to 10 minutes to each theory segment and 10 to 15 minutes each to activity and testing.

Types of Sessions

As introduced in Chapter 3, three types of training formats are: theory, skills, and lectures (see Table 3-3). Unlike the theory session model (see Figure 3-1), in which you create an activity by observing whether participants have attained the training objective, in the skills session model (see Figure 5-5), you readily observe the trainees performing the task and directly applying the content you have provided. The skills session is all about physical activity (the behavioral component of the objective).

Figure 5-5. Skills session model.

Introduction ⟶ Show • Show and Tell • Check for Understanding • Practice ⟶ Conclusion

The body of the skills session can be broken down into its three components as well. The introduction aims to gain participants' interest, check their current knowledge, and orient them to the training. The body is for show, show-and-tell, and practice. The conclusion links material together and clarifies issues. Therefore, in organizing the skills session, you break the task down into a series of closely linked steps requiring physical activity. By having the participants repeatedly practice those steps, you give them the chance to perfect the task (measured in terms of time it takes and quality of output).

To help determine if you have explained the task successfully, figure that the trainees should be able to perform it in less than 10 percent of the total length of the session. Again, using the example of a 45-minute session, you would want the participants to learn a four-and-a-half-minute task.

Active Teaching Tools

If you remember only one thing about the conclusion, it is to make it memorable. Use body language to indicate that you have finished your presentation. Nod and step back briskly from your speaking position. You might say something like, "I enjoyed being with you. Thank you for your attention and your participation. Best of luck to all of you."

But first, begin the conclusion by briefly reviewing your topic and the major points, and provide a summary of the training. Here is a list of techniques that assist in summarizing the learning content. You may do one or more of these steps, in sequence or simultaneously. Make your choice by considering the topic, the participants' abilities and accomplishments, and the participants' preferences:

- Appeal for action by stating what you want the participants to do.
- State your conclusions.
- Relate the conclusion to the introduction.
- Ask a question.
- Use a dynamic quotation.
- Stress the relationship of your topic to the participants' interests.
- Pay your audience a compliment.

Review the course and participant objectives, pointing out accomplishments. Refer back to significant moments in the training. Take out the pretraining needs assessment, and review it. Go around the circle, and ask participants to identify a significant event for each day of the training. Discuss memorable learning.

Similarly, take care of remaining housekeeping issues. Make sure you have done all of your tasks, critiques, forms, and rosters. If you have promised to send materials, announce an arrival date. Mention how long you will remain in the room for help or questions. Summarize all of the learning that occurred in the training. Point out how much the participants have achieved using the topic name. Praise their perseverance, their effort, and their hard work. Then end with a story that motivates and encourages lifelong learning.

Be sure to give participants a reason to practice what they learned in the course. Make sure your conclusion is real. If it has a joke, be sure it's an original. Don't preach or significantly change your personal style. Your last words should be "thank you" to the participants, telling them how much you have enjoyed the experience. Don't ruin the moment by adding anything more!

A power close includes everything: a summary of the content, an opportunity for a dialogue or exchange, and individual reflection and sharing. The final point should end with some type of graphic display. For example, a group picture, a review of the individual goals' chart, or the circle of sharing. Using a strategy that collects all of the information together to develop a summary, invite reflections to ensure successful training transfer.

And when you are planning, organizing, and rehearsing your presentation, be sure to include how you will leave the speaking area, as well as what you will do immediately upon leaving. You have several options:

- To sit in the chair from which you were introduced
- To stand on stage to greet people
- To move around the room to greet people
- To go into the hall to greet people
- To leave the area so that the group can proceed to another activity

Remember, the power close is a memorable time. All learners like to participate in something that brings the training to closure. For some, the training has been a wonderful experience; they have met a lot of great folks, and they have learned plenty. Even the "fence sitters" will participate during the closing because it's a positive event. Participants start to mentally check out about 30 minutes before the announced ending, so about

30 minutes before the end, begin making it clear that it's almost over. As for delivery, keep these tips in mind:

- There's no way to fake a good closing!
- Don't memorize it.
- Allow enough time at the end of the event to deliver it well.
- Stay on schedule.
- If they ask, "Can we go now?" You can bet you didn't close it well!

Secrets for Presentation Success

Audience Management

What if your worst fears are realized and your audience is looking around the room, and not at you—or worse, they seem to be falling asleep? If you find yourself in this situation, risk more not less. Make your delivery more dramatic. Identify a few sympathetic-looking faces, and work with them. Communicate an increased level of caring about your audience. For example, ask the learners to share their concerns or discuss the situation with you. It's best for everyone concerned that you know what's going on—best for the learners to know that you know that they know and that you want to understand and solve the problem.

One method for managing the audience is to use the SEE factor:

- **Spontaneity.** Respond immediately when there are concerns or concepts that need clarification.
- **Enthusiasm.** Be genuinely glad to be facilitating the learning situation; welcome questions or comments. If the matter is not appropriate, agree on a time for discussion.
- **Eye Contact**. Be an active listener by looking at the person talking, and be an active presenter by focusing on the audience. Don't look over their heads or at your notes. Be engaging.

Teaching people is like holding a conversation with friends. Provide a structure for the conversation, and direct the dialogue so that it is open and satisfying for everyone involved. Most of the time, we have to make inferences about the participants, and your participants will make those inferences about you, too. The first 10 minutes are the most critical. In a friendly way, present the training according to its logical four parts: introduction, topic information, practice, and feedback.

1. **Introduction**. To engage learners at the outset of the training requires meticulous attention to the way you begin your event. Preview the training, and be specific as to what the participants are going to learn.
2. **Topic Information**. To keep on track, pay attention to sequencing; make sure that every detail is structured to achieve the overall objective. Make sure the training targets the learners' reasons for being there. Also, think about the various learning styles and how to match up the style with the need. Note the three types of learners in the audience. The auditory learner will not take notes, just listen with a consistent stare; don't be alarmed about this because these learners are concentrating on what is being said. Don't ask if they are "with you." They are with you—they are processing the information. The visual learner will furiously take notes, draw pictures, use colored pens, and ask you to describe or give examples that explain the concepts. These learners will also be engaged and active. The affective learner will be calm and comfortable unless confronted. If something does happen, the affective learner will act to make things okay for everyone else.
3. **Practice**. Create opportunities for the participants to try out the new concepts or skills. Actively involving them will hold their interest. Develop a demonstration, tell a story, or give an example of how the concept or skill works back on the job. Once the learners understand how to connect the concept and the example, the opportunity to practice will keep them interested in the training.
4. **Feedback**. Design feedback opportunity into your session. The more learner-centered your training is, the more your learners will

be with you. Think of yourself as the coach, and establish learning contracts with your participants.

Handling Difficult Situations

Keeping the monkeys off your back is an important part of being in control and feeling calm during the training sessions. If you know the typical things that can go wrong, you are prepared if they do. There are three categories of difficult situations:

1. When things go wrong . . .
    - Remain calm and think of something proactive you can do.
    - Even if the best of techniques goes wrong, laugh at it.
    - Keep your sense of humor. Your ability to laugh at yourself or the situation will increase the participants' positive opinion of you and your expertise!
    - Do not place blame. Focus on the solution, not the problem.
    - Don't spend time rehashing what's happened. That's reactive behavior!

2. If participants complain . . .
    - Don't automatically agree with the participant; remain neutral.
    - Ask the other participants for solutions.
    - If participants can solve the problem, and it's okay, empower them!
    - Find the appropriate person to solve the problem; you don't have to handle all of the issues!

3. If the participant is right . . .
    - Remain neutral.
    - Find an immediate common ground.
    - Look for a solution that helps the situation now!

Question-and-Answer Sessions

Most presentations build a question-and-answer session into the end. This session allows the conversation you are having with the participants to move in the direction trainees might want to go. Plan ahead for this by having answers to questions that you anticipate the audience will ask.

However, what do you do if the unthinkable happens and no one asks a question? You have several options:

- You can avoid the appearance of no questions by planting a colleague or two in the audience who will ask questions. Sometimes that one question will encourage other people to begin asking.
- You can ask a question yourself: "Someone once asked me. . . ."
- You can end the presentation gracefully, "Seeing that there are no questions, let's end for today."

Additionally, audiences have a variety of reasons for asking questions. Don't assume that all those who ask questions are seeking information. People may ask questions to test you, show their own knowledge, make points, or get your approval. Following are some tips for managing your audience during the question-and-answer sessions:

- Receive all questions in an open, friendly manner. Don't react or be defensive, even if someone is trying to put you on the spot.
- Listen carefully and restate the question to make sure you understand it and the entire audience hears it.
- Think before you answer. Consider the following processing points before providing a response: Why is someone asking this question? How does this question fit with my purpose? How can I answer as briefly and as well as possible?
- Use the KISS (Keep It Short and Simple) principle. However, do not answer simply yes or no; answer with a short, to-the-point statement, perhaps supported by a brief example.

- Admit to not knowing an answer, and offer to find out the answer and then follow up with the answer.

Memorable and Motivational Training

There are three lesser known ways that really help you get the learners' attention. These fun events are usually memorable and leave people talking about them long after the training is over.

1. **Ring a bell**. Agree at the beginning of the course that you will quietly ring a bell when it's time to reconvene or end an activity. Or stop the music that you have been playing during the activity.
2. **Use real-life examples**. If you can relate your organization's, or another company's, situation or a well-publicized example to the training subject, do so. Also, customer or client stories work well.
3. **Tell a story from your own experience**. If you are trying to explain a complex theory, tell a success story from a previous training. Or give examples of what you have observed. Try to relate the training to problems learners have had when back on the job.

Additionally, there are two basic types of memorable training techniques that are free of cost and simple to use, as shown in Table 5-2. Environment techniques use the physical setting to catch learners' attention. Get-to-know techniques help you bridge the distance and reach reluctant learners.

Ideas for Greater Retention

The successful transfer of training is not just the trainer's job, it is also the learner's responsibility. However, as the facilitator, you can help that transfer take place. Table 5-3 lists some retention strategies you can use during your sessions.

Table 5-2. Memorable training techniques.

Environment Techniques	• Put phrases on the back of the tent cards. • Hang quotes around the room • Ask participants to write motivating phrases on an index card. Pass the index cards around, and then hang them on the wall.
Get-to-Know-Participant Techniques	• Seek out those who seem distant, and talk with them to make them feel welcome. • Help the shy learners get to know others in the classroom; arrange chairs so that they have someone to sit with. • Provide a "lunch chat" session for anyone who wants to eat with the trainer.

Table 5-3. Retention techniques.

Technique	Characteristics
Outline your course on the first day, immediately during the introduction.	Make sure the outline flows from one idea to another. Think about these points: • Daily outline defines what is to be covered during that day. Don't skip anything, and don't add anything on. • Post the outline on the wall; refer to it often.
Look for sequence of process.	Teach in logical progression. For example, use steps, general to specific and specific to general.
Use diagrams and flowcharts.	• Each chart should contain icons that represent the most important information sections of the course. • Repeat the course outline in the participant notebook. • Ask the participants to draw a flowchart that will represent the information being covered in class.
Conduct daily review sessions.	Use session reviews to reacquaint participants with the items covered the previous day.

Conclusion

Following are key points to remember when you prepare to implement your training:

- Training delivery is like holding a conversation with your audience.
- The most important and time-consuming step of training implementation is planning the delivery.
- Understanding the relationship between content and training methods helps you select the correct materials and format for your delivery.
- How you organize your training determines whether you use theory or skills sessions.
- You successfully manage your audience by paying attention to the group, and by fulfilling your contract to deliver on time and in the allotted time.

Use the presentation checklist in Table 5-4 to ensure you have prepared each stage of the presentation.

You can monitor the progress of your presentation by asking summarizing questions or using a checklist posted on a flipchart. If you use a wall chart or learning map, make sure you refer to each item on it. If you use a checklist, check off the items as you complete them.

In this chapter we discussed the implementation of the training design, the result of which is successful training, with the participants gaining new skills or greater information. Whether they take that information back with them to the job is best measured by feedback and evaluation—the topic of our final chapter.

Table 5-4. Presentation checklist.

Item	Date Completed
Accept invitation to delivery training.	________
Write the title.	________
Determine the purpose.	________
Prepare the instructional objectives.	________
Identify your audience.	
Learn about the physical setting in which you will deliver training.	________
Research the content.	________
Organize your material and determine the exact content.	________
Plan the body.	________
Plan the conclusion.	________
Plan the introduction.	________
Plan the visual aids.	________
Engage a full-service shop to execute the visual aids.	________
Receive professionally prepared visual aids.	________
Type your notes.	________
Rehearse for yourself.	________
Rehearse for others.	________
Conduct a dress rehearsal.	________
Write an outline of the presentation each night.	________
Review the answers to any questions, quizzes, tests, instruments, or surveys.	________

CHAPTER SIX

Measure the Effectiveness

We have looked at defining, designing, and developing the training program. Now we need to see if it does what we want it to do. This is another phase during which the course designer has less control—much as with the defining phase (Chapter 1). This is also when the instructor and the learners have the most accountability and when the training is most visible. Thus, this chapter focuses on the evaluation of training programs and their subsequent learner outcomes. Specifically, we review the critical importance of evaluation and the accomplishment of objectives—that is, whether job performance and organizational results have improved.

Formative and summative evaluations are discussed and compared, and the reasons for evaluation are identified. The process of evaluating a training program is outlined, and the outcomes used to evaluate that training are described in detail. Donald Kirkpatrick's well-known training model incorporating the four major levels of evaluation is highlighted, as well as the five major categories of outcomes possible.

Another important issue—that of how good the designated outcomes are—is also discussed. Perhaps most important evaluation designs and the preservation of internal validity are reviewed, as well as calculations of the return on investment (ROI) for training dollars. In an environment of increased accountability, knowledge of how to show ROI is invaluable.

The Terminology of Training Effectiveness

Let's begin by reviewing the definitions of some key terms and processes that pertain specifically to evaluation. You should have become familiar with these because of their use in earlier chapters of this book, but they particularly pertain here:

- **Training effectiveness** refers to the benefits that the company and the trainees experience as a result of training. Benefits for the trainees include acquiring new knowledge, learning new skills, and adopting new behaviors. Potential benefits for the company include increased sales, improved quality, and more satisfied customers.
- **Training outcomes or criteria** refer to measures that the trainer and the company use to evaluate the training.
- **Training evaluation** refers to the collection of data pertaining to training outcomes, needed to determine if training objectives were met.
- **Evaluation design** refers to the system from whom, what, when, and how information is collected, which will help determine the effectiveness of the training.

Because companies have made large dollar investments in training and education, and they view training as a strategy to be more successful, they expect the outcomes or benefits of the training to be measurable. Additionally, training evaluation provides a way of understanding the investments that training produces and provides the information necessary to improve training. Figure 6-1 shows the interlocking nature of training evaluation.

Figure 6-1. Interlocking nature of training evaluation.

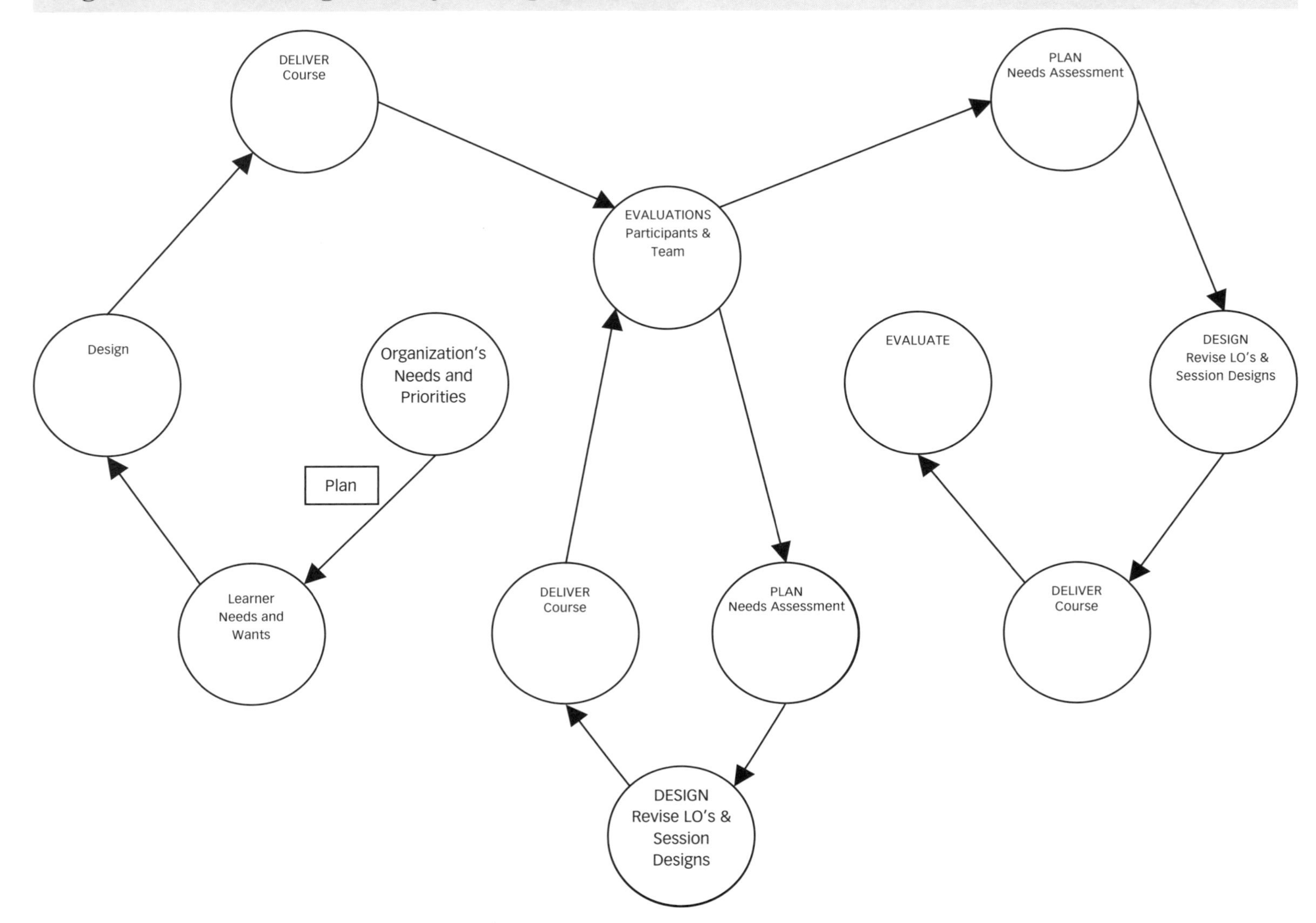

The Evaluation of Training

We end this book as we began, discussing the success of a training program. From the start, all efforts to define a need for training, through design and implementation, were aimed at achieving measurable success. It's time to review the process for determining that success. Ultimately, the evaluation leads to improvements in the program (content, instructional strategies, pace, or sequencing).

Thus, evaluation is a significant part of the design and development process. While we usually think of evaluation as something that takes place during or after the training, it really is critical to the entire process. And the heart of evaluation is the assignment of value and the making of critical judgments. The evaluation process measures what changes have resulted from the training, how much change has resulted, and how much value can be assigned to these changes.

The Levels of Evaluation

Because evaluation is so closely entwined with implementation, the methods of evaluation need to be built into the delivery of the training. There are two types of evaluation, as shown in Table 6-1—formative and

Table 6-1. Two types of evaluation.

	Description	Method
Formative	Assesses program before full implementation. Usually done by instructional designer with small focus group.	Try out and revise the process as needed. Then test the materials and instructional methods at each phase of the development.
Summative	Assesses the final training after implementation. Four levels.	Determine the degree to which objectives were met and the results after widespread use of the training.

summative. Each type provides different information to be sure that training is on track, and the table presents methods for obtaining that information.

The *formative* evaluation assesses programs before their full implementation, usually by the instructional designers using a small focus group. This involves trying out and revising the training process along the way, testing the materials and instructional methods at each phase. The *summative* evaluation assesses the training after implementation, setting up the means to determine the degree to which learning objectives were met and how widespread the use was of the training.

Within the summative evaluation are four levels, as introduced by Donald Kirkpatrick (1994) as a simple model, summarized and adapted in Table 6-2.[1]

Based on these four levels, I present in Table 6-3 the evaluation techniques and guidelines for their use. Let's look at each of these levels in turn.

Level 1: Learner Reaction

It's easy to determine a learner's individual reaction to the training. You can conduct an ongoing evaluation of the training during the sessions or

Table 6-2. Four-level Kirkpatrick evaluation process.

Level	What Is Evaluated	Description
1	Learner reaction	How did the learner react to the training?
2	Learning	How well did the learner apply the new skills and knowledge?
3	Training transfer	What changes in job behavior resulted from the training?
4	Organizational impact	What were the results of the training on the company's bottom line?

Table 6-3. Guidelines for evaluation techniques.

Evaluation Level	Techniques	Guidelines
1. Learner reaction	• Reaction sheet • Spontaneous feedback • Focus groups	• Have varied time frame—end of each day or last day of training. • Use planned session to collect feedback. • Make questions very specific to avoid subjective information based on trainees' moods and energy.
2. Learning	Test items measured during class time: • performance tests • knowledge tests • product tests	Make sure test items are appropriate, doable, and match objectives.
3. Training transfer	Checklists and other techniques to use to measure on-the-job improvement.	• Need upfront planning. • Need management communication and commitment from beginning of project. • Need agreement on how job should be done.
4. Organizational impact	Questionnaires and other techniques to determine training effect on organization.	• Need upfront planning. • Need management communication and commitment from beginning of project. • Other factors besides training may impact company results.

after the sessions. Did the learner enjoy the session? Was the learner enthusiastic? Did the learner learn quickly and perform the task correctly? Although these questions call for subjective responses, it's important that they are answered so you can determine if you did your job in building actions, developing skills, changing behaviors—and had an impact during the training program.

Measuring learners' reactions to group sessions (conferences and lectures) is more difficult. However, if your plan is for training over a period of times you can check learner reaction as you go along so that you can improve future sessions, if necessary. Checking on the responses to group training is most often done via questionnaires. The results are compiled and form the basis for making modifications to the training program. Figure 6-2 is a sample questionnaire, with possible questions that yield

Figure 6-2. Sample feedback questionnaire.

DIRECTIONS: Circle the appropriate response to questions 1–5 below, then use space provided to respond to question 6.

1. What is your overall reaction to the training?

   Very Good   Good   Fair   Poor

2. How well did the material presented in the program relate to your job?

   Very Good   Good   Fair   Poor

3. Will you be able to use and apply the material presented in your daily duties?

   Definitely   Probably   Maybe   No

4. Would you please give your overall reaction to the way the instructor presented the session?

   Very Good   Good   Fair   Poor

5. What is your reaction to the visual aids that were used?

   Very Good   Good   Fair   Poor

6. What suggestions do you have for improving this session?

the answers you want. Responses are commonly given on a numbered scale (0 = bad, 5 = good) or with fill-in spaces for writing comments.

Level 1 evaluations measure participants' feelings about the training, either ongoing or at the end of the course through participant feedback. The goal is to gather data that can be used in assessing training outcomes. Thus, each question posed usually deals with one aspect of the training at a time. Even when a rating scale is used, there should always be space at the end of the assessment for open-ended responses. Figure 6-3 is a sample of Level 1 evaluation questions with simple "agree" and "disagree" choices, but with space at the bottom for greater feedback.

Figure 6-3. Sample learner reaction questions.

DIRECTIONS: For questions 1 and 2, circle the word that best reflects your feelings regarding the training you have received. Then add any comments as a response to question 3.

1. The trainer's instructions were easily understood.

   Agree   Disagree

2. The location of the training room was assessable to me.

   Agree   Disagree

3. What is the most beneficial information you received during the program?

Level 2: Learning

There are many ways to evaluate whether the learner has met the learning objectives. Level 2 evaluation can include both formal and informal strategies. Formal evaluation involves testing for that knowledge; informal evaluation uses the learners, peers, and course instructors to measure how well the objectives were met.

In essence, this level of assessment measures participants' change over the duration of the training, so it is easy to anticipate the assessment during the design phase of the training program. Specifically, you use the statement of learning objective and outcome for each module to write an evaluation question. This question can then be given to the participants as a written exercise or used during a discussion as part of a review process. Remember, each question that you design should measure mastery of content. Don't test to determine if a learner remembers everything; reserve testing for those points that are critical to job success. Test to see what the learner can apply directly to the job. Figure 6-4 shows two sample questions for this level of evaluation.

Figure 6-4. Sample learning questions.

1. Name the 5Ws that we discussed during this session, and when do you use them?

   a.

   b.

   c.

   d.

   e.

2. How do you define the term *evaluation*? What are the major components in your definition of the term *evaluation*?

But let's take a closer look at each of these types of Level 2 evaluations:

Formal Evaluations. Tests come in many forms. You select the type of test you want to use based on the nature of the training content, its critical nature, the training setting, and any corporate or federal guidelines regarding certification or licensing. Knowledge and skills testing is sometimes done prior to the training (to determine how much the learner knew before training) and then after the training to measure results. The difference in test scores indicates a gain as a result of the training provided. Table 6-4 shows three types of formal tests, with guidelines for their use.

Table 6-4. Three types of formal testing.

Type of Test	Description	Guidelines
Performance	Measures how well a person performs in a given situation. Performance tests can be as varied as the individual training needs. These skill tests can range from simulations, to interactive tryouts, to hands-on repair in a specific workshop setting.	The key to performance testing is to make the situation and test environment as close to the real job as possible.
Product	Evaluates whether the learner can explain, use, describe, recommend, and demonstrate certain products.	This testing should be done in conjunction with selling skills performance tests or product specialist/customer service training. In addition, it is often important to have learners compare products and identify features, functions, benefits, and product audience.
Knowledge	Evaluates how much information a learner has retained. Often a knowledge test is not useful for skill testing because it focuses on what the learner can recall. Unless the learner's job includes recalling information without job aids, you should limit the amount of knowledge testing that you do.	Written knowledge tests come in a variety of formats. These include multiple choice, fill-in-the-blank, true or false, and essay.

Many learners are uncomfortable with any type of testing, so it is important to set the stage before administering a test. Explain the purpose and use of the test, as well as the results, in a clear and timely manner. Take care to validate all tests to be sure they measure the appropriate skills and knowledge before they could be used for promotion or demotion. Table 6-5 offers some advantages and disadvantages for using these Level 2 evaluation strategies.

Informal Evaluations. Often, there is no formal testing, owing to the subject matter and noncritical nature of the content. But that does not mean that Level 2 evaluations are not used. Frequently, the learners will self-evaluate their learning or use their peers or classroom instructors to help measure their transfer of information.

Level 3: Training Transfer

This level of evaluation measures participants' application of the newly learned information to the job. The way to measure whether the learners transfer their new skills or knowledge when back on the job is best evaluated through personal observation or testimony. Say, through supervisor or learner input, you heard how an employee performed previously (sloppy work habits); you can now compare those behaviors to the behaviors following the training (correct methods, clean work area). If behaviors have significantly changed, you can probably attribute that to the effect of training.

Some ways to measure Level 3 changes in behavior include follow-up surveys sent to participants after the training, on-the-job surveys, testimonials by peers or supervisors, and performance comparisons with untrained peers. Responses to these techniques are the feedback from participants who relate stories of their successes in applying the new concepts or, if the learners had signed a contract at the start of the program that promised they would apply the concepts, you have a date for

Table 6-5. Evaluation of learning guidelines.

Strategy	Advantages	Disadvantages
Written tests/ assessments (could be pre/post)	Provide documentation and immediate feedback Reinforce knowledge Are easy to administer Are flexible in timing Advance the organizer Reinforce knowledge content	Create anxiety/stress Are difficult to construct Could have legal implications
Performance tests/assessments	Allow for self-discovery Allow for application Can be an instructional strategy (case study, role play, etc.) Reinforce course content and skills Provide immediate feedback Are behaviorally oriented Simulate the job	Require time Could have legal implications Require trained observers/ assessors Can affect performance more than training (pretraining skills)
Skill tests/ assessments	Replicate the job Separate levels of dexterity Support job standards Provide immediate feedback Allow for direct application of knowledge and skills Reinforce skills	Determine level of performance Imply level Require equipment Require equipment room Require trained observers/assessors
Work product tests/assessments	Replicate the job Allow for direct application of knowledge and skills Link to field supervisors/leads Support job product standards Involve subject-matter experts Reinforce skills	Require equipment Disrupt work environment Have high visibility or high risk Could have legal implications Can be time-consuming May take equipment out of service impacting production Require trained observers/assessors May be difficult to construct and assess

checking back and a date for completion of the contract. Typical forms of evaluation for Level 3 include:

- Checklists
- On-the-job surveys
- Mystery customers/shoppers

Level 4: Organizational Impact

Evaluating the effect of training on the organization is the process of determining how much and how well the training led to increased organizational productivity or improved customer satisfaction, or how much it contributed to realizing the organization's strategic business plan. When we use the term *impact evaluation*, we are usually referring to ROI. However, the term can mean other things as well, such as cost/benefit or intangibles. Essentially, the "results evaluation" examines the impact of training on learners' work output.

There are two types of ROI for trainings, as shown in Table 6-6: forecasting ROI and cost–benefit analysis. The first is done prior to initiating a training program, to determine whether to go ahead with the plan; the second is done after implementation as a way of evaluating results.

Table 6-7 then considers the purpose of each of these evaluation levels in terms of what is measured, when, and with what instrument. Note

Table 6-6. Evaluating the impact of training on organization.

Type of ROI	What It Means
Forecasting ROI	Determines the desired results of a training so as to make a go/no-go decision before investing in the training.
Cost/benefit analysis	Compares after-the-fact costs of training to after-the-fact benefits realized from training.

that the table includes the fifth level of evaluation, the program's monetary value to the organization. This table will prove valuable when you are trying to make decisions about what to measure and what tool to use.

Table 6-7. Purpose of the evaluation levels.

Level Number	When to Measure	What to Measure	Measurement Instrument
1	During program (end of day) End of program	Reactions Pace and sequence Relevance (content) Instrument strategies Interaction Facilitators' style Level of discussion Objectives met Environment Knowledge of facilitator Participant interaction Registration process	Questionnaires Individual responses in class Follow-up interviews
2	During program Pre and post	Is learning taking place, and to what extent? Teaching of content Knowledge of participants	Knowledge tests Performance tests Role plays Case studies Checklists Product tests
3	After program A few weeks to three months	On-the-job change	Performance records Performance contracts Action plans Interviews Observation with checklists
4	After program Three months to one year	Impact on organization	Action plans Interviews Questionnaires Focus groups Performance contracts
5	After program Three months to one year	Monetary value of impact	Control groups Trend line Participants' estimates Supervisors' estimates Management's estimates Extant data External studies

Evaluation's Ultimate Value

The hierarchy of evaluation, shown in Figure 6-5, adds another level to the process: ultimate value. Presented as a pyramid, with ultimate value at its base, this system measures the outcomes and effectiveness of training, with its foundation being the affect of training on the organization over time.

This view of the assessment process provides a variable time line; it might take six months, a year, or even longer. You gather the data that reveal how the organization or individuals have been affected over time as a result of the training. Once you establish your data point, you can validate the change and establish that the change was a result of the training. Then, if possible, you can calculate the dollar value of revenue lost if the actions were not addressed and the changed behavior did not

Figure 6-5. Hierarchy of evaluation.

FOCUS		TIME FRAME/ WAYS OF MEASURING
What did the participants like or dislike?	REACTION	Measured during the course or immediately following: participant evaluations
How did the participants change by the end of the program?	LEARNING	Measured during the course or immediately following: trainer observations; pre- and post-course self-assessments
How much participant change subsequently affected job behavior or performance?	BEHAVIOR	Measured three to six months following the course: on-the-job demonstrations
What are the results produced by behavioral change?	RESULTS	Measured six months to a year following the course: statistical data; personnel evaluations
How do results affect the organization or individual over time?	ULTIMATE VALUE	Measured one year or more following the course: evaluation of organization strategy; evaluation of career progress

occur—this is a simple form of ROI. Figure 6-6 is a simple back-home exercise that you can provide your participants so they can record the transfer of training back on the job.

Figure 6-6. Sample back-home exercise.

DIRECTIONS: Answer each of the following questions, based on your recent training experience.

1. Given the five levels of evaluation that you reviewed during your recent training, describe a situation in which you might be able to immediately integrate one of the levels of evaluation.

2. Write a short description of the situation:

3. Describe the suggested action you would take:

The Methods of Evaluation

There are many ways that you can assess training outcomes. Listed below are various techniques and short explanations on how to use the techniques in your training.

➤ **Questionnaires.** This is the most popular evaluation instrument that trainers use. Questionnaires can be a short reaction form or a detailed follow-up survey. In short, they can be used to obtain information at all levels of evaluation. For the questionnaire to elicit accurate data, however, the participants need to have good reading and writing skills.

There are two types of questions you can ask on a questionnaire: (1) open-ended questions, which give unlimited possibilities for responses;

and (2) close-ended questions, which allow participants to select from predetermined choices.

➤ **Surveys**. This is a specific type of questionnaire, with several applications for measuring results at all levels. It can be used to gather information about perceptions, policies, procedures, work habits, and values. Note, however, that it is difficult to measure attitudes toward the training; that is better done though interviews or observations.

The survey is not a research tool per se. However, it can serve as a means of collecting data as part of a longitudinal study, or can be a quick check on participants' responses to training with respect to materials, facilitation, and transfer back home.

➤ **Tests.** This form of evaluation may be best used to judge the effectiveness of skills-based training, not necessarily human relations training. Tests allow you to collect information on all levels of evaluation.

➤ **Observations.** This process can be used before, during, or after a training session to obtain information for all levels of evaluation. The desired behavior should be determined at the beginning of the training, with changes recorded. Observers should be trained in proper observation methods and be knowledgeable about their subject matter.

➤ **Interviews.** This process can be time-consuming, yet it can yield valuable information that you would not get from surveys or questionnaires. Develop the interview questions before you conduct the interviews, and make sure you use the same questions for each interviewee.

Types of Evaluation Data

Various types of statistics or data can lend credibility to your study. The following data sources can also serve as points around which to design and develop the training.

➤ **Accident Rates.** Statistics on on-the-job accidents can provide a frame of reference for developing your training. The only caution for using this information is to make sure that the statistics are accurate and that you use them appropriately. This information can be used to demonstrate why training is necessary.

➤ **Quality Indicators.** These are used in the evaluation process for both formative and summative assessments to determine if the training achieved the objectives and purpose of the course. That is, quality indicators are used to justify training. However, be mindful that the use is appropriate. If you do not have a baseline for the quality indicators, create one using industry standards, then develop your own organizational benchmarks for training.

➤ **Test and Retest Scores.** Test scores can produce data backup to support your training, especially when the retest scores show marked improvement. You can use preliminary test scores to guide your training design and help establish training outcomes. Be careful to use tests appropriately, however; don't test for topics or processes that do not require tests or outcome documentation.

➤ **Pre- or Post-Training Data.** Data that show improvement can serve as guidelines for learning and also for establishing learning goals. The pre- and post-training data should not be used inappropriately or serve as judgment of someone's learning potential.

➤ **Follow-Up Training.** This is a popular strategy for ensuring that an ROI exists. Design your follow-up campaign to include the supervisors and managers of those you have trained. In the follow-up training, gather the data using a reaction form similar to that shown in Figure 6-7 or the sample follow-up questionnaire shown in Figure 6-8.

The Validation for Your Training Program

After a training has been completed, there are many ways to validate your training design. Table 6-8 is a checklist for ensuring that you have

Figure 6-7. Sample post-meeting reaction form.

Directions: Carefully read the statements below and rank-order each using the following scoring process: use 1 to indicate least useful and use 5 to indicate most useful. For each question, first identify the statement you would rank 1, then the one item you rank 5, then 2, 3, and 4. Note: We've shown one sample question here; depending on the nature of your meeting, add more questions to solicit the information you need.

1. During the meeting, participants were

   ( ) uninterested and uninvolved.

   ( ) in need of help.

   ( ) involved in process issues.

   ( ) strictly task oriented.

   ( ) involved in learning.

2. Additional questions. . . .

Figure 6-8. Sample follow-up questionnaire for program participants.

Name of Course: ______________________________ Date: _______________

Directions: Answer the following questions, based on the training you received. There are no right or wrong answers; honest responses are appreciated and will be used to improve this training program.

1. Which of the topics covered have you applied directly to your work since you attended the training?
2. Describe how you used what you learned in the training:
3. How successful do you think you have been in transferring what you learned to your performance on the job? (Circle one)

   Very successful   Successful   Not very successful

4. What changes in or additions to the training format would you recommend?

Table 6-8. Checklist for validating your training program.

	Data to Collect	Notes
Learners	• Timing • Materials easy to use • Instructor's directions easy to follow • Individual and group activities completed • Learners' questions and confusions • Incorrect or misleading information • Difficult areas, terminology, sequence • How well objectives were achieved	
Instructor	• Timing • Difficult explanations of content • Used interactive techniques • Answered learners' questions • Sequence • Led learners to achieve objectives	

collected all the relevant data, from both learners and instructors. Check off the items on the list and make appropriate notes in the right-hand margin if you need to follow up on any you have missed. The checklist proves especially helpful because it targets the two dimensions of training: learner achievement and instructor facility with the content.

Ensuring the Transfer of Training to the Job

Many factors are important for successful learning and training transfer, but perhaps the most important are learner motivation and expectations, effective training design, trainer personality and skill, opportunity to use the information, support from supervisor and peers, and an organizational culture that supports training. Because the goal of your training program is to ensure training transfer, this is paramount from the point you begin to design a training program.

According to Barbara Carnes, a leading consultant on training, keep these three concepts in mind when designing a training:

1. **Consider the critical time frames**. There are three points in time that influence training transfer: before the training, during the training, and after the training. The most important of these are before the training, when positive expectations of the utility of the training and supervisor support should take place; and during the training, when the trainer/instructional designer skill and personality are used.

2. **Identify the barriers.** There are several barriers to successful training transfer: no opportunity to use the newly acquired skills, no support or encouragement from the supervisor or the rest of the organization, training received that is not applicable to the job, low or poor expectations prior to the training, supervisor or peer pressure to ignore the new skills, and no motivation to use the new skills.

3. **Integrate the education.** (TIEs) are easy-to-use teaching methods for before, during, or after the training that increase the chances that training transfer will take place. These techniques are within the control of the trainer, although they may also involve the trainee or the supervisor, and they can be incorporated into any training program, regardless of content.

The following are 12 techniques that you can use to ensure training transfer.

1. Target objectives

    - Start with SMART (Specific, Measurable, Achievable, Relevant, and Time-based) instructional objectives.
    - Invite personalization.

- ➤ Include supervisor.
- ➤ Use pre-work, in writing.

2. Success stories and lessons learned
   - ➤ Use before, during, or after the training.

   BEFORE: Previous graduates share success stories on using their new skills

   DURING: Trainer shares these stories

   AFTER: New graduates share success stories and lessons learned

   - Use e-mail or voicemail.
   - Use a memo of success stories, and make connections.

3. Training buddies
   - ➤ Use before, at the beginning, at the middle, at the end, and after the training.
   - ➤ Assign or let participants choose.
   - ➤ Share goals.
   - ➤ Agree to support, help, and hold accountable.
   - ➤ Combine with other TIEs.
   - ➤ Reinforce.

4. Picture yourself
   - ➤ During: Trainer leads visualization: "Picture yourself with these new skills. . . ." Trainees draw pictures of themselves using the new skills. Trainees discuss benefits.
   - ➤ After: Discuss/visualize the application. Trainer leads visualization: "Draw a picture of how you are going to use this new training."

5. Training tickets
   - ➤ Before: Send ticket or memo to introduce content, outcomes, expectations, and access prior to learning. Collect ahead of time to customize the class. Send to supervisor, too.

- During: Start the training with them. Use to assign training buddies. Trainer says, "To gain admission, bring it with you or send it in. Ask the boss to complete it for you to identify mutual goals."

6. Application check
   - During: Several times during the training have participants write how they will use what they are learning.
   - After: Send to participant to remind and reinforce.

7. Measure it
   - Before: Pre-test for prior learning. Give feedback results to participant.
   - During: Give feedback to instructor and participant.
   - After: Post-test to determine learning six weeks to nine months later to determine transfer, and include their managers.

8. Transfer trivia
   - Measure learning informally.
   - Use board games, index cards, or paper.
   - Write your own content questions, or borrow them from course materials such as post-course tests or review questions.
   - Award prizes.
   - Before: Use as pre-test or introduction.
   - During: Reinforce or test learning.
   - After: Test learning or transfer.

9. Critical mass feedback
   - Chart to show how many in the work unit or department have been trained.
   - With manager, set completion goal: 100%, 75%, etc.
   - Before: Feedback to supervisor and trainee to motivate enrollment.
   - After: Show progress toward goal, and stimulate future enrollments. Post or send via memo or e-mail.

10. Use it or lose it checklist
    - During: List or have participants list specific things to do back at work to apply the training. Send their supervisor a copy.
    - After: Follow up. Recognize/reward completed checklist.

11. Play bingo
    - After: On each box on the card, list one activity to apply training. Get managers to help identify activities. Customize for different departments. Offer prizes for blackout. Do electronically.

12. Action plan
    - Use before, during, or after.
    - List activities or actions to take after training.
    - Have trainee, supervisor, and trainer sign.
    - Write formal contract with commitment to learn and use (trainee); guide and support (supervisor and trainer).
    - Give copies to all: trainee, trainer, and manager.
    - Follow up.

Linking the Training to the Bottom Line

Today there is a call for accountability in training. Measuring the effectiveness of training, its business value, and its ROI are frequent topics of conversation when training plans are being reviewed or funded by upper management. Thus, evaluation of training results is vital for reinforcing the value of training. It is also a vital link between you and the client organization or its stakeholders.

Training represents a change project in any organization, and correspondingly there are levels of training evaluation in regard to any change effort:

- The first level measures how well each task is performed within the total project scheme before any changes or training is performed.

The goal is to determine the performance of each individual involved.

- The second level is the observation of individuals, units, and departments to determine how they handle the new processes dictated by the change project.
- The third level is the measurement of the impact of meta-tasks and how these tasks impact the organization.

Let's look at each of these levels.

Short-Term Evaluation

The first level mentioned above consists of short-term projects within the larger change process. This usually involves analyzing the implementation of a challenging task, and it provides the change team with necessary feedback on how well the project is progressing. It can provide feedback on how the project is being managed and can indicate if anything needs to be added, adjusted, or eliminated. During this level, adjustments to the project can be made.

Given the fact that there are individuals working on the change project team, an evaluation tool is used merely to provide these individuals with an opportunity to share their experiences, get help, hear from others, and come to some mutual agreement as to what the present state of the project looks like. There are two tools that are recommended to conduct this short-term evaluation: oral reviews and project sessions.

Oral Review. An oral review is a series of well-framed questions. You want to have each of the change team members and other managers or supervisors deemed necessary to explain what they see in the project that needs attention. When you design the questions, structure them around a key project indicator or action step. This creates strong redundant data patterns. Also, never answer your own questions because that allows the participants to stop thinking, and it defeats the purpose of the review.

When conducting the oral review, do not tackle large tasks or chunks of material at once. Break down the information you want to gather in short, simple sentences. Also, keep the review short and to the point. Don't let the review become a gripe session. Look for effective redundant loops of information. Be consistent. Review regularly, and don't miss a chance to review. Develop a schedule, and stick to it.

Reviews only provide feedback and evaluation of what the impressions are of those involved, so try to quantify the information they provide. To enlist people to attend the oral review, summarize the feedback that members have provided and give a perspective on what they have done and what is the next step. This process keeps everyone in the habit of reviewing the project on a regular basis and prevents surprises.

Project Session. A project session is a meeting of all members involved in the change project. There are several ways to conduct the session. For instance, ask each person to bring a critical incident in the project (a critical incident is an event that the individual recently experienced that was crucial to or had a significant effect on the task performance). Collect the incidents, choose the most germane, and assign groups to work on evaluating and solving the incident.

Another type of project session is the case history, usually structured around a single large problem that must be solved. If there is a persistent problem with a task, assign the group most immediately involved to write a case history. The case is then presented, and the entire group studies the situation and comes up with solutions.

Immediate Application

The second level consists of medium-term feedback loops that are evaluated during the change process. This usually consists of observing the performance of a task within the project. The performance evaluation focuses on ensuring that the tasks are completed appropriately, and that the individuals completing the job know what they are doing and why they are performing the task. The aim is to gather feedback from those doing the specific task. Just as in the first level, findings now can lead to adjustments to the project. There are four steps to follow in conducting the second level of evaluation:

1. Review the action plans in the job setting. At the completion of each task, have the task leader use an evaluation technique to assess if the individuals working the plan know what they have done. This assessment might consist of having the individuals write a simple synopsis of what they did and then sharing it with the group. This activity checks for understanding of the action plan being put into place.
2. Set key variables or techniques. Develop a technique with the group that they must use while putting the action plans into operation. Check with the group to see if they used the technique and if they modified it. If there was a degree of modification to make it their own, this is an evaluation that the group is applying the technique they learned on the change project.
3. Let the project team know that at some future date they will be asked to respond to a survey. Ask them what type of questions they think would be important to ask in the future. If the questions are appropriate for evaluating progress, use them in the survey.
4. Let the group know that you have planned to hold group sessions during well-spaced intervals. This provides the opportunities for individuals to offer input and to hear from others working on other tasks. You can use an assessment tool, case studies, project studies, dialogue, or role-playing events.

The second level really focuses on the individuals who are taking the project action back to their own units, programs, or departments. It's important to provide structured events to have them share their experiences of working on tasks and to hear from others.

Bottom-Line Evaluation

To move from a reactive to a proactive status, the team must become an integral part of the organization's strategic planning. This means that the change project must be evaluated in terms of the bottom line. If the change is to have a positive effect on the organization, there needs to be evidence of both qualitative and quantitative data.

The first thing that the change team must consider, if they choose to adopt this level of evaluation process, is how to establish a relationship between costs of the existing situation and costs as a result of the change. This is not a matter of justifying costs; it is an exercise to prove that there is a reason for initiating the change. It has to consider, therefore, the opportunity cost of *not* making the improvement. Thus, the third level is a measure of the impact of change on the organization at large. The proposed change can relate to the mission statement, a budget difference, department goals, or other outcome of making a change, but its purpose is to assess how the change project will succeed and how that success will be measured. Ultimately, the change team discusses the impact of the third level and determines if it is an action that is necessary to performance.

Closing Activities

All training programs come to an end. Below are closure techniques and activities you can use to end your training.

Inter-Twined

This activity demonstrates the effect of team members' actions on one another. It is a good closure to teambuilding workshops.

1. Break participants into groups of four or five, and give each a ball of twine.
2. Read the following:

   DIRECTIONS: Consider yourselves a team. Cluster together. Be no farther than an arm's length from the teammate next to you. One person takes the ball of twine, holds onto the end of the twine, and passes the ball to a teammate. That teammate holds onto a segment and passes the ball to another teammate—it can be the teammate next to you or across from you. Keep the twine taut without breaking it. You are encouraged to make complex, multiple loops around each other. You can loop the twine around one or two other teammates. Your looping pattern will demonstrate how creative you are as a team—and you are creative. Continue this process until every member of the team is holding the twine at some point.

3. When the team is all connected, tell them to try these actions in sequence, one after the other:

    - One teammate moves hand to the right.
    - Another teammate moves to the corner of the room.
    - Another teammate sits down.
    - Another teammate moves back to where the exercise began.

4. Reconvene the large group, and lead a discussion on how the exercise demonstrates the effect of one person's actions on others in a group, such as work teams or committees.

Participant Summaries

Typically, trainers end a program by summarizing their training program. These summaries have the potential to be disengaging and dry. One way to counteract this potential is to have participants create their own summaries. The primary purpose is to provide participants with an opportunity to evaluate the information they have learned and present it in a meaningful way. The secondary purpose is to provide trainers with immediate feedback on the course and know that the participants gained the ability to integrate the information they have learned.

Use this closer, which takes 90 to 120 minutes, for longer nontechnical trainings such as leadership development, professional development, safety management, or process improvement. The materials you will need include flip charts, a box of markers, computers with presentation software, scissors, and tape. Follow these directions:

Step 1. Divide participants into groups. Use your judgment as to the makeup of the groups. Consider the complexity of course content and participant representation, such as organization, roles, level, and expertise. Each group will focus on one main area of content.

Step 2. Assign each group a topic or allow groups to select their own. Each group creates a 20-minute review of their topic using any format. Formats could include presentation, role-play, panel discussion, or facilitated discussion. Participants should be encouraged to be creative. Provide the following:

INSTRUCTIONS: Your group has 15 to 20 minutes to lead a review session on your topic. Ensure your review is interactive and involves the other participants. Consider the following items in your review:

- Explain the most important aspects of your topic.
- Describe how your group will use the information on the job.
- Describe how your thinking has changed as a result of the training.
- Explain what you will do differently as a result of the training.
- Demonstrate how to apply tools or concepts.
- Share what conclusions you have reached.

Step 3. Provide groups with 45 to 60 minutes to prepare their review. This is a self-directed activity, and the trainer should only be available to answer questions.

Step 4. Have groups lead their reviews. The other groups are participants and should ask questions and follow directions.

Step 5. Lead a debriefing by asking the following types of questions:

- What was the process like for creating your own course review?
- What types of skills did you use in leading your reviews?
- What did you like about other groups' reviews?

Poetic Experience

This is a good concluding activity for any length class and also serves as a fine lead-in to the level one evaluation. The purpose of this closer is to provide participants with an opportunity to express their reactions to the class.

For this activity, which will take 40 minutes, you need poetry magnets or slips of paper with a variety of words typed on them and card stock or cardboard and tape.

Step 1. Break participants into groups, and provide each group with a box of magnetic poetry words and a piece of card stock. Inform participants that they are to work together, using the words provided, to create a poem about their reactions to the class or to the content of the program. Share the definition of a poem, such as this one: "Writing that formulates an imaginative awareness in language chosen to create a specific emotional response." The poem can be humorous or serious, but it should reflect the group's opinion of the training. To get things started, the trainer can provide a poem example that describes the class. Allow 25 minutes for the activity.

Step 2. Participants can spend 10 to 15 minutes reviewing the poems.

Step 3. Lead a debriefing session by asking questions such as the following:

- How did the group develop the process of creating its poem?
- Did you notice any themes emerging in all of the poems?
- Why did your group choose its topic?

Step 4. Take a picture or make copies of the poems so you have evidence to supplement an evaluation report or as the basis for future classes.

Blended Learning in the Work Environment

When more than one delivery mode is used, with the objective of optimizing the learning outcomes and the cost of administering the program, this is termed *blended learning*. However, it is not the mixing and matching of different delivery modes that makes this program style significant but, rather, its focus on learning and business outcomes. Blended learning gives participants valuable ways to assess, focus, measure, and reinforce the knowledge they gain by delivering targeted and actionable content at key stages. The goal of blended learning is long-term retention, improved mastery of subject matter, and markedly greater on-the-job performance.

There are various feedback devices that you can use to assess the success levels that will result from blended learning. These devices provide valuable information that alerts you to any need to adjust the training while ongoing, so you don't have to wait until the end to uncover problems with presentation.

1. **Pre-Training Assessments**. Prior to the training, participants use online tools to assess their subject-matter knowledge, identify areas of potential development, and create an individualized learning plan that focuses their learning on those goals.
2. **Instructor-Led Seminars**. Most learning is acquired during a live course led by an instructor who is an expert in the field. During this phase, learners refer to the learning plan they developed in pre-training assessments.
3. **Post-Assessments**. After the instructor-led training has concluded, participants complete an online post-seminar assessment to measure what they've learned.

4. **Tune-Up Courses and Other Online Resources**. Retraining and subsequent building on new knowledge is the first step to achieving subject-matter mastery. Any remaining knowledge gaps are identified in the post-seminar assessments and are eliminated with targeted online tune-up courses.
5. **Measurements**. Through comparisons of pre- and post-assessments, the training program designer can measure the transfer of learning and report the effectiveness of the training to the organization, thereby demonstrating a return on the training investment.
6. **Lasting Resources for the Employees and the Organization**. Months after the program has ended, participants can go online to select refresher topics and apply them to the job.

Attributes of Blended Learning

Originally, the term *blended learning* was applied to the linking of traditional classroom training to e-learning activities. However, it has evolved to encompass a much richer set of learning strategies. Today, a blended learning program may combine one or more of the following dimensions, although many of these have overlapping attributes.

Offline and Online Learning

Blended learning sometimes combines online and offline forms of education, where *online* usually means "over the Internet or intranet" and *offline* happens in a classroom setting. For example, a program may provide study materials and research resources over the Internet while using instructor-led classroom training as the main medium of instruction.

Self-Paced and Live Collaborative Learning

Self-paced learning implies solitary, on-demand learning at a pace that the learner manages. *Collaborative* learning, on the other hand, implies dynamic communications among several learners. Thus, this form of blended learning may include individual review of important literature on a regulatory change or new product, followed by a moderated, online, peer discussion of that material's application.

Structured and Unstructured Learning

Not all forms of learning involve a structured program with organized content, presented in a specific sequence like chapters in a textbook. In fact, most workplace learning occurs in an unstructured form, such as in meetings, in hallway conversations, and through e-mail. A blended program captures conversations and documents from these unstructured situations and places them in knowledge repositories where content is available on demand—paralleling the way workers collaborate at work.

Custom and Off-the-Shelf Content

Off-the-shelf content is, by definition, generic, so it cannot cover an organization's unique context and meet specific requirements. However, it is much less expensive and frequently has higher production values; that is, greater results from more money being spent on design, development, delivery, and production of training than custom content. Generic, self-paced content can be tailored to suit an organization's needs with a blend of live experiences (classroom or online) and limited content customization. Industry standards such as SCORM (Shareable Courseware Object Reference Model) can offer greater flexibility in blending off-the-shelf and custom content, thereby improving the user experience while keeping costs at minimum.

Work and Learning

The true effectiveness of learning for any organization is the paradigm of inseparable work (such as business applications) and learning, whereby learning is embedded in the business processes, such as hiring, sales, or product development. That is, work becomes a source of shared learning and learning is a constant in the workplace. In this paradigm, constraints of time, geography, and format that we associate with the traditional classroom are no longer valid. Even the fundamental organization of a training course can be transformed into an ongoing learning process.

Ingredients for Today's Blended Learning

Blended learning is not new. However, in the past the ingredients were limited to formats used in traditional classroom formats (lectures, labs, books, or handouts). Today, trainers have myriad learning approaches, including but not limited to the following:

- Synchronous physical formats: instructor-led classrooms and lectures, hands-on labs and workshops, field trips
- Synchronous online formats (live e-learning): e-meetings, virtual classrooms, Web seminars and broadcasts, instant messaging
- Self-paced, asynchronous formats: documents and Web pages, Web/computer-based training modules, assessments/tests and surveys, simulations, job aids, online learning communities and discussion forums

As mentioned above, the concept of blended learning is rooted in the idea that learning is not just a one-time event but, rather, a continuous process. Blending provides various benefits over using a single learning type because it avoids the limitations of a single delivery mode. For example, a scheduled classroom training program limits access to those who can participate at that time and in that location, whereas a virtual classroom is inclusive of a remote audience and when supported by a recorded version (the ability to replay a recorded live event) can be revisited for review or greater clarification.

Getting Started with Blended Learning

The training designer or instructor needs to approach blended learning as a journey rather than a destination. The first steps are to build content experience with self-paced learning techniques and live e-learning, thereby understanding their strengths and weaknesses in your training context. The good news is that this initial step consistently demonstrates quick financial payback and strong user acceptance.

The next step is to experiment with dimensions of the blend. You may find it useful to link self-paced content with live learning activities. Whichever elements you decide to blend, approach the design as you would in making any significant organizational change. That is, ensure that the following project criteria can be met:

- There is clear, high-value business justification to achieve executive sponsorship.
- Executive sponsorship will provide the resources and management support required.
- A committed project team will execute the project regardless of obstacles.
- A change management strategy exists to anticipate and overcome resistance to change.
- There are responsive vendors to provide resources and expertise.
- You have a deadline that helps you maintain focus and commitment.

Learning-design theory states that learning is an outcome. Instructional theory is the process of arranging material directed to a learning outcome.

E-Learning and Technology for Blended Learning

As with all instructional strategies, technological innovations for training purposes have their own strengths and limitations. In general, technology-based learning systems require more upfront work and more money than traditional methods and will usually be more complex to implement and manage. However, once the systems are up and running, they can be convenient and cost-effective ways to deliver learning.

There is a lot of talk these days about e-learning. Most people consider e-learning to be learning via electronic or online means, using a computer. Actually, the scope of e-learning goes a bit deeper than that. SmartForce, a large provider of online learning systems, considers *e-learning* to mean "to experience learning." The company applies it to other "e-words," such as *enterprise*, *excellent*, *everywhere,* and *electronic.* People using advanced "definitions" of e-learning understand that adult learning principles are at the heart of their total learning solution.

Simply put, e-learning is used to meet the demands of today's organizations and today's individual learners. It is viewed as the best technology to deliver learning that meets all of the following criteria:

- Flexible (can be configured quickly to meet different learning needs)
- Fast and available (can often be started immediately, and instruction "comes" to the learner)
- Convenient (can often be done at the learner's location and at the learner's convenience)
- Tailored to the learner (can be adapted to suit the learner's abilities, interests, and existing knowledge)
- Economical (usually far less costly than face-to-face training and reduces or eliminates travel costs)
- Interactive (can be an engaging and effective way to learn)
- Enterprise-wide (can be standardized for use across the organization)
- For everyone (can be accessed by more people than traditional settings)

Components of Learning Technology

To take advantage of the power and flexibility of learning technology, e-learning experts recommend you build a variety of learning methods into a comprehensive solution. This total-solution concept supports the greatest range of needs and learning styles. Whichever methods you choose, however, consider each of these components of learning technology:

➤ **Asynchronous Content Delivery**. There needs to be a way for learners to receive and explore the content whenever they have the time. *Asynchronous* means that the learner is not required to connect with the material at the same time as an instructor or other learners. Instead, the interaction is with the computer and the material that others have previously made available. Examples of asynchronous content delivery include Web-based learning modules, CD-ROM programs, structured courseware, Web site links, and libraries of published articles. None of these requires direct interaction with another person.

➤ **Synchronous Content Delivery**. It is often helpful for a learner to be able to ask questions of the instructors, experts, or peers, and to learn more than the programmed instruction allows. Attending online classes, meetings, or presentations provides this synchronous, or same-time, two-way communication, usually via chat-based classes, video or satellite classes, or Web meeting classes.

➤ **Supplemental Learning Resources.** Collaboration is an advantage of the e-learning environment. Learners can discuss problems, work on joint assignments or projects, and gain a sense of community through bulletin boards, online chats, discussion groups, and instant messaging sessions. Job aids are another type of learning supplement that helps learners apply what they learn.

➤ **Work Applications**. To be effective at improving performance, e-learning solutions need to help learners transfer the learning to the job. Often, opportunities for this transference need to be designed into the total solution, as it is not a component of the course itself. Examples of work applications include on-the-job projects or assignments, links of the material to real-work situations, and expectations of accountability for using what the person learns.

▸ **Support Methods.** In the e-learning environment, learning is not limited to a set class period or training session. Learners can get ongoing help, support, and advice through online coaching and mentoring, help files, frequently asked questions files, and organizational teaching support.

▸ **Assessments**. Online tools allow learners to complete pre- and post-training skills assessments, as well as surveys that customize the course to their needs and abilities. For certification or qualification programs, the computer can be programmed to automatically administer, score, and record the certification tests.

Limitations of Learning Technology

Most new training technologies are an improvement over the static classroom methods used in the past, largely because they create a more positive learning environment. However, developmental costs can be high and programs can become obsolete quickly.

To decide whether to integrate technology into your training program, consider the monies and time needed for product development, the geographic location of prospective individuals and learning groups, and the inherent difficulties in getting employees to attend training sessions. Also, consider which methods best support the organization's business strategy and produce effects that can be used on the job. Below are some disadvantages to using technology in the training program:

- Learners must be computer-literate and have routine access to computers. In most cases, the learners also need routine access to the Internet, the organization's computer network, or both.
- E-learning frequently requires a larger upfront cash investment than traditional methods, often involving software licenses and customization courseware (if needed).
- The planning, design, and implementation of e-learning require coordination across training and IT functions.

- Custom course development using technology involves more detailed work and usually costs a lot more (up to ten times more, for detailed multimedia) than traditional learning methods.
- Computer-based instruction is inherently limited in the complexity it can handle because all options must be programmed into the courseware. This makes it less suitable for practice of social-interaction skills (coaching, leadership, sales), where every interaction is different.

Implementing an E-Learning Program

Making the move from classroom training to a mix of classroom and e-learning requires a shift in expectations and skills sets. For the effort to be successful, the organization needs to accept changes in its culture. Here are some of the keys essential to implementing e-learning:

➤ **Learning Expertise.** It should be no surprise that the organization needs experts who understand how people learn. Sound knowledge and application of adult learning theories drive e-learning as much as (or more than) traditional learning attempts.

➤ **Learning Experts Who Understand Technology**. The learning expert must not only understand how the technology works but also be aware of its strengths and limitations. In the e-learning environment, technology is the medium and the training content is the message. Many organizations have found that relatively few trainers can make the transition to online delivery. Training skills sets and competencies are different in the e-learning environment.

➤ **Clear Judgment**. Organizational decision makers need to remain focused on the learning and performance-improvement goals. E-learning should not be done just because it can be done or because other organizations are doing it. Make sure that it is a good choice for the learning needs and the situation.

➤ **Infrastructure.** The organization must have the commitment of the IT group and a stable and reliable organizational computing network.

The learners must also have routine access to networked computers on which to access and do the learning.

▸ **Upfront Budget**. Licensing software and building an e-learning infrastructure almost always entail an upfront charge. The cost savings can be great when compared to traditional training logistics, but organizations should expect the initial investment to be higher.

▸ **Time to Become Used to New Methods**. For e-learning to be accepted, there needs to be a strong organizational commitment to training and learning.

Learning Technology Success in the Blended Learning Application

To ensure success for your blended learning applications, consider the following criteria in evaluating the learning technologies available to you.

1. **Ease of Navigation**. How easy is it for learners to get to the learning site and to find their way around within the learning package? Look for clear, simple navigation tools, bookmarks, and the option to skip ahead or go back to review material previously covered.
2. **Content/Substance**. What is the quality of the instructional content itself? Look for references to models and theories that are supported with research, as well as demonstrations of practical utility. Does the content reflect proven principles, or is it based on a fad? How easily can content be added, deleted, or upgraded by your training staff and technical support?
3. **Layout/Format/Appearance**. How well does the package present a clean, professional appearance? Look for graphics and a visual style that enhance learning points. Also look for sound and animation options, where appropriate to the learning need. Would learners take it seriously at first glance?

4. **Interest.** How well does the instructional content keep learners' interest? Look for frequent opportunities for the learners to click, type, move, or otherwise interact with the software in a meaningful way. Instruction that allows learners to generate their own ideas and use them in the instruction meets adult-learning principles better than page-turner packages.
5. **Applicability**. How applicable is the instructional content to the specific need and situation your learners face? Look for a strong connection between the course content and what your learners need to actually do on the job.
6. **Cost-Effectiveness/Value**. How cost-effective is this learning package when all supporting costs and licenses are figured in? Can the package be charged on a pay-as-you-go plan, or is a large user-license fee required? Does the package require hosting on a server? If so, who will provide that? What kind of support is necessary and included?

Note

1. Donald L. Kirkpatrick, *Evaluating Training Programs* (San Francisco: Berrett-Koehler, 1994).

Appendix

Tips from ASTD Presentation Masters

In her *Training and Development* article "Presentation Tips from the Pros," Donna Abernathy, of the American Society for Training and Development, comments that "all presenters and trainers aren't techno wizards, but because presentations are increasingly going digital, they [trainers] have to keep up with new technology. The demand for high-quality presentation media, such as animation, audio, and video, is on the rise, according to the International Association of Presentation Professionals [IAPP]. Seventy-five percent of IAPP members are involved in some form of Web site development or online show-and-tell."[1]

There is still debate over whether technology is more of a help or a hindrance for trainers. Does PowerPoint come between a presenter and the audience? Does checking miles of computer cables and multimedia wire rob a presenter of valuable prep and connection time? At its heart, a presentation remains a decidedly human event. Whether you're new to the training field or are an experienced conference speaker, here's help from the seven best presenters, according to the American Society for Training and Development.

Preparation

1. Overprepare. Know your content inside and out so that if you get nervous, you can focus on the "how" of your delivery.
2. Don't just do a mental rehearsal. There's nothing like a physical walk-through to build your confidence and help you perfect the timing.
3. Know why you were asked to do the presentation. That will give you the new perspective you're expected to bring to the event.
4. Stay up-to-date. Read continually in your area of expertise so you can add fresh anecdotes, statistics, and insights.
5. Create new concepts, processes, or applications. Don't borrow other people's material or ideas and try to make them your own. You can't build your credibility on someone else's work.
6. Design your presentation from an audience's perspective. Review your materials from an audience's point of view and ask yourself, "So what?" If the answer isn't clear, you should consider revising the materials or the sequence.
7. Limit the content. When you're new to training, you may become content-centered. As you grow more confident, you'll understand that it's better to learn one or two things effectively than more ineffectively.
8. Get professional help. Every budding trainer should take a one-day acting course. If people don't buy the messenger, they won't buy the message.
9. Rejuvenate your presentation skills. Attend a National Speakers or Toastmasters meeting. Find associated industries in which you can gain exposure to the top presenters. You can also listen to tapes during your travels.
10. Stay motivated. Read more, learn more, and stretch beyond your comfort zone. Doing the same things, in the same way, every day and expecting a different result is commonly viewed as a definition

of insanity. With the Internet playing such an active role in your research, there's no excuse for not staying current.

11. Be prepared. Master the content, and manage your time.
12. Once in a while, learn something totally out of your area of expertise. That will remind you of what it's like to be a beginner and will keep you sensitive to participants as they struggle with content that you may find basic.
13. Watch experienced speakers.
14. Take improvisational theater classes.
15. Give back. Do free speeches for good causes.

Openings

16. Begin before the beginning. Use the time before your presentation to meet people as they come into the room. Arrive in time to set up and test your equipment and still have 20 minutes to talk with people.
17. Plan the beginning. Most often, the success of a presentation depends on the first five to 10 minutes. That's the amount of time that most people take to decide whether to stay.
18. Have the room ready 20 minutes before the first participant arrives. This ensures that problems are solved before participants are in the room.
19. Spend the next 15 minutes greeting participants and making them feel welcomed. Then, you present to an audience that you've already connected with.
20. Cover housekeeping in small chunks or just before the first break. Demonstrate to participants that their time will be well spent.
21. Have people line up at the session, beginning by their level of knowledge or experience in the subject. They can do that through discussion with each other. Or, as a twist, ask them to do it nonverbally. Then, have participants count off so that they're divided into groups of five to seven. That will help ensure an even distribution of knowledge and experience, and allow you to add their expertise to your own.

Presentation

22. Don't become a slide narrator. Beginning trainers or speakers, in an attempt to have adequate prompts at hand, tend to use too many slides and put all of their key points on them. Don't let the slides become the presentation.
23. Don't talk at people; talk with them. Consider a speech to be a conversation with an audience larger than one person. Interact.
24. Customize, customize, customize. Canned comments don't work. You need to dialogue with the audience. You need to get to know the organization, its values, its language, and its culture (even the dress code—respect it and live it, if needed).
25. Continually work for interaction. A reflective question followed by a long pause can give participants time to examine a new idea, rather than play three games without having put their brains in gear.
26. Stir your passion for a topic. If you don't feel passionate about what you want an audience to do, neither will the audience. Genuine emotion almost always comes through—positively and negatively.
27. Teach what you love, and live a life that shows it.
28. Open up. Be authentic, positive, and vulnerable, and your audience will do likewise.
29. Keep it simple and to the point.
30. Reinforce for learning. Reinforce each point with theory and research, experiential exercises to integrate the point, a true story to provide anecdotal evidence, and open discussion.
31. Keep it alive. Use a continual flow of visual, auditory, and kinesthetic learning.
32. Have fun. Your audience will, too. Learning and laughter go hand in hand.
33. Make it relevant. Create an action plan for and with participants to help them incorporate the learning points in their lives.
34. Remember that you are the presentation. Generating and maintaining energy are critical. No matter how effective your visuals, you

carry the responsibility for the audience's experience. Your voice and body are important tools. Modulate your tone. Speak loudly to emphasize important points. Be dramatic to draw attention, and speak softly as a contrast. Move around.

35. Never give away any answers. Most likely, someone in the audience will know as much or more about the topic as you do. And most people will know something. Use that. The more an audience is involved in the presentation, the easier and more fun it is for the presenter and the more effective it is for the audience.
36. Don't read the slides. Give the audience a chance to read your visuals before you start speaking. During the few seconds that they're not listening to you, acknowledge that. Ask them to look at the slide and then to refocus their attention on you.
37. Remember that context is powerful. There is a great cartoon that shows two fish in a fishbowl. One says to the other, "Water? What water?" The clearer the context in which you place your ideas, the more powerful the impact. Paint the big picture as well as the details.
38. Be a provocateur, not a presenter. Deliver most of your content through a series of questions rather than statements. For each visual you use, develop a provocative question that will unveil facts or lead people to answers or points you want to make.
39. Be illustrative. Stories and examples bring concepts to life. Use situations from the audience.
40. Remember that timing is everything. Don't fill up the allotted time with so many stories and examples that there's no time at the end for questions or a summary.
41. Practice, rehearse, and drill. In one study, people were asked to rank their fears in order. Sixty-eight percent said death was number one; 32 percent said public speaking was number one. That means that one-third would rather die than speak. Many trainers feel the same way. The only way to overcome such fear is to practice. You never lose the fear; learn to control it.

42. Stay at it. The more you present, the easier it gets. There's a lesson to learn every time.
43. Concentrate on the process. Be creative, devising ways to increase participation. Watch the pros; see how they work the crowd. Then modify some of their techniques for yourself.
44. Take a break. Trainers and presenters burn out, so reserve personal time for you to recharge your batteries. For example, you can use a conference as a sabbatical to stay in a nice hotel, learn something new, and network with some exciting people. It's called becoming a student again.
45. Be practical. Deliver what is needed.
46. Focus on performance. Teach to the objective; test to the objective.
47. Deliver effectively. Listen and process.
48. Facilitate learning. Appropriately access the four roles of the training professional: instructor, facilitator, coach, and consultant.
49. Create vision. Deliver new information each time.
50. Organize. Raise your organizational skills to an art form.
51. Listen to hear.
52. Care for each person.
53. Be credible. Remember that credibility takes intention and work.
54. Make your handouts interactive. Have participants add a caption or fill in a key word to increase their attention, retention, and participation.
55. Be instructor-led but participant-centered. Help participants develop their own answers, apply tools and techniques, use reference materials, and tap resources (their own and their colleagues') to reach solutions that work in the session and back on the job.
56. Have at least two ways to teach everything. That allows you to change your presentation to keep it fresh for yourself while still covering content that participants need.

57. Have your visuals available in at least two formats. If PowerPoint goes down, have overheads on hand or copies of all the overheads in handouts. The medium isn't the message; the medium supports the message.
58. Put one-third of the content you plan to cover in an appendix. If you end on time, participants will feel they're getting a bonus when you cover the appendix.
59. Use interactive activities.
60. Be yourself. Be willing to be vulnerable.
61. Remember that silence is as important as speaking.
62. Love what you do.
63. Control your environment.
64. Keep taking risks.
65. Mentor your trainers. They can teach you a lot.
66. Take time to renew yourself.
67. Be an instrument of something larger than yourself.

Endings

68. Summarize. Provide a summary of learning points and a special closure that celebrates participants' learning.
69. Begin and end on time.
70. Be available afterward. You are there for your audience.

Evaluation

71. Evaluate everything. Examine every presentation and ask, "What could I do next time to make it more effective?" Have a friend give you some positive feedback so that every event is a learning event. And don't work in front of a video camera at first; you're not a professional actor. Video is unforgiving and can give you negative feedback too early in your development.

72. Change. Doing the same program day after day can be boring. Constantly ask how you can do it in a new, fun, and exciting way, and revise.
73. Watch and listen. Watch yourself on video, and listen to yourself on audio.

Additional Reading

Aldrich, C. "Global learning, 2008." *The AMA Handbook of E-Learning: Effective Design, Implementation, and Technology Solutions*. New York: AMACOM, 2003.

Austin, M. "Needs Assessment by Focus Group." *Infoline* 259401 (1998).

Balaguer, E. "Facing the future: 5 questions." *Training and Development* 60, no. 1 (2006).

Barbazette. J. *Managing the Training Function for Bottom Line Results*. San Francisco: Pfeiffer, 2008.

Barnnick, M. T., and E. I. Levine. *Job Analysis: Methods, Research, and Applications for Human Resource Management in the New Millennium*. Thousand Oaks, Calif.: Sage, 2002.

Bennis, W., W. W. Burke, G. Grey, W. M. Juechter, G. Rummler, and N. Tichy. "What lies ahead?" *Training and Development* 57, no. 1 (2006).

Bernthal, P. R., K. Colteryahn, P. Davis, J. Naughton, W. J. Rothwell, and R. Wellins. *ASTD Competency Study: Mapping the Future.* Alexandria, Va.: ASTD, 2004.

Blanchard, P. N., and J. C. Thacker. *Effective Training Systems, Strategies, and Practices,* 2nd ed. Upper Saddle River, N.J.: Pearson, 2004.

Boyatzis, R. E. *The Competent Manager*. New York: John Wiley, 1982.

Brethower, D. M. "Rapid Analysis Matching Solutions to Changing Situations." *Performance Improvement* 36, no.10 (1997).

Broad, M., and J. Newstrom. *Transfer of Training*. Reading, Mass.: Addison-Wesley, 1992.

Bunker, K. A. "When a Classroom Revolt Is a Good Thing." *Training and Development* 60, no. 1 (2006).

Caffarella, R. *Program Development and Evaluation Resource Book for Trainers*. New York: John Wiley, 1988.

Center for Army Lessons Learned Named in Info World 100 for 2008 Top IT Solutions. Retrieved from http://usacac.army.mil/cacz/call/index.asp; accessed March 30, 2009.

Chyung, S., and M. Vachon. "An Investigation of the Profiles of Satisfying and Dissatisfying Factors in E-Learning," *Performance Improvement Quarterly* 18 (2005).

Clark, R., and R. Meyer. "Learning by Viewing versus Learning by Doing: Evidence-based Guidelines for Principled Learning Environments." *Performance Improvement* 47 (2008).

Cohen, S. L. "The Case for Custom Training." *Training and Development* 52, no. 8 (1998).

Cole, S., S. Gale, S. Greengard, P. Kieger, C. Lachnitt, T. Raphael, D. Shiut, and J. Wiscombe. "Fast Forward: 25 Trends that Will Change the Way You Do Business." *Workforce* 82, no. 6 (June 2003).

Coombs, S. J., and I. D. Smith. "Designing a Self-Organized Conversational Learning Environment." *Educational Technology* 38, no. 3 (1998).

Cooper, K. C. *Effective Competency Modeling and Reporting: A Step-by-Step Guide for Improving Individual and Organizational Performance*. New York: AMACOM, 2000.

Davenport, R. F. "Future of the profession." *Training and Development* 60, no. 1 (2006).

Dolezalek, H. "Virtual Vision," *Training,* October 2007.

Draves, W. A. *Energizing the Learning Environment*. New York: Learning Resources Network, 1995.

Dubois, D. D., and W. J. Rothwell. *The Competency Toolkit,* vol. 1. Amherst, Mass.: Human Resource Development Press, 2000.

———. *Competency-Based Human Resource Management*. Palo Alto, Calif.: Davies-Black, 2004.

Dunn, R., and T. C. DeBello. *Improved Test Scores, Attitudes and Behaviors in America's Schools.* Santa Barbara, Calif.: Praeger, 1999.

Eiffert, S.D. *Cross-Train Your Brain: A Mental Fitness Program for Maximizing Creativity and Achieving Success.* New York: AMACOM, 1999.

Filipczak, B. "Difference Stokes: Learning Styles in the Classroom," *Training,* March 1995.

Fitz-enz, J. *The ROI of Human Capital: Measuring the Economic Value of Employee Performance.* New York: AMACOM, 2000.

Furjanic, S. W., and L. A. Trotman. *Turning Training Into Learning: How to Design and Deliver Programs that Get Results.* New York: AMACOM, 2000.

Galagan, P. "Second That," *Training and Development,* February 2008.

Gerson, G., and C. McClesley. "Numbers Help Make a Training Decision That Counts." *HRD* 43 (November 1998).

Hannum, W., and C. Hanson. *Instructional Systems Development in Large Organizations.* Englewood Cliffs, N.J.: Educational Technology Publications, 1989.

Harris, P. "Outsourced Learning: A New Market." *Training and Development* 57, no. 9 (2003).

Jackson, T. "The Management of People Across Cultures: Valuing People Differently." *Human Resource Management* 41, no. 4 (2002).

Jensen, E. *Brained-based Learning.* San Diego: Brain Store, 2000.

Johnson, D. W., R. T. Johnson, and K. A. Smith. *Active Learning: Cooperation in the College Classroom.* Edina, MN: Instructional Book Company, 1991.

Kaye, B., and B. Jacobson. "True Tales and Tall Tales: The Power of Organizational Story Telling." *Training and Development,* March 1999.

Kirkpatrick, D. "Techniques for evaluation training programs." *Training and Development* 33, no. 6 (1979).

———. *Techniques for Evaluation Training Programs. More Evaluating Training Programs.* Alexandria, Va.: ASTD Press, 1987.

Kolb, D. *Experiential Learning.* London: Financial Times/Prentice Hall, 1983.

Kraiger, K, "Transforming Our Models of Learning and Development: Web-based Instruction As Enabler of Third-Generation Instruction. *Instructional Organizational Psychology* 1, no. 4 (December 2008).

Kronhert, G. *Basic Training for Trainers,* rev. ed. Sydney, Australia: McGraw-Hill, 1994.

Kules, J., and M. Smith. "Produce It or Purchase It!" *Technical & Skills Training* 8, no. 3 (1997).

Lacey, K. "Building Bridges—Making Mentoring Happen." *Training and Development in Australia*, October 1999.

Laird, D. *Approaches to Training and Development*. Reading, Mass.: Addison-Wesley, 1985.

Langdon, D. "Are Objectives Passes?" *Performance Improvement* 36, no. 9 (1997).

———. "Selecting Interventions." *Performance Improvement* 36, no. 10 (1997).

Lawson, K. *Improving On-the-Job Training and Coaching*. Alexandria, Va.: ASTD Press, 1997.

Loughner, P., and L. Moller. "The Use of Task Analysis Procedures by Instructional Designers." *Performance Improvement Quarterly* 11 (November 1998).

Lucas, R. *The Creative Training Idea Book: Inspired Tips and Techniques for Engaging and Effective Learning*. New York: AMACOM, 2003.

Mager, Robert. *Preparing Instructional Objectives,* 2nd ed. Belmont, Calif.: Fearon, 1975.

Marquardt, M. *Action Learning in Action: Transforming Problems and People for World-Class Organizational Learning*. Palo Alto, Calif.: Davies-Black, 1999.

Marshall, V., and R. Schriver. "Using Evaluation to Improve Performance." *Technical & Skills Training*, January 1994.

Mayer, R. "Applying the Science of Learning: Evidence-based Principles for the Design of Multimedia Instruction. *American Psychologist,* November 2008.

McArdle, G. *Conducting a Needs Assessment*. Menlo Park, Calif.: Crisp Publications, 1998.

———. "The AMA Trainers' Activity Book." *Problem-Based Learning: A New Teaching Tool*. New York: AMACOM, 2004.

———. *Training Design & Development,* 2nd ed. Alexandria, Va.: ASTD Press 2007.

McLagan, P., and P. McCullough. *Models for Excellence: The Conclusions and Recommendations of the ASTD Training and Development Competency Study.* Alexandria, Va.: ASTD Press, 1989.

McLean, P. "Brainblog: News About Our Knowledge of the Brain and Behavior." http://neuropsychological.blogspot.com, accessed January 10, 2008.

Meier, D. *The Accelerated Learning Handbook: A Creative Guide to Designing and Delivering Faster, More Create Training Programs.* New York: McGraw-Hill, 2000.

Miller, C. L. "Design, Implementation, and Evaluation of a University-Industry Multimedia Presentation." *Journal of Instructional Delivery Systems* 12, no. 2 (1998).

Moallem, M., and R. S. Earle. "Instructional Design Models and Teacher Thinking: Toward a New Conceptual Model for Research and Development." *Educational Technology* 38, no. 2 (1998).

Montier, R., D. Alai, and D. Kramer, "Competency Models Develop Top Performance." *Training and Development,* July 2006.

Murphy, S., "Ritz Camera Focuses on Web-based Teaching Tools." *Chain Store Age,* December 23, 2008.

Nacheria, A. "Robots in the Room." *Training and Development,* November 2008.

Parry, S. "Organizing a Lesson Plan by Objectives." *Technical Training* 9, no. 4 (1998).

Perkins, D. *Outsmarting IQ: The Emerging Science of Learnable Intelligence.* New York: Free Press, 1995.

Phillips, J. J. *Handbook of Training Evaluation and Measurement Methods.* Houston: Gulf, 1991.

Plattner, F. "Instructional Objectives." *Infoline* 259712 (1997).

Ricks, D. M. "Challenging Assumptions That Block Learning." *Training* 34 (November 1997).

Roberts, B. "Hard Facts about Soft-Skills E-learning." *HR* magazine, January 2008.

Rose, C., and M. J. Nicholl. *Accelerated Learning for the 21st Century: The Six-Step Plan to Unlock Your Master-Mind.* New York: Dell, 1998.

Rossett, A. *The ASTD E-Learning Handbook: Best Practices, Strategies, and Case Studies for an Emerging Field.* New York: McGraw-Hill, 2001.

Rothwell, W. J. (ed.). *ASTD Models for Human Performance Improvement: Roles, Competencies and Outputs.* Alexandria, Va.: ASTD Press, 1998.

Rothwell, W. J., and H. C. Kazanas. *Mastering the Instructional Design Process: A Systematic Approach,* 2nd ed. San Francisco: Jossey-Bass, 1998.

Rothwell, W. J., and H. J. Sredl. *The ASTD Reference Guide to Workplace Learning and Performance: Present and Future Roles and Competencies,* 3rd ed. Amherst, Mass.: Human Resource Development Press, 2000.

Russell, S. "Training and Learning Style." *Infoline* 258804 (1998).

Russo, C. *The Early Bird Guide to ASTD Professional Certification: Your Jump Start to CPLP Certification*: Alexandria, Va.: ASTD, 2005.

Rylatt, A. *Learning Unlimited. Practical Strategies for Transforming Learning in the Workplace of the 21st Century,* 2nd ed. NSW Australia: Business + Publishing, 2000.

Schuler, R. S. *Human Resource Management,* 5th ed. Cincinnati, Ohio: South Western College Publishing, 1996.

SHRM. *Learning System Certification Guide.* Alexandria, Va.: Society for Human Resource Management, 1997.

Silberman, M., and Carol Auerbach. *Active Training.* San Francisco: Jossey-Bass, 2006.

Silberman, M., and K. Lawson. *101 Ways to Make Training Active.* San Francisco: Pfieffer, 1995.

Spitzer, D. R. "The Design and Development of High Impact Interventions." *Handbook of Human Performance Technology.* San Francisco: Jossey-Bass, 2000.

Spitzer, I. "Value-Minded." *Workforce Management,* July 2005.

Steadman, S. V. "Learning to Select a Needs Assessment Strategy." *Training and Development,* January 1980.

Stinger, D. "Case writing 101." *Training and Development,* 1999.

Sugrue, B., and R. Rivera. *2005 State of the Industry Report.* Alexandria, Va.: ASTD Press, 2005.

Swanson, R. A., and E. F. Holton. *Results: How to Access Performance. Learning, and Perceptions in Organizations.* San Francisco: Berrett-Koehler Publishers, 1999.

Tampson, O. "Training Ties That Bind." *Technical Training* 9, no. 2 (1998).

Thiagarajan, S. *Thiagi's Interaction Lectures.* Alexandria, Va.: ASTD Press, 2005.

Thilmany, J. "Passing on Knowledge." *RH* magazine, June 2008.

Thompson, C., E. Koon, W. H. Woodwell Jr., and J. Beauvais. *Training for the Next Economy: An ASTD State of the Industry Report on Trends in Employer-Provided Training in the United States.* Alexandria, VA: ASTD, 2002.

Tyler, K. "15 Ways to Train on the Job." *HR* magazine, September 2008.

Van Buren, M. E., and W. W. Erskine. *State of the Economy: ASTD's Annual Review of Trends and Employer-Provided Training in the United States.* Alexandria, Va.: ASTD Press, 2002.

Vygotsky, L. S. *Mind in Society: The Development of Higher Psychological Processes.* Cambridge, MA: Harvard University Press, 1978.

Waagen, A. K. "Task Analysis." *Infoline* 259909 (1998).

Walter, K. "Bring on the Entertainment." *Personnel,* July 1995.

Weinstein, D. "Managing the Magic." *Training,* July/August 2008.

Weinstein, M. "Winning Games." *Training,* April 2007.

———. "Wake-Up Call." *Training,* June 2007.

———. "A Better Blend." *Training,* September 2008.

"What Does It Cost to Use a Virtual World Learning Environment?" *Training and Development,* November 2008.

"What Is Web-Based Training?" Retrieved from www.clark.net/pub/nactive/fl.html.

Wilson, D., and E. Smilanich. *The Other Blended Learning.* San Francisco: Pfeiffer, 2005.

Zemke, R. "How to Do a Needs Assessment When You Think You Don't Have Time." *Training* 35, no. 3 (1998).

Zemke, R., and Zemke, S. "What We Know for Sure about Adult Learning." In L. Ukens, ed., *What We Know for Sure about Adult Learning.* San Francisco: Pfeiffer, 2001.

Index